advance praise for

TIME OFF!
THE UPSIDE TO DOWNTIME

"Happiness in this country is on the decline and depression has spiked. We desperately need to change our beliefs about the centrality of work to our lives. *Time Off! The Upside to Downtime* will help Americans begin to deal with the fear of unemployment, the fear that keeps us paralyzed with inaction, leading us to accept the control the workplace has over our lives. Everyone thinks that someday we'll start living. *Time Off!* helps you to start now."
> ~ **Cecile Andrews, author of *The Circle of Simplicity: Return to the Good Life* (www.cecileandrews.com)**

"The only thing more important than making a living is making a life. So do something radical—take a sabbatical. But first read this savvy and surprising book. *Time Off!* is the ultimate guide to leisure with a purpose."
> ~ **Daniel H. Pink, author of *A Whole New Mind* and *Free Agent Nation* (www.danpink.com)**

"Leisure Team gave the San Francisco Bay Area something to cheer about with their first book, *Time Off! The Unemployed Guide to San Francisco*. Now they've created a colorful guide to leisurely living for the rest of us: *Time Off! The Upside to Downtime*. Read it slowly, follow the advice and start living a more balanced life—today."
> ~ **John de Graaf, national coordinator, Take Back Your Time Day (www.timeday.org) and co-author, *Affluenza***

"Taking a sabbatical is a time-honored tradition. *Time Off!* shows how these breaks (whether voluntary or not) can be a blessing. It's a common-sense guide, with sound advice and great travel ideas."
> ~ **Larry Bleiberg, travel editor, *The Dallas Morning News***

"You're going to work more than five-hundred months in your lifetime. Don't you want them to be as joy-filled and purposeful as possible? In their book, *Time Off! The Upside to Downtime*, authors Kristine Enea and Dean LaTourrette give you the guided path you need to find the career, the worldviews, and the optimism we crave for the journeys ahead."
> ~ **Hope Dlugozima, co-author, *Six Months Off: The Sabbatical Book***

"What will you accomplish when there is no one to tell you what to accomplish? Kristine Enea and Dean LaTourrette know that this is an important question. You can climb hierarchies, impress your boss and plan for the future but if at some point you don't step outside the structure of what others expect, you will never know your true nature. Learning to make the most of your leisure time means nothing less than learning to be in charge of your own destiny."
~ **Ethan Watters, author of** *Urban Tribes: Are Friends the New Family?* **(www.urbantribes.net)**

"*Time Off!* not only convinces you how important it is to take control of your life, but shows you how to do it. The art of leisure and its value was never so clear as in these pages. Buy the book and release yourself!"
~ **Larry Habegger, executive editor, Travelers' Tales books (www.travelerstales.com)**

"Not too many people on their death beds wish they'd worked more. But lots of departing souls regret not taking more time off to travel, play and share with loved ones. Downtime can restore and renew, enabling us to be more creative and productive and to see what really matters in our lives. *Time Off! The Upside to Downtime* shares savvy strategies to create, savor, and make the most of these times in your life."
~ **Michael Shapiro, author of** *A Sense of Place: Great Travel Writers Talk About Their Craft, Lives, and Inspiration*

"Wake up America! The time has come to seize the moment, get laid off, take a vacation, capitalize on being fired, or simply play hooky from work. All who claim boredom shall be shamed. *Time Off!* is the ideal action antidote for couch potatoes, stress addicts and slackers alike—with a healthy dose of soul-searching thrown in."
~ **Amanda Jones, travel writer and photographer (www.meanda.net)**

"This book reminds us that the leisure class is a mindset and not a socioeconomic status. The authors creatively suggest ways any of us may realize the benefits of downtime, and revitalize ourselves in the process. *Time Off!* is a whimsical, fun-filled yet purposeful invitation to join the leisure class, which I plan on doing—right after my nap."
~ **Bill Anthony, Ph.D., founder of The Napping Company (www.napping.com), author of** *The Art of Napping*, **and co-author, with his wife Camille Anthony, of** *The Art of Napping at Work*

"An excellent read that not only offers practical ideas, but helps put everything in the context of the incredibly fast-growing international 'slow down' movement. It's now time for things that are not only good for people but the planet as well. The Work Less Party wholeheartedly supports this book."
~ **Conrad Schmidt, founder, Work Less Party (www.worklessparty.org)**

"This book is loaded with words, sentences, punctuation, and indentations! It's also chockfull of great motivational advice for anyone who wants to put some positive upswing into their downtime."
~ **"Odd Todd" Rosenberg, creator, oddtodd.com and author** of *The Odd Todd Handbook: Hard Times Soft Couch*

rave reviews for TIME OFF!
THE UNEMPLOYED GUIDE TO SAN FRANCISCO

"I wish I could be Mayor of San Francisco forever but even us politicos need a break once in a while. *Time Off!* has given me a wealth of ideas for enjoying life after City Hall and the book beautifully represents San Francisco."
~ **Former Mayor of San Francisco, Willie L. Brown, Jr.**

"Authors Dean LaTourrette and Kristine Enea dissect all that's cheap, free, and otherwise beneficial for the unemployed, from the city's best happy hours to window-shopping to public pools to the science of a good garage sale."
~ *The Wave Magazine*

"With impressively researched lists detailing cheap happy hours, free art, and ways to stop feeling guilty about taking a giant loan from Mom and Dad, this exhaustive tome eloquently preaches the love of leisure and the importance of wise financial planning. Dean LaTourrette and Kristine Enea offer enticing suggestions for what to do with your extended free time."
~ *SF Weekly*

"If you're touring on the cheap, read *Time Off!* for some good tips on saving cash."
~ *Razor Magazine*

"The book is a hip, friendly bundle of ideas and information for the purposefully—or accidentally—unemployed."
~ *San Francisco Downtown*

TiME OFF!

THE UPSIDE TO DOWNTIME

TiME OFF!

THE UPSiDE TO DOWNTiME

KRiSTiNE ENEA
DEAN LATOURRETTE

leisure team
productions

Time Off! The Upside to Downtime

Published by Leisure Team Productions, LLC
First printing 2005

10   8   6   4   2   1   3   5   7   9

Distributed in the United States by Publishers Group West
Distributed in Canada by Publishers Group Canada

Publisher's Cataloging-In-Publication Data

Enea, Kristine.
    Time Off! : the upside to downtime / Kristine Enea, Dean LaTourrette.

    352 p. : ill. ; 22 cm.
    Includes bibliographical references and index.
    ISBN: 0-9741084-9-9

    1. Leisure—Guidebooks. 2. Conduct of life. 3. Satisfaction. I. LaTourrette, Dean. II. Title.

GV14 .E54 2005
790.1   2005926648

Edited by Jennifer Birch, Nalani Jay and Jennifer Jeffrey
Cover design by Jamie Leap Designs
Illustration by Sara Irvin, Romnee Pritchett, Kathryn Otoshi and Jamie Leap
Printed and bound in the United States by Malloy Incorporated

*This book is dedicated to
the leisure seekers of the world.*

FOREWORD
A FEW WORDS FROM DR. LEISURE

WAY back in 1919, when criticized for continually arriving late for work, the Irish nobleman Lord Castlerosse retorted, "But think how early I leave!" Now I don't know about you, but I like this guy's attitude. Going to work late and making up for it by leaving early prevented Lord Castlerosse from becoming an unhappy workaholic. Undoubtedly, he enjoyed more free time than most workers of his era. Moreover, he knew how to live a better-balanced lifestyle than most people do today.

Most people don't know how to truly live and enjoy themselves in the present. Adopting a more relaxed and carefree attitude, as displayed by Lord Castlerosse, would do wonders for their overall well-being.

Here's another favorite story of mine to get you tuned up—not only for this great book, but for the rest of your life. I often share it with happy, leisurely individuals whenever they tell me that they might have become millionaires by now, if only they had sacrificed their balanced lifestyle to work a lot harder. This story helps them put life back in proper perspective. It may help you do the same.

A wealthy entrepreneur from New York went on a two-week seaside holiday on the coast of Costa Rica. On his first day there, he was impressed with the quality and taste of the exotic fish he bought from a local fisherman. The next day, the American encountered the native Costa Rican fisherman at the dock, but he had already sold his catch. The American discovered that the fisherman had a secret spot where the fish were plenty and the quality superb, but he caught only five or six fish a day.

The New Yorker asked the local fisherman why he didn't stay out at sea longer and catch more fish.

"But Señor," the fisherman replied, "I sleep in late, until nine or ten every morning; I play with my children; I go fishing for an hour or two; in the afternoon I take a one- or two-hour siesta; in the early evening I have a relaxing meal with my family; and later, I go to the village and drink wine, play guitar, and sing with my amigos. As you can see, I have a full, relaxed, satisfying, and happy life."

"You should catch a lot more fish," the American declared. "That way you can prepare for a prosperous future. Look, I'm a businessman from New York and I can help you become a lot more successful in life. I received an MBA from Harvard, and I know a lot about business and marketing."

The American continued, "The way to prepare for the future is to get up early in the morning and spend the whole day fishing, and go back for more in the evening. In no time, with the extra money, you could buy a bigger boat. Two years from now, you can have five or six boats that you can rent to other fishermen. In another five years, with all the fish you will control, you can build a fish plant and even have your own brand of fish products.

"Then, in another six or seven years," the American rambled to the increasingly bewildered fisherman, "you can leave here and move to New York or San Francisco, and have someone else run your factory while you market your products. If you work hard for fifteen or twenty years, you could become a multimillionaire. Then you wouldn't have to work another day for the rest of your life."

"What would I do then, Señor?" responded the fisherman.

Without any hesitation, the wealthy American enthusiastically proclaimed, "Then you'll be able to move to a little village in some laid-back country like Mexico where you can sleep in late every day, play with the village children, take a long siesta every afternoon, eat meals while relaxing in the evening, and play guitar, sing, and drink wine with your amigos every night."

The moral of this story is pretty obvious: most success, as defined in Western society today, costs too much in terms of blood, sweat, and tears. What's the point of working hard for so many years, sacrificing happiness and well-being along the way, when you can have happiness and well-being today by *not* working so hard, or by not working at all for a year or two?

Loafing has a bum rap in our culture. Someone who's loafing around is seen as lazy, unproductive, and unmotivated. Yet there's a concept I like to call "creative loafing." I believe loafing is crucial for all of us, not only to rest and rejuvenate, but to spark our creative spirit. Some of my greatest spiritual revelations and best business ideas have come during what others might describe as my "laziest" moments.

I have been, for all intents and purposes, in temporary retirement or semiretirement since I was in my late twenties. Somewhere along the way, I found myself in a writing and consulting career, and I discovered the power of intellectual property. It's money you can make while you sleep. So I joke with people—that's why I sleep until noon and take afternoon naps!

As the author of numerous books on enjoying life, retirement and overall happiness, I am often asked, "What is the true 'joy' of not working?" To me, it's all about freedom. As I stated in both *The Joy of Not Working* and *How to Retire Happy, Wild, and Free*: You will have attained true freedom in this world when you can get up in the morning when you want to get up, go to sleep when you want to go to sleep, and in the interval, work and play at the things you want to work and play at, all on your own pace.

In the event that you don't have some underlying perverse need to complicate your life, and are instead looking for a relaxed way toward prosperity and well-being, then the principles advocated by Dean LaTourrette and Kristine Enea in *Time Off! The Upside to Downtime* are for you. These principles will not only help you attain more success, they will also help you attain a freedom not experienced by most people in the Western world. Dare to follow these principles and you can become a more creative, more insightful, more productive, more playful, and happier human being. All this, by working less and enjoying life more!

Ernie Zelinski, a.k.a. "Dr. Leisure"
author of the international bestseller *The Joy of Not Working*
master of **The Joy of Not Working** website
(www.thejoyofnotworking.com)

TABLE OF CONTENTS

INTRODUCTION

Every man who possibly can should
force himself to a holiday of a full month in a year,
whether he feels like taking it or not.

~ William James, *psychologist and philosopher*

HARD work is part of the American dream. We all know that in order to succeed, you must pull yourself up by your bootstraps, put your nose to the grindstone, work, work and then work some more. Over the last couple of decades, this push to work has grown from an encouragement to innovate and create to a soul-sapping force driving people to 80-hour weeks chasing careers they may not even find satisfying. And the real cost for all these extra hours? Many people can no longer relate to their friends, participate in the political process or even keep themselves sane. Legions of burned-out workers volunteer to be laid off so they can get "the package" and try to catch a breath. It's misemployment madness! Someone needs to cut us a break.

So who's going to provide it, business? The government?

Nope. We are more or less on our own these days. Workers used to rely on employers or lawmakers to dictate work hours, vacation time, pay scales, and job types. Increasingly, however, it's up to each individual to decide how many hours to work, what type of benefits to demand, and how and when to take time off. Those who haven't yet adapted to this new economy are vulnerable to allowing others to dictate their work-life balance. You've heard about managing your career, but what about managing your need for free time?

We wrote *Time Off! The Upside to Downtime* to help you give *yourself* a break, to help you figure out how to work *and* live. Think of time off as not only just as important as work, but also as a way to refresh and rejuvenate that enables you to work more effectively, and with greater fulfillment. In fact, "time off" and "downtime" are in some sense misnomers. There is perhaps no greater potential for the human spirit to be "on" or "up" than during a break from work.

WHAT IS TIME OFF?

More of a philosophy than a fixed, pre-planned period, time off comes in many forms, and how to get it depends on your situation.

The most obvious path is to take a sabbatical from a job that you can return to. More and more companies are instituting formal sabbatical programs as a reward for loyal service (remember that concept?). If you want a sabbatical but your company doesn't offer one and you don't have enough savings to fund your own, look into volunteer vacations and short-term internships.

Perhaps you don't like your job at all. Quit! Or start saving and planning to. And never forego vacation days. Remind your reluctant employer that the Europeans work a much shorter year than we do but their jobs still get done when they're on vacation. The world doesn't crumble and employees return to work refreshed and ready to contribute. They work harder before they leave, too, knowing that they have a break to look forward to.

If you're already *Non-Employed*, don't pressure yourself to get back to work right away if you don't have to. Decompress. Learn to enjoy your time off. Believe it or not, even getting the axe can lead to greater peace of mind in the long run, especially if you have a bit of savings. No money tucked away? You are in the toughest spot of all—but there are ways to shore up your pocketbook via odd jobs, low-income utility programs, free health clinics, affordable insurance, and other tips from the many valuable resources available to you. Remember that if you lost your job, you're not alone, your life is not over and there's nothing wrong with you. You still need and deserve a life beyond the job hunt.

A break from work invites you to imagine an entirely new future, one that could be the polar opposite of your past. If you were (or are) miserable behind a desk, maybe you need more adventure. Why not commercial fishing, substitute teaching or your own freelance business? If your checkbook tells you to get right back in the ring, you can learn to work smarter instead of harder—and fit in downtime as often as possible. In all cases, look for work that you enjoy even if it doesn't pay the most—you'll feel like you've added hours to your day. Whether you love your job or hate it, have a nest egg or not, are taking time off as the result of careful planning or turning a surprise layoff into an accidental sabbatical, aim to make the most of any break from routine.

Time off doesn't have to be lengthy or formal. All it requires is a desire to transcend your daily obligations for a year, a month, or one savory afternoon. Time off can work wonders for your psyche when overwork has turned you into a psych-o (not to mention what it will do for the psyche of everyone around you!). So even if your non-employment was a surprise and you need a new job *right now*, strive to find the free time you need.

Rich or poor, famous or obscure, working or not—everyone needs time off. And everyone can get it.

LEISURE

"Time which one can spend as one pleases," says the Oxford English Dictionary. "Time free from the necessities of work," said Aristotle. Some scholars view leisure as a distinct period of time, to be enjoyed only as a luxury or by an elite leisure class; others see it more as goofing off. One thing's for sure, the daily grind is consuming too many hours these days to leave much room for leisure.

Many Americans believe that leisure awaits them only in retirement, but a growing number of us see leisure as something deeper—a way of living life to the fullest, and closer to the heart. We see leisure as an attitude and a lifestyle. It is this belief that led us to write this book.

WHO THIS BOOK IS FOR

You don't have to quit your job to enjoy *Time Off!* If you *are* out of a job, you're perfectly poised to rediscover what's important to you. If you merely aspire to take a break, we hope to tip the scales in favor of gaining a new perspective on the familiar.

Maybe you have a job but it's part-time or project-based. If you're not into hustling 60 hours a week for *The Man* and would rather save some daylight hours for feeding your own soul, this book is for you too. And if you're lucky enough to like your job, or have a secure job and want to keep it—well, what's wrong with playing a little hooky now and then? Even workaholics need a vacation day once in a while.

Whether you were "downsized" or are gainfully employed, proactively taking a sabbatical or reacting to a sudden layoff, you'll find hundreds of ideas in *Time Off!* on how to take advantage of and savor your free time, without burning through piles of money.

FORMAT OF THE BOOK

Time Off! is divided into three parts: preparing for leisure, making the most of your free time, and transitioning back to work.

Part One makes the case for taking a break, and lays out strategies for overcoming financial and psychological hurdles.

Part Two steers you through your Unemployed Odyssey, suggesting ways to not only rediscover your hometown and yourself, but to see the world, explore your edgy side, boost your health and fitness levels, volunteer to your heart's content, and deepen your connections to family and friends.

Part Three focuses on easing back into career-mode. You can change course by going back to school, or just learn to balance fun and play in your job hunt, and then bring a little leisure with you back to the office. We invite you to join the push for more leisure by telling you how you can plug into the fast-growing Leisure Movement.

Spread throughout the book are celebrations of **Great Moments in Unemployment**. If you see a term that you're not familiar with, edify yourself with our **Leisure Lingo** glossary in the back of the book. Recommended resources are shown in bold as well as indexed alphabetically in the back; recommended reading is in the back too.

People who asked to remain anonymous are referred to by a made-up first name only. But you should know who *we* are: childhood friends, travel aficionados, and survivors of the dot-com boom and bust. Dean digs surfing. Kristine has a thing for movies and pets. Corporate refugees and grad school geeks, we'll be your "instructors" throughout this Leisure School lesson.

Time Off! is not "life on the cheap," although we *are* big fans of free fun. It's not a career manual, although we do share some unconventional means for landing a new job and finding leisure at work. And it's not a travel book or self-help tome, although we offer plenty of tips on both journeys within and trips to lands afar.

It *is* a fun and practical guide to creating a healthier, more balanced life by taking a break from work, whether by design or circumstance. Consider it your Leisure School primer. We hope our ideas will enrich your time off and propel you forward into the wonderful world of leisure.

UPDATES

Although all of the information herein was current as of the publication date, it's always a good idea to double check to see if websites, phone numbers or any other information has changed. Please share your ideas or feedback by emailing us at info@leisureteam.com. We'll publish updates and other breaking news at www.leisureteam.com.

Enjoy, and share the leisure!

LEISURE LEO THE SEA LION

Every school needs a mascot.
For Leisure School, that's me. Take a page from my
book: I eat, I bag rays, I honk—and sometimes I
dunk my little brother in the drink—but I don't think
too much about work. I'll be barking you on during
your Unemployed Odyssey.
~Leo

PART ONE
CHARTING YOUR COURSE

CHAPTER 1
THE ART OF LEISURE

*Leisure, some degree of it, is necessary
to the health of every man's spirit.*
~ Harriet Martineau

*When you have time off from school or somewhere you're
supposed to be, you want to do things that are fun.*
~ Jason, *first grader, leisure prodigy*

ASK some people what they would do if they won the lottery and their answers mostly *sound* like leisure—shopping in exotic locations, driving fast cars to happening nightclubs, and basically living like a rock star. For others, "leisure" is a weekend time-share or a cookie-cutter vacation, or some other pre-packaged pricey getaway that's too short to truly refresh. Yet quick-fix vacations and lottery dreams that focus on the cost-intensive, media-driven image of leisure—with its misleading promise of sex appeal, status and fulfillment through spending—aren't particularly realistic or satisfying in the long run. In fact, they miss the mark completely.

Consider, for a moment, leisure as a grander concept, one more holistic in nature. Just imagine the feeling of having all the time and money in the world—even though you don't. The consumer-economy version of leisure is fine for what it is and at times can hit the spot as conveniently as an all-inclusive resort or a double latte, but true leisure has little to do with how much money you spend, and everything to do with how you spend your time.

Researchers confirm what we already know—most leisure takes place in and around the home, and what's most important to the majority of us are interactions with our loved ones and activities we've invested in. You don't need big bucks in order to get together with your family and friends, learn a musical instrument, or improve your basketball game. Just like love, many of your greatest moments will be experiences that money just can't buy.

While leisure doesn't depend on money, it *does* depend on time. It may sound like the same thing, but that's only because we're used to hearing the "time is money" mantra. Taking a break can be crucial if you find yourself needing a new direction or even needing to learn how to live.

Leisure means much more than just being out of the office. It means enjoying life and living richly. It means living life in balance, both at work and at play. With the right mindset, a little planning, and a healthy splash of creativity, leisure turns mere day-to-day existence into a life worth living.

WHAT IS LEISURE

Anthropologists have observed tribes that mix work and leisure across every aspect of life, but most societies sharply distinguish the two: work is what we must do, leisure is what we want to do. Scholars believe that leisure did not exist until we humans, as a species, were able to meet our basic survival needs.

Well, are we there yet? We're way beyond gathering our basic scratch yet our concept of leisure hasn't changed much since the times of the ancient Greeks when philosophers expounded that only the elite were entitled to downtime, often gained at others' expense. The Romans "democratized" leisure with the Circus Maximus but it turned out that "bread and circuses" was designed by the politicos to divert social protest and sedate the masses with entertainment. Today's mass entertainment diversions—television, shopping, video games—have the same potential for sedation: sapping energy from endeavors that can be more satisfying and significant, such as working on that fast ball with your kid or putting in your two cents at the city council meeting. After all, you have only so much room in your closet for "bargains" from the television shopping channels, don't you?

SIZE YOURSELF UP

You're not alone if you identify closely with your job or feel guilty when you're not working. Americans have always been wary of leisure.

Almost a hundred years ago, the German sociologist Max Weber identified the link between capitalism and the self-denying ethos of Protestantism, and dubbed it the *Protestant Work Ethic*. This conviction tells us that wasting time is evil and the grindstone clears the path to salvation. The concept of "nose to the grindstone" has been ingrained into the American psyche ever since.

Yet, the average American workplace runs rampant with depression, chronic fatigue and burnout. Most workers don't get the proverbial two-week vacation, much less use all the vacation days they do get. People are volunteering to get laid off just to get a break from the grind. Despite the evidence all around us, our culture continues to cling to the notion that material success symbolizes divine favor and that our purpose on earth is to work for *work's* sake.

What's wrong with this picture?

identity check

If any of these statements have passed your lips, take them as a sign to get yourself to Leisure School, pronto!

I'm not at the top of my game.
I can't balance work and family.
I never have enough time.
I am so tired I can't think straight.
I've become someone I don't like.

self-worth ≠ net worth

Self-worth does not equal net worth, promotion does not equal success, and life really isn't a competition to see who can climb highest on the corporate ladder.

you ≠ your job

Taking time off makes you no less smart, attractive, funny, kind, or any of the other things that define you. You're still the same person—maybe even a better person—if you're on sabbatical or under-employed. Saying no to more work allows you to renew relationships and become a better citizen of your community. Non-employment presents an opportunity to rediscover your best self.

THE LEISURE COMMANDMENTS

Thou shalt enjoy at least one sustained period of unemployment during thy career.

Thou shalt switch careers to do something thou really enjoyest, even if it means taking a pay cut.

Thou shalt pursue one secret childhood dream without regard to status or the judgment of others.

Thou shalt party until dawn on at least one weeknight.

Thou shalt lounge around thy house in thy pajamas.

Thou shalt create, experiment, and ponder.

Thou shalt reconnect with thy community.

Thou shalt partake of the great outdoors.

Thou shalt travel and explore, beginning with thine own hometown.

Not enough downtime, that's what. Every hour of overtime is an hour that you don't spend playing, singing, dancing, learning, or enjoying the company of others. It's an hour that you're not spending on an experience that you choose purely for its own sake, whether or not anyone rewards you for it. All work and no play, as the saying goes, makes Jack a dull boy. Well, Jack needs mental space to create and grow. Jack needs a break.

If overwork has turned you into someone you don't like—you don't want to know yourself and no one else does either—take a deep breath and repeat this mantra: "I am not my job. I am *not* my job." Then remember that you can't reminisce with the friend you never had, you won't be telling fish tales about the adventure you never found, you can't enjoy the satisfaction of volunteer work that you never did. Trust us, you will not be on your deathbed wishing you had spent more time in the office. When you think in terms of what you might have lived or done, leisure becomes nothing less than crucial. The art of living will never be perfected without practicing the *Art of Leisure*.

LEISURE REDUX

When we say "leisure" we mean more than unoccupied time. We mean the freedom to pursue whatever activity it is that revitalizes you. If you lack autonomy in your day job, take matters into your own hands by launching your own business. If you're tired of navel-gazing, step outside yourself and volunteer to help others. Not happy with where you're at in life? Take off on a personal journey of self-discovery and contemplation. Got cabin fever? Feeling just plain lifeless? Hop on a jet plane and start a torrid international love affair.

GREAT MOMENTS IN UNEMPLOYMENT

GAME AFTER GAME AFTER GAME

During the Depression of the early 1930s, an unemployed salesman living in Pennsylvania developed a strange new board game while struggling with odd jobs to support his family. The inventor? Charles Darrow. The game? None other than Monopoly. Parker Brothers bought the rights to Monopoly in 1936, but Darrow shrewdly negotiated a royalty payment for every game sold. Darrow's entrepreneurial instinct and refusal to buckle despite being out of steady work made him a millionaire, the first game developer ever to have made as much money. ••• Unemployed Michael Wurstlin created the layout, design and logo for the iconic board game Trivial Pursuit. His payment? Five shares in the company. By 1986, those five shares were valued at two-and-a-half million dollars. ••• Alfred M. Butts, an unemployed architect looking to play a game that required equal amounts of skill and chance, created the predecessor to Scrabble in 1931. It would take until 1948 for him and his business partner to get the word out and begin manufacturing Scrabble in its modern form. The game has since become an international phenomenon—over 100 million sets have been sold in 121 countries—and early royalties to Butts allowed him to retire. Although Butts enjoyed playing the popular board game until his death in 1993, he wasn't a particularly good player. The reason? Por speling.

Leisure activities that demand intense attention and effort, such as taking an art class or playing a competitive game of racquetball, can provide the feeling of accomplishment and rigor that might be missing in your lackluster *McJob*. On the other hand, playing, relaxing, socializing, entertaining, taking in the sensual pleasures of life—activities that you choose for their own sake—can provide the release from mental or physical tension that overwork spawns.

We strongly support lounging around—in fact, it's one of our commandments. Moreover, downshifting while the world rushes around you is hardly unproductive. Research has repeatedly found that people who spend less time at the office are more productive than those who spend extra hours at work. Even pure loafing can relax the body and mind to a state where new ideas blitz you from all directions. Bring *that* creativity to the boardroom, why don't you?

Be it childlike and light or serious and competitive, as short-lived as an amiable conversation or intense enough to send you into that frame of mind where you're so absorbed in what you're doing, you don't think about anything else—leisure means doing what comes naturally, and engaging in intrinsically rewarding activities.

The best work is work you want to do; the best leisure involves a conscious decision to improve your life or at least your state of mind. Leisure and work can be one and the same if you choose what fulfills you and then pursue it for all you're worth—and that's *self*-worth, not net worth.

YOU'LL GET NOTHING AND LIKE IT

Out of 168 countries surveyed, a healthy number guarantee family-friendly benefits:

Paid leave for new mothers	163
Paid leave for new fathers	45
Paid sick leave	139
Paid annual vacation leave	96
A maximum limit on the workweek	84
Paid time off for parents when children are sick	37

But the U.S. guarantees none of the above to any worker.

WHO HAS LEISURE?

Workers around the world today have less free time than our ancestors did. In fact, no group enjoys less leisure than today's Americans. Ancient Romans, by contrast, designated over a hundred days a year "unlawful for judicial and political business" and medieval Europeans took off three to five months every year, including long vacations for Christmas and Easter and weeks-long "ales" to celebrate marriages, deaths, harvests and other special occasions. Pre-industrial societies might have been less wealthy but they were far more relaxed.

The year-round workweek is a relatively modern invention, introduced during the Industrial Revolution, which saw American work-hours balloon to nearly 80 per week. The workweek contracted through the Great Depression, but the end of the World War II created a new boom in the standard of living and consequently a new boom in the working hours required to achieve it. Between 1969 and 1987, the average employee added almost a month's worth of hours to the working-year. Most Americans today work more than 55 hours a week, not counting housework or childcare.

In Japan, a society that takes its work ethic to the extreme, the literal English translation for "I work for Nissan" is "I am Nissan." Never mind getting too caught up in your work—in Japan, apparently you *are* your work! Yet Americans now work longer than even the Japanese, by almost two weeks a year.

we're number one!
(but do we want to be?)

Americans have longer workweeks and less vacation time than workers in any other industrialized country, according to the United Nations' International Labour Organization.

American workers average almost 2,000 hours a year. This substantially exceeds the workweeks of industrial Europe: the British work 1,731 hours a year, the French 1,656, the famously industrious Germans only 1,560 hours, and those lucky Norwegians—1,399 hours.

The countries with workweeks most similar to ours are the developing nations—Sri Lanka, Thailand, Malaysia—where underpaid workers are scrambling to improve their quality of life.

We, on the other hand, have no such excuse. So much for "first world" evolution!

Long hours aren't America's only burden. Family-friendly work policies barely exist in the U.S., even though 61% of young families say they spend too much time at work. Today, fewer than half of Americans can take advantage of the 12 weeks of unpaid leave provided by the Family and Medical Leave Act of 1993. About a third of female employees earning less than $40,000 a year receive no paid vacation at all. The only bright spot is that American employers are more likely to offer flex-time than are employers in other advanced industrialized nations, although part-time workers generally don't receive pro-rated benefits.

wasted leisure time

Too often, the burned-out ooze home, spend four unproductive hours in front of the television, and drag themselves back to the office the next morning. Work becomes an escape from home and home an escape from work.

"I kept going for more money," former work-junkie Mary Mangold told us. "I got a really nice apartment, lived in a good neighborhood, bought designer clothes, with no energy to do anything. When I came home it was time to sleep. I might as well have been living in a closet."

This is not a minor problem. This is a tragedy, and the underlying syndrome has been dubbed *Wasted Leisure Time*. Inoculate yourself!

TIME KEEPS ON SLIPPING...

As unemployment has gone up, so has overwork. Survey respondents recently told Expedia.com that they'll be taking 10% less vacation than in the year past—too much work to get away. Many Americans take no more than a long weekend. Five years ago, all but 5% of U.S. companies offered at least some paid vacation. Today, almost 15% offer none. American employers offer the most miserly vacation allotment in the industrialized world—just 8.1 days off after one year on the job and 10.2 days after three years.

Yet, most Americans say they would trade money for more free time. It's not hard to see why. Email, instant messaging and cell-phone calls pervade our lives, nagging us at all hours with unfinished business. We hurry everywhere and begrudge anyone who intrudes into our space. The more we work, the less likely we are to eat dinner with our family, spend enough time with our pets or even vote. Our short vacations leave us more stressed-out than before, and we use up the rest of our paid time off taking "mental health days." The Chinese word for busy has two characters—one means heart and the other means killer—and indeed, the perpetual time crunch can cause weight gain, weight loss, insomnia or anxiety attacks. "I can see the difference between me and my co-workers," says Bob, a computer programmer who takes regular sabbaticals. "They have lots more gray hair."

wake up call

One survey in the U.K. (where workers log in more hours than anywhere else in the European Union) revealed that given an extra hour in the day in bed, most respondents would rather sleep than make love. Now that's just not right!

The laid-back Australians get four weeks a year guaranteed by law; Americans are guaranteed zilch, zero, the big goose egg.

And it's not even a golden goose egg. Overtime is now the norm, frequently without any extra pay. Subtract from your pay the costs of your commute, the professional clothes you have to buy, your lunches at the deli downtown, and the childcare bill you pay each week. Add to your work-hours the hours you spend every week getting ready for work, going to and from work, and then winding down after work. Divide one by the other. How much is your true hourly wage? Overwork doesn't benefit business, either. American business loses $300 billion a year in job stress-related costs, not including the billions spent replacing absent workers.

WHAT HAS HAPPENED TO LEISURE?

Working long hours and being plugged into the office at all times (cell phone implant, anyone?) blurs the division between work and personal time. Some people work longer hours on weekdays and try to squeeze in the rest of their life on Saturday and Sunday. But by Friday night the weekend warriors are so exhausted that it's all they can do to get ready for work again by Monday. Others toil away their whole youth in a misguided attempt to save their leisure for retirement. Somehow a gargantuan mortgage slips in, medical bills from a premature stress-related disease, college tuition for kids who you don't really even know, and you're too far in debt to retire in luxury like you planned. What kind of leisure savings account is that?

off-peak driving   Take regular breaks.

Use a headset.   TACKLE THE HARD STUFF FIRST.

Keep an overnight bag packed.   ten minutes a day

DoNotCall.org

SPEED DIAL

☒ junkbusters.com   Plan your route.

You gotta ♥ clogs.   Clean up as you go.

Do it now.

Make a list.

FREE YOUR TIME

One subject per email.   Freeze the leftovers.

Log on for a specific purpose.

Measure twice, cut only once.   no-phone zones

smartertravel.com   SCREEN CALLS.

Be selective.

Have a place for things.   Schedule downtime.

SPEED CLEANING   Prioritize.

Break a challenging task into small pieces.

Set goals.   Get rid of things you don't use.

Turn commute into exercise.   just one junk drawer

MORE LEISURE, MORE LEISURE, MORE LEISURE!

We are bombarded with thousands of messages a day telling us first to spend, then to consume, then to spend again. We can't sustain that kind of consumption without then going to work, work, work to pay all the bills, and loans, and…and…. ENOUGH!!!!!!!!

Whew! The work-spend-consume cycle is *exhausting*. It's time to get Jane off that crazy train and onto the leisure locomotive.

If working too much causes all that harm, what happens when you get more leisure? Is it like playing a country song backwards—you get your dog back, you get your friends back…?

Yes! Leisure will bring you all that and more.

Playing and dabbling are not only hedonistic and relaxing, but can also generate new ideas. All the major arts and sciences, especially the humanities, developed from the creative use of leisure. Constructively used, free time leads to cultural, societal and individual enrichment, all crucial to the evolution of advanced society. Just take a look at the **Great Moments in Unemployment** throughout this book for some examples. Goofing around can be serendipitous, the source of accidental discovery and spontaneous invention.

Bill Coleman, a CEO who grew his software company to a billion-dollar run rate after just five years in business, shared one of his most important management secrets with us. "I ask all my employees to take off at least two weeks in a row each year," he told us. "I get my best ideas during time off, including the idea for this company." If it worked for him, it can work for you. Bring on the Art of Leisure!

Taking a "time out" can help you to re-create yourself after a lengthy tour of duty in corporate America. Working hard may or may not have swelled your bank account. It may or may not have advanced you up the proverbial ladder. But there is no maybe in the effect your tour has had on your family, your neighborhood, and your community. They want you back! The energy you have diverted toward work will be a tremendous gift when directed toward them.

Free time allows you to figure out who you are and how you relate to the people around you, whether they're former colleagues or family members, and to give more thought to where your efforts will be most productive in the long term. The skills you have learned in the workplace can be put to use in many other aspects of your life. Management and organizational skills can help you run a civic league, coach a softball team, even run for local office. Negotiating skills can help you start your own business, raise money for a local non-profit, or serve as a Big Brother or Big Sister.

Leisure isn't a luxury to squeeze in after taking care of your basic needs. Leisure *is* a basic need. You need to get away from it all and recharge yourself in order to handle life's many obligations.

LEISURE SCHOOL

If you're starting to burn out, you need to enroll in Leisure School!

The first lesson is all about attitude. Convince yourself that you truly need and deserve leisure, and that you and everyone around you will be better off for it. You're on your way to becoming an honor student once you begin to adopt this mindset, since leisure is as much a state of mind as it is a function of free time.

Freeing your time is important, though—one unhurried step at a time. Life is about making memories. Are most of your memories packaged in a gray cube and tagged with a sticky note?

Take this simple quiz: Have you taken a significant break from work in the last several years? Do you make yourself available by cell phone at all hours of the day? If you're looking for work, should you really spend every waking hour searching for a job?

If your answers are "yes," don't worry—this is the most enjoyable course of study that you'll ever take! Start small by remembering that you don't have to be "scheduled" every minute of the day. Decide which goals are most important and let the least-pressing ones go. Don't rush around just for speed's sake. Take a risk—unplug from the World Wide Web and get out to see the wide wonderful world! It's time to launch your very own *Unemployed Odyssey*.

The rest of this book is full of ways to free up time and make the most of it. These ideas can work whether your sabbatical is by choice or circumstance; whether you're working full-time, part-time, or no-time.

Don't worry if you can't just snap your fingers and be leisurely. Remember, you're fighting the tide of culture and history, and change takes time (oh the irony). Leisure is a process that most of us need to adjust to slowly and in stages.

So get out your number two pencil and start taking notes—right after your siesta!

CHAPTER 2
ADJUSTING TO TIME OFF

I slip from workaholic to bum real easy.
~ Matthew Broderick

*I'm trying to free your mind, Neo, but I can only
show you the door. You're the one that has to walk
through it.... You have to let it all go, Neo—fear,
doubt, and disbelief. Free your mind.*
~ Morpheus, *The Matrix*

WELCOME to the School of Leisure, where every day feels like Friday! We know a bit about you, simply because you're reading this book. You're either non-employed or you're thinking about taking the big non-employment plunge. Perhaps you've just been laid off from your job, and find yourself taking an accidental sabbatical—pausing to reassess your work and personal life, even though you weren't the one to initiate the sudden change in status. Or maybe you're completely burned-out at work and are conspiring to make the break and treat yourself to a well-earned hiatus.

Welcome—and congratulations! Whether by design or circumstance, you've already taken a big step forward in freeing yourself from the culture of overwork, and for that we salute you. You may feel ill at ease with the concept of taking time off but that's perfectly normal in our work-centric society. Remember, just because you want or need to take a breather from the grind does not mean that you plan to never work again, or that you'll have any greater difficulty landing a job in the future. It does mean that until you're ready to work again—and work is ready for you—you can unwind, have fun, and make good use of your freedom. So put your watch away, chuck your PDA into a drawer, and learn to embrace a leisure lifestyle by launching your Unemployed Odyssey, guilt-free.

FREE YOUR MIND

Reactions

You hear countless stories about individuals who retire only to be bored out of their minds with no job or career to occupy their time. Erik's dad got laid off and decided to stay retired rather than find new work. He got so restless, he resorted to vacuuming his driveway—with the hose attachment! At the other end of the non-working spectrum, Drew Jordan of San Jose, California, suffered from strong bouts of guilt. "I hated being unemployed," he told us. "I felt a lot of guilt that my wife (and really most of the rest of the world) was off working away, and I was home in my pajamas screwing around on the Net."

Obstacles

Clearly, the health of your financial position is critical to your peace of mind, which is why we devote the entire next chapter to getting your money house in order. "I think it's really important that you can cover [a break from work] financially," says Tess Roering, a marketing executive who recently took a six-month break to travel and volunteer. "I think it would be extremely stressful to try and relax and enjoy the time if you didn't know how you were going to pay the rent."

Experts, however, say that it's usually *psychological* barriers that keep people from enjoying a break—or even taking one in the first place. "I just don't have the money," or "I'm not independently wealthy," or "That's nice for other people," are excuses you hear all the time. But the professionals say that financial obstacles typically exist as a *result* of mental constraints, not the other way around.

"People think that money is going to be the biggest problem in taking a sabbatical, but our findings were that it really isn't money," says Hope Dlugozima, sabbatical expert and co-author of *Six Months Off.* "People can find their ways around money once they really start focusing on things. It's usually fear, more the sense that 'I just can't really do this,' 'this is too weird,' or 'I'm going to screw up my career going forward' that keeps people from doing it."

Paydirt

Most of us only dream about what we would do if we didn't have to work. So why, when that wish is granted even temporarily, do we have difficulty seizing the moment? "Most of us have an innate love of security, even if we envy someone who doesn't have that as their main goal in life," says Hope. "Doing things out of the norm is a really hard thing to do, even if philosophically you think you're in favor of it. It's like jumping off a cliff, and it's really hard to make that first jump.

"But once you do it," she adds, "it's exhilarating. Things start to fall into place, and all kinds of energies and drives you didn't even know you had, all of a sudden they're right there because you took that one big step first."

This holds true whether your break is planned or not. You're definitely not alone if you don't hit a groove right away, but sooner or later you'll learn to take downtime in stride.

POST-EMPLOYMENT HOUSEKEEPING

Sometimes we forget how many personal benefits are covered by a full-time employer. Psychological challenges aside, non-working newbies should deal with several logistical issues right away. Leaving the employed world, even if for a short time, can trip up the unsuspecting neophyte. Here are a few tips to smooth your transition.

Severance

If you're unfortunate enough to have suffered a layoff, did you negotiate a severance package when you were hired? (Or in *Aspiring Retired* mode?) It might not be too late, either to start from scratch or to improve the one you have.

Your severance package should cover not only the severance amount but also things like benefit continuation, pro-rated bonus, and vesting of a portion of any stock or options—as well as spelling out the circumstances under which you'll be entitled to receive severance in the first place.

Get it in writing. Severance can occur after a takeover, a new boss, an economic downturn or any other job-changing event, and can be paid either as a lump sum or a salary continuation.

pink slip: fact or fiction?

Getting the "pink slip" has long been a euphemism for getting fired. The term is even in most dictionaries. But has anyone ever actually gotten one?

Traditional lore says that companies issued employee termination notices on pink slips of paper. At the Henry Ford Motor Company, managers reputedly placed slips of paper in workers' cubbyholes at the end of each day—white meant that their work was acceptable, pink meant that they were out the door.

Neither theory has been verified, according to *Snopes.com*, a popular website that researches urban legends.

Snopes reports that Peter Liebhold, a curator at the Smithsonian Institution's National Museum of American History, has searched for ten years to find an actual pink slip but so far hasn't found one.

So while the concept of "getting the pink slip" is very real to certain unlucky workers, the origins of the term remain a mystery.

Know Your Rights

Do you suspect you were unfairly laid off? **Nolo** (800-728-3555, www.nolo.com) has released the sixth edition of the popular book *Your Rights in the Workplace* by Barbara Kate Repa. Nolo offers a few nuggets of free legal advice on their website, too. Consulting either of these sources might help you size up whether your employer followed the rules when sizing down.

Direct Deposit

If your paycheck used to be deposited directly into your bank account, you may get socked with monthly fees once those direct deposits end (curses to fake-free-checking banks!). A quick phone call can let you know whether your bank will be charging you fees and whether you can avoid them by switching to a different type of account.

Health Insurance

Whether you are leaving of your own accord or are a victim of downsizing, parting ways with a full-time employer usually terminates your healthcare plan. Unless you're willing to roll the cosmic dice, you'll need insurance to protect yourself against major injury or illness, regardless of the duration of your break.

If you're leaving a company that offered a health insurance plan, you qualify for COBRA, the national program designed to ensure continued coverage for workers after they leave a company. Paying a monthly premium will guarantee you the same coverage you were receiving before you left, for up to 18 months after you leave. The rub? You have just a brief window of time to decide whether you want CO-BRA coverage. The good news is you can decide, retroactively, to enroll in the coverage up to 60 days after your company plan terminates. For tips on whether to elect COBRA or some other kind of insurance, see **Chapter 3**.

Stock Options

You may or may not have been offered stock options at your former job. If you were, you'll normally have a fixed amount of time to exercise vested, unexercised stock options after you leave a company, or forfeit them altogether.

For publicly traded stock, your decision is straightforward: if the current stock price is higher than your option "strike" price, exercise the options. You can either sell them all immediately and bank the profits; sell just enough to cover the cost of exercise (a partial-sale); or, if you can afford it, hold all the stock until you want to sell.

If the company is pre-IPO (Initial Public Offering), the choice is less obvious. To exercise the options, you'll have to cut your company a check with no immediate chance to recover any costs by selling. If the company never goes public, the stock could end up being worthless. Double-check your paperwork to verify how much time you'll have to decide. You may want to wait until the

pink slip: fiction or fact?

The layoff stories we've heard involve methods a lot wackier than pink slips of paper.

Software veteran Andrew Riley's boss lured him to his favorite bar, and then laid him off between sips. Account manager Mary Mangold showed up one morning to find her desk cleared and her computer missing. "That was my first clue," she said, "that something wasn't quite right." And a whole group of high-tech employees who got canned in one fell swoop were then marched over to a table in the corner where the local newspaper offered them a special deal: half-price subscriptions for the recently unemployed.

Layoffs didn't take graphic designer Steve by surprise. He got tipped off that they were coming the next day, so he brought a disposable camera to work to document the scene. "I hid the camera under the table while the flash was warming up," he told us. "The shots didn't turn out too clear but they sure caused a stir." Management complained to no end that Steve was trying to "make a case"—for who knows what.

last minute to see how the company is faring—particularly if you left as part of a large layoff!

Keep in mind that exercising stock options represents a taxable event, whether the company is publicly traded or privately held. That means you could have a substantial tax liability even before you sell. Your tax burden will depend on the fair market value of the stock on

BEFORE TURNING IN YOUR BADGE

If you're facing an impending layoff or have just plain had it with your job, take these important steps before you walk out the door:

• *Transfer Your Contacts.* Whether it's a pile of old business cards or a comprehensive database, your contact information could be the most important asset you leave work with. Back up this information so that you can access it once you're no longer with the company—provided, of course, that your employer's confidentiality policy allows you to do so.

• *Transfer Your Personal Files.* If you're like most workers, you have personal files mixed in with business files. Separate them out and take them with you. Security policies might apply here, especially if you're walking out the door with a box of documents. Discs will fit nicely into your pockets. You can also email stuff to a personal email address.

• *Set Up a Personal Email Account.* If you haven't already, get a personal email account and let friends and associates know before you leave that your contact information will change.

• *Settle All Financial Reimbursements.* If you can, have the company cut you a check for any money they owe you before you walk out that door. This includes salary, travel expenses, or any other reimbursable expenses you've incurred.

• *Don't Sign Anything!* Don't sign a parting agreement—including a severance package—that you're unsure about until you've had a chance to review it thoroughly. At a minimum, take it home with you to evaluate outside of your work environment. Better yet, have a lawyer look it over and advise you on how to proceed.

the date that the options are exercised and whether your options are qualified ("ISOs") or non-qualified ("NSOs"). You'll want to consult a tax adviser, preferably one who has experience with stock options (not all do). Remember to keep exact records of when you exercise your options, and how many shares you bought. For more on taxes, see **Chapter 3**.

Retirement Plans

If you had a 401(k) or some other retirement plan with your former employer, you might be forced to do something with the funds. Many plans or companies will continue to administer your retirement funds if they exceed a minimum threshold amount. Otherwise, you should consider rolling over the funds into an IRA to avoid early withdrawal penalties.

FIVE STEPS OF UNEMPLOYMENT GRIEVING

Ever heard of "The Five Stages of Grief" from Elisabeth Kübler-Ross's book, *On Death and Dying*, or seen the movie *All That Jazz*? If you feel like you're going through a similar mourning process, it's because you are. You're mourning your former employed self.

Those who find themselves suddenly out of work usually do go through some sort of grieving process to get over the shock of joblessness. The good news is, the unemployment grieving process has a much happier ending. It goes something like this:

1-Denial. Denial is fairly common for people who feel pressured to work constantly and feel unproductive if they're not. Some people lie to themselves; others experience such shame that even if they don't outright lie to family and friends, they conveniently fail to mention that they've quit or been laid off.

DENIAL
I'm not unemployed—I'm simply "between jobs."

ANGER
*That @&%$ employer! I never liked working there anyway. I hope that f****** organization goes under.*

2-Anger. Some people get angry about their predicament, lashing out at former employers, the economy, the government, or anyone else in range. Instead of embracing and enjoying time off, they expend a great deal of energy being mad at the world.

BARGAINING
I'll trade you half my old salary for my previous job.

3-Bargaining. Many try to bargain their way out of unemployment, either trying to hang on to their old job under less desirable circumstances or settling for a job that's beneath their abilities.

4-Depression. Depression afflicts the newly-unemployed more than any other emotion. Don't fall for it!

DEPRESSION
This sucks—I'll never find another job.

5-Acceptance. Acceptance is your goal if you want to get the most from your non-working time. It's a Zen mindset that will come fairly naturally when you've become versed in the Art of Leisure.

ACCEPTANCE
I'm at peace with my non-working status. Now, please pass the hookah.

DEALING WITH GUILT

Guilt is evil. Guilt is your enemy. Guilt stands between you and your happiness and could be your greatest obstacle in reaching time-off enlightenment. You must fight it off at all costs! We implore you, do not let it grab hold of your psyche; it can spoil an otherwise savory time of relaxation and self-fulfillment, and cause you to cut this precious time short.

Give yourself a break, both figuratively and literally. This is your time and your life. As long as you can maintain financial stability, you're entitled to do as you please. Transitional times are tough enough without assigning unnecessary and destructive blame.

AVOID THE COMPLEX

Guilt is one of the most common emotions associated with unemployment, says Rochelle Teising (www.rochelleteising.com), psychotherapist, life coach, and co-founder of the San Francisco-based consulting group Success at Work. "It's really hard for people to see the gift in not working," she says, "because they often think that they've done something wrong. They don't let themselves enjoy the time off."

Many of her clients try to alleviate this guilt by immersing themselves in their job search, not allowing time for leisurely activities, and driving themselves crazy in the process. Don't let that be you!

Liberate yourself from the "must-work" mentality and instead of berating yourself for your current status, congratulate yourself. *Sit* for a while. Celebrate your standing in the non-working world!

THE UNEMPLOYMENT TIME-SPACE CONTINUUM

The *Unemployment Time-Space Continuum* is a loosely formed concept that goes something like this:

* You will be late.
* You will forget non-essential appointments.
* You will be transported to an alternate parallel universe where...this is okay.

Time becomes much more fluid when you're not working, and you'll find yourself on a completely different clock. Don't be alarmed if you're convinced it's Monday when it's really Tuesday. A severe case will have you thinking it's a weekend when it's not—lucky you! Just don't expect any sympathy from your working friends.

It's also normal that you won't make it to every appointment or task that you set for yourself. The reality is, you don't *have* to do anything—at least not in a work sense—and human nature tends to breed apathy in the absence of necessity.

Again: this is okay. Don't get overly upset or feel guilty, but do monitor your personal flake factor. Skipping out on your friends or colleagues is hardly anything to aspire to during a sabbatical.

SLOW DOWN, YOU MOVE TOO FAST

If you want to truly break away from a set schedule, try telling your friends and others ahead of time that you're going off the clock for a bit, and not to expect immediate responses from you, or your presence at every gathering. Remember, there's nothing wrong with taking a break from social obligations in addition to work obligations, especially if your goal is to slow down your pace of life.

Speaking of slowing down, there's something of a movement afoot in this country and around the world. Advocates call it the Slow Movement, but we prefer to call it the "move at your own pace" movement. Carl Honoré, recovered "speedaholic" and author of *In Praise of Slowness: How a Worldwide Movement Is Challenging the Cult of Speed*, went through his own personal transformation to arrive at a more leisurely pace. "I just couldn't slow down," he told us. "I was speed reading *The Cat in the Hat* to my son. Then, while reading a newspaper at an airport, I saw a series of books called *The One-Minute Bedtime Story*—which is an appalling idea, but I was like 'Great! That's what I need.' And that's when I saw the lightbulb. As a journalist, the first step is to write, so I started writing about it." Sounds like the write stuff to us, but we're sometimes a bit slow ourselves.

GETTING OFF THE GRID

No, we're not talking about saving on electricity, but the concept of "unplugging" from a number of modern life's communications and conveniences. Technology provides us with a fantastic array of devices that enable us to stay connected to people and places like never before. But this technology can come at a price: an over-stimulation of media and messages, and ever-accelerating demands on our time from an increasing number of people. We're not just talking about work, either. Between cell phones, email, instant messaging and text messaging, our social lives can become a rapid-fire succession of stress-inducing stimuli.

John de Graaf, a Seattle-based author and television producer, runs an advocacy group called **Take Back Your Time** (www.timeday.org), organized to fight overwork and what they call "time poverty." "Technology is playing a factor in making lives busier around the world," says de Graaf. "It's all the more necessary to find ways to protect people's time off because you're on this electronic leash all the time."

Consider cutting the cord on some or all of this technology for a set period of time. Trust us, it's extremely refreshing. If you're packing up and hitting the road during your break (see **Chapter 4**), you may have no choice, particularly if you're traveling to some far-flung corner of the world. But even if you're hanging out in your own community, give it a whirl and see how it goes. The peace of mind you gain from not answering your cell phone or email for a few weeks (do we hear a month, anyone?) can be enough to recharge your batteries—and that's *personal* batteries, not cell phone batteries.

"One of the most refreshing breaks I ever had was when my girlfriend and I took a vacation, but then ended up not going anywhere," Dane Larson told us. "We actually didn't plan it that way, but at the last minute we decided not to travel, yet didn't tell any of our friends. It became an adventure—no phones, no email, no responding to messages of any kind for over a week. We just cruised around town and did whatever we wanted, whenever we wanted."

AFTER THE HONEYMOON

If you're like most non-employed people, it's been a long time since you've had your weekdays free. After a few weeks of waking up with boundless energy for carefree, pure enjoyment (the *Unemployed Honeymoon*), you might start to wonder what retired people do with themselves. You run the risk of losing motivation, getting too much sleep and (doh!) actually watching daytime television. Here are better options.

daytime specials

Weekdays suddenly free? Then you'll have plenty of time for court appearances (we know, they can really pile up). Challenge those parking tickets! Those who do are often rewarded just for showing up. Any small claims you'd like to collect? A pesky misdemeanor or two to clear up? Your local or state court can guide you through solving your "problem." (I drank. I fell down. What's the problem?) Even jury duty might become a weekday "to do." You can't really say no to it now!

Have you heard? Runs to the DMV no longer take up an entire afternoon. Make medical appointments, dental appointments, or any other appointment that you'd normally have to squeeze into your lunch hour, and cross them all off of your list.

When you run out of your own errands, take care of your friends and neighbors: pick up their dry cleaning, walk their dog, or watch their kids. You'll score big-time brownie points, and make some serious deposits in the favor bank. If they later offer to help you out by, say, buying you dinner, it will be more like reciprocation and less like charity.

Personal Maintenance

Ever wish you had a personal assistant? Now you do—yourself. Spend some time on your personal life maintenance. And no, we're not talking about manicures, pedicures or bikini waxes (ouch!), but activities that hopefully go a little bit deeper than the skin.

Start with getting "stuff" done. Clean the closets. Shine your shoes. Alphabetize the spice rack if you've been wanting to. Everyone keeps a running tally of "nice to do's" that aren't urgent but can stack up like dishes in a sink. Checking them off of your list will clear your mind (or at least the table!) for more advanced leisure pursuits.

Rob DeWaters multitasked his job-search time in front of the computer by digitizing his entire CD collection and portions of his friends' collections. The fruits of his labor amounted to over 40 gigabytes of music files and paid huge dividends more than two years later when the iPod was introduced to the market. That's a lot of burning, ripping, and otherwise organizing your love for music. "Investing the time that otherwise would have been spent at work allowed me to pull this off while simultaneously looking for a new job," Rob told us. "Alan Greenspan has no idea how productive the computer has made me!" Try tackling *that* project while you're working full-time.

Setting Goals

Once you've come down from the initial euphoria of your freedom from work, you may want to set some goals for yourself. Wait a minute, set goals? Whoa, you say, I didn't take a sabbatical so I could set goals. If this sounds a bit ambitious, keep in mind that worthy non-work goals can range from such lofty pursuits as travel or reading as many classics as possible, to hanging a hammock in the backyard—seriously, it takes several steps!

The point is—and you've heard the saying before—time flies when you're having fun. Before you know it, you'll be facing the prospect of work again. So outline what you'd like to accomplish, as grandiose or as simple as it may be, and prioritize your leisure.

For more on goal setting and exploring new directions, see **Chapter 7.**

PREPARING FOR CHALLENGES
Talking To Your Family

Families can be a real challenge when it comes to not working. Consciously or unconsciously, most families expect financial and career success of their members, and don't see taking time off as a way of furthering either.

Are your parents on your case? Maybe they were raised in an era when unemployment carried even more of a stigma than it does today. To their generation, work was a large part of a person's identity and it was uncommon to leave a job without having a new one. For the most part, that generation didn't face the level of layoffs and employee turnover that characterize today's

preemptive strike

One non-employed gentleman we know took the bull by the horns, as had always been his secret yen (you'll see...).

He was so tired of fielding questions on what he was doing for work and his plans for the future that, in anticipation of a friend's wedding, he drafted a one-page personal fact sheet. The sheet mockingly explained that he had left his last job to "pursue other interests," including his "dream to someday be a rodeo clown."

He handed out copies at the beginning of the reception, forcing everyone in attendance to focus on other areas of interest in his life—whether they wanted to or not! While it might not have dramatically changed anyone's opinion of him, he did manage to score a date with a cute coed.

working environment. Constant change became a way of life toward the end of the baby boom—the U.S. Bureau of Labor Statistics reports that people born between 1957 and 1964 changed jobs an average of 10 times by the time they were 36 years old. It's a new type of generation gap, one that can leave you feeling like a disappointment to your parents.

Being married can also make time away from work more stressful. Many who are not working fear that their spouses will see them as lazy or inept. Whether real or imagined, this perception can create barriers, conflict and even resentment between partners. "There's the stigma of job loss to deal with—will your spouse think you're a failure? Your kids? Your parents even?" says Peter Hannah (www.changingforgood.com), a one-time victim of technology layoffs who now counsels others on the topic as a trained therapist.

GREAT MOMENTS IN UNEMPLOYMENT

TAKING THE PLUNGE
Dan Briody was an account executive for Purdom Public Relations, a small high-tech PR firm in Northern California. In 1995, he informed his boss, Ned Purdom, that he was quitting his job and moving to Hawaii, with no plan and no job. Ned informed him he was committing career suicide. Briody's "career suicide" involved publishing the critically acclaimed bestseller *The Iron Triangle*, followed by *The Halliburton Agenda*, both about the Carlyle Group's business dealings with the Bin Laden family. Ned was then featured in Michael Moore's incendiary *Fahrenheit 9/11*. If this is suicide, sign us up!

"I personally shared more with my partner and less with my parents when I got laid off."

Add kids and your obligation to support them into the mix, and you could have a real disaster. "There may also be an internal drive to hide real-world problems from the kids, to try to insulate them," says Peter. "Kids are pretty wise though—the older ones figure things out, and the younger ones can sense that something is wrong."

Career counselor Rochelle Teising claims that communication within families is often poor during times of unemployment. Some of her clients who are laid off are so ashamed of losing their jobs that they keep it a secret! "The irony," says Rochelle, "is that these people need to connect with friends and family more than ever."

So, take your *family* to Leisure School! Explain to them your goals and intentions. Tell them why you're taking time off—even if it *is* largely to goof off. Your goal is to make them more comfortable with your non-employment, even if they don't necessarily agree with the concept, and to circumvent those awkward moments at the dinner table. For more about time off-in-the-family, see **Chapter 8.**

What To Say To Friends

Chances are, your friends will be more understanding than your family when it comes to taking time off. Ted Witt, a 35-year-old operations director, claimed that most of his friends were happy for him when he lost his job. "They knew I was miserable at work, and that I wanted to go and travel anyway," he says. "My parents, on the other hand, didn't quite see it the same way."

In many instances, though, even your true friends will think, "You should be working like me," or "When are you going to go out and get a job? *Coaster!*"

Don't let unemployment come between you and your friends; use it to re-connect. Not only will you have more flexibility but you'll be getting reacquainted with your non-work self—the self that your friends might have been missing. Eileen and Alexia had fallen out of touch after college but they picked up right where they left off after Alexia quit her demanding day-job. "Eileen's a mom whose free time is when her daughter's at school," Alexia told us, "so she's got a lot of good ideas about how to have fun during the day."

Being open with friends is the best way to combat any resentment. Without explanation, your friends could translate "not working" into "lazy" or "spoiled"—or both! They might jump to the conclusion that you have a large trust fund, for example, when in reality, you were smart with your money and saved. Or maybe you do have a leisure patron—offer to help find them one too! (See **Chapter 3** for tips on how.) Who knows, you might even convince one of them to join you on your Unemployed Odyssey!

♪ ...Tell me why, I don't like Mondays--tell me why!

~*Boomtown Rats*
"*I Don't Like Mondays*"

Mondays

Conventional wisdom holds that Mondays are the toughest day of the week for the working set. Yet, Mondays can be strange for the non-working, too. Others go off to work, but not you. Your weekend simply continues.

Nearly all of the people we spoke with who used to work nine-to-five experienced some sort of anxiety around Mondays. "Sometimes it's the best day and sometimes it's the worst day," says Dave Casuto, a human resources coordinator who was unemployed for six months. "It's the worst day because everyone's going to work, and you feel kind of useless. It's the best day because on Sunday night, you get that instinctive pang about work the next day, until you realize, 'Oh yeah, I don't have to go to work tomorrow.'"

Fiona, a software executive who quit her job to travel for a year, says the first few Mondays were the weirdest. "I was so used to waking up early that for about a month after I quit, my internal alarm clock was still going off at 6am. I would wake up with all this restless energy that I didn't know what to do with. What on earth do people do before 6am besides go to work?" Undaunted, Fiona set to the task of re-learning how to sleep in. Ah, the perks of leisure!

Turn what could be the worst day of the week into the best. Make it your bonus day. Go to your favorite café and read a good book. Partake in your preferred workout. Do whatever it is you care to do, and set the tone—or the tune—for the rest of the week.

Having free Mondays is not only okay, it's cause for celebration. Embrace it! Revel in it! If you can conquer the Monday Blues, you'll be well on your way to reaching a higher time-off plateau.

CURES FOR THE BLUES

Being on sabbatical can open up new worlds of freedom for you. Or, you might find yourself sleeping too much, missing appointments and letting your laundry pile up.

Beware! While we are all in favor of moving a little to the right on the *Unemployment Time-Space Continuum* (see p. 29), we do want you to *feel* like a million bucks, even if you don't actually have a million bucks.

Everyone's got a favorite cure for the blues. Working out is one. According to many experts, all forms of regular exercise combat depression, anxiety, stress, and sleeplessness through a massive release of the same chemicals in the brain that produce "runner's high" (see *Chapter 7* for fitness ideas). Taking responsibility for another living creature also works. "It's not for the faint of heart," Marsha Converse told us after getting a dog, "and it was a long-term commitment, but it got me out and about in the neighborhood every single day."

Rochelle Teising recommends music and dance, noting, "You cannot be depressed when you're dancing." Chinyan Wong changed her tune with new music. "I started listening to more classical music," she said. "My dad left his radio alarm clock in my bedroom which is set on the local classical station. It's actually a very gentle and soothing way to start the day."

And Rob DeWaters went to the beach once a week, weather permitting. "Seeing beautiful women in various forms of undress always had a way of keeping my spirits up," he quipped.

If you can't seem to break out of a funk, you might need some professional help. We can't make that call but mental health specialists can. They'll help you see the *Layoff Blues* for what they are—tired old tunes that you can do without.

"what do you do?"

??????????

This all too familiar inquiry haunts the leisure seeker. Perhaps no other question is more indicative of our workaholic culture. It might come during a first meeting at a cocktail party or from an uncle at your brother's wedding but it always implies the same thing: what do you do for *work*?

The "what do you do" question clearly subscribes to the tired old work-as-identity doctrine, implying that working is the one and only way of "doing."

"It's funny, when people ask me what I do," said Tess Roering during an extended break from work. "I always just say 'nothing,' which takes people a little bit by surprise."

Next time someone asks what *you* do, whether you're working or not, try out the following responses to help turn the tables:

Play ignorant.
"About what?"

Tout your favorite hobby.
*"I climb mountains.
How about you?"*

Get philosophical.
*"I enjoy life.
And what do you do?"*

Holidays and Special Occasions

Ah yes, the holidays. If ever a time was rife with societal and familial pressures, this would be it. You should be working, you should be dating, you should be marrying, you should be having kids! Whatever you should be doing, you should be doing it doubly over the holidays, making November through January the most challenging months for the non-working set.

According to counselor Peter Hannah, there's also financial stress to contend with. "Christmas is a time where we want to give gifts, where we may feel we need to match the gifts others give us. It's definitely an easy time to feel 'poor' when finances are constrained."

If you can avoid succumbing to traditional pressures, however, the holidays can actually be the best time to not have a job. Think about the bright side— stress-free Christmas shopping! (Or *reverse* shopping, see **Chapter 4**.) Leslie Gonsalves, a recruiter who was out of work for four months beginning one November, savored the holiday season. While her friends could take off only an afternoon here and there, she could shop every day, enjoying the company of a different friend each time.

And beware of special occasions. Birthdays and weddings can unite you with extended relatives and friends who'll want to know what you're "up to" or will toss you the infamous, "What do you do?" Because holidays and special occasions can be such trying times, we recommend these tactics to minimize the damage:

Stay Out of the Corner
Watch for family traps like the inevitable two-on-one gang-up. The minute you sense the conversation at the dinner table turning against you, bob and weave, anticipate and avert. Change topics quickly, and deflect questions about your time off by asking your own questions in return.

> *Your mother:* So, are you even *looking* for a job?
> *You:* Mom, this cranberry sauce is fantastic. Did you make it from scratch?

Be Proactive
The best defense is a good offense. Being the initiator means you won't get caught off guard and sound defensive. Have stock answers ready for questions about your transitional time, and offer information to head off awkward lines of questioning. It's the "nothingness" that makes people uncomfortable.

> *Transitioning between careers, or thinking about it?*
> —I'm taking a class.
> —I'm doing some research.
>
> *No such ambitions?*
> —I'm exploring my creativity.
> —I'm writing my memoirs.

Know Your Allies
Know who will rush to your defense in tight situations. Your protectors are usually the people who know you best, and they can help fend off the work-centric attacker from advancing within your comfort zone. Defense in numbers is almost always more effective than a solitary defense. Unite with the Leisure Team!

Losing Friends from Work
One potential side effect of being job-free is losing your friends from work. You could be surprised to discover that your relationships with these people you spent so much time with were bound by the job and not much else. This realization can be unpleasant, particularly if much of your social life was wrapped around your workplace.

"I had a hard time filling the social void after I quit," Fiona told us. "I had spent so much time on the job that my non-work relationships had all but disappeared."

Be prepared to confront this issue by making an extra effort to keep in touch with former co-workers. This is your chance to put more energy into friendships outside of work, too. (See **Chapter 8** for ideas.)

Too Much Sleep

Sleeping too much can leave you drowsy all day and lead to depression. Try to get up on the early side and start your day with something physically active to get your blood pumping. There's no need to imitate the army (you know—getting more done before 9am than most people do all day) but there's nothing wrong with getting one thing done early—wash last night's beer mugs, maybe? At least take a shower!

The January Effect

January is to the year what Monday is to the week. The holidays are over. Vacations have ended. People have gone back to work. This can be unsettling for the aspiring leisure seeker.

Although Leslie Gonsalves enjoyed having time off during the holidays, the opposite was true once January rolled around. Low on funds and with potential employers back at work, she no longer had any excuse to put off her job search efforts.

Stand fast and do not waver, for yours is a mission of quality of life, not of logging in as many work hours as you can. January can be the month to use your flexible schedule to set personal goals and decide how you want to spend your free time for the rest of the year.

Tailor your New Year's resolutions to what you want to accomplish over the coming months: pledge to transition to a new career by taking classes or applying to graduate school, for example, or just resolve to enjoy your time off!

SURPRISE!

Don't worry, time off also brings plenty of pleasant surprises. Besides being able to catch up with old friends, you'll feel more relaxed and you'll probably become a kinder, gentler person. Your refreshed demeanor can lead to many other subtle benefits, such as improved restaurant service, better rapport with law enforcement officials ("You don't really need to write me that ticket, do you officer?"), and smiles from strangers on the street.

HOW MUCH TIME?

Wondering how long to stay off the work clock? That's easy—as long as possible! If you have financial stability, peace of mind, and a good story to go with it, you can justify almost any length of time away from work. Employers are gradually changing their attitudes about extended breaks and that's something we can all be glad for.

Jamie Alfaro, a human resources specialist and professional recruiter for the past ten years, says that the amount of time off employers view as "acceptable" depends on the circumstances. "In a challenging job market," Jamie says, "hiring managers wouldn't even question a candidate whose job search took a

top ten accomplishments of the recently non-employed

10 Ann Marsh, a writer going through a career transition, went on more than 100 dates in six months, and found her man!

9 John Donnewald saw his son off to kindergarten every day and performed a self-scribed song with his daughter's 7th grade chorus in front of a live audience—to a standing ovation!

8 Leslie Gonsalves got her carpets as "clean as they've ever been" by cleaning them for *three days straight.*

7 Steve Friedman, a former software VP, furnished his entire vacation house— with furniture he built by hand.

6 Anastasia Shilling moved to the central coast of California and became the local "chocolate fairy."

5 Cheryl Beck sold a couple of scripts to a children's TV show taping near her home—which might lead to a full-time job.

4 Dana Magenau, on a one-year trek around the world, climbed some of the world's highest peaks in Africa, South America, and Asia.

3 Scott Phillips, on a partially paid sabbatical, moved to his wife's hometown in Prague for a year, road-tripping across Croatia along the way.

2 Nelson Hyde Chick wrote a novel; was awarded one patent and filed three more applications; and got a beagle, noting that people with dogs live three years longer, statistically speaking.

And the number one accomplishment of the recently non-employed...
[go on, flip the page!]

> **1** Marlo Sarmiento got hired as an independent contractor by his former employer for more money than he was making before he left, went scuba diving three or four days a week, completed his underwater photography portfolio, and won a photo contest sponsored by *Smithsonian Magazine*. **Congratulations, Marlo!**

year or more. In a red-hot economy, however, a candidate should have a very clear explanation for time off, and be able to talk intelligently about it."

In a stagnant economy, less than six months is almost self-explanatory. Between six months and a year, you should probably have a good story about why you haven't taken a job sooner.

Most employers consider travel a legitimate use of six months. Being able to afford your respite also sells well. Matt Green, a former software sales executive, says, "I always mentioned in interviews that I could afford to take time off. Once people heard that, they understood, and I also gained credibility that I had made a little money in my life."

After a year, according to most career experts, you'll be better off having either completed some kind of project or taken care of a medical or family situation. The bright side of taking a year off is that you'll be thoroughly rested for your next job. The challenge, if you simply enjoyed yourself while living off your savings, will be finding a compelling way to describe it.

THE PIGGY BANK

Did we mention savings? It's obviously a key factor. Don't give up too easily if you want to take a long leave but wonder whether it'll fly financially. Even if you have a financial goal beyond covering your cost of living—such as buying a house—set a minimum under which you won't let your savings drop, then enjoy yourself until then.

Whatever you decide, you will need to get a solid grip on your expenses—the fear of running low on cash or missing your financial goals can seriously bum your hiatus high. Read on for tips on how to cut costs, as well as generate some interim lounging lucre.

CHAPTER 3
FINANCE

Money frees you from doing things you dislike.
Since I dislike doing nearly everything, money is handy.
~ Groucho Marx

I have enough money to last me the rest of my life,
unless I buy something.
~ Jackie Mason

MONEY. Whether you can't get enough of it or think it's the root of all evil, probably no single factor troubles (or eases) the unemployed mind more. It's no fun to be off work if you're broke. If you're going to take time off, you're going to need some money—it's as simple as that.

In the best case scenario, financial planning for time off starts while you're still working. Saving money for a rainy day (or better yet, a sunny day!) is a critical step to enjoying your non-working time. That said, a budget will come in handy whether or not you were able to plan ahead. The first section of this chapter, **Finance 101**, covers these topics.

In the worst case scenario, unemployment comes unexpectedly and sticks you in a financial bind. Don't panic. Even if you have just a small financial cushion, there are many ways to maximize your standard of living without a steady paycheck. You can scale back your discretionary expenses and, with a little more discipline, cut some of your fixed expenses too. You can even reduce your tax bill! If you have debt, you can deal with it proactively. **Finance 202** covers all of these ways to "play defense" and conserve your cash.

Finance 303 gets to the offense: bringing some funds your way. We include information on an array of funding sources—from severance packages and unemployment insurance to odd jobs—plus information on loans, grants, and proceeds from selling your things.

Be prepared—this is one looonnnnnng chapter. Give yourself plenty of time to digest it. It's dense, but it's important, so cancel all your plans and get your slide rule handy.... No, not really, but if you do need a break, sneak a peek at the fun stuff in **Part Two: The Unemployed Odyssey.**

FINANCE 101

Planning & Budgeting

Most financial advisors recommend stashing three to six months' salary in the bank to protect against the unexpected. Gina Clark, a New York writer who used to teach in an inner city public school, followed that advice.

"My initial time off was definitely an 'employment divorce' and it has lasted a little over six months," Gina told us. "Fortunately, I was not completely unprepared for it and thus able to pay the critical bills."

Gold star for Gina! How much do you have? How much will you need?

Your sabbatical budget will depend on how long you want to take off and how you want to pass your time, especially if you want to travel. If you're currently unemployed, you'll need to know how long you can milk your savings. If you're a member of the *Aspiring Unemployed*, you will want to know just how long you'll have to save up before you can cut loose.

Libraries are full of good books on personal financial planning. Check out *Living Well On Practically Nothing* by Edward Romney, *Life or Debt* by Stacy Johnson, or the out-of-print but still priceless *Blindsided: Financial Advice For The Suddenly Unemployed* by Edie Milligan (available used at Amazon.com). Any of these resources can help you get a handle on your current spending, and each offers ways to cut back.

come to taxmama

If only personal financial planning could be as warm and fuzzy as a big hug from Mama. *TaxMama (www.taxmama.com)* says it can be!

In the words of Eva "Tax-Mama" Rosenberg, MBA, EA and author of *Small Business Taxes Made Easy*, here are the simple A-B-C-Ds of how-to planning for time off:

A Figure out your base living costs for a year. That includes your rent/mortgage, utilities, insurance, auto costs, and food and clothing costs.

B Decide if you're going to be renting out your home while you're away on sabbatical. (Most people go away that year.) And if you are, how much you really, honest-to-goodness expect to collect as rent.

C Find out what your travel costs will be for the whole family, including the costs of enjoying yourselves.

D Don't worry about taxes since you won't have any income (unless your employer arranges some kind of leave savings plan.)

what comes after "D" again?...

...still saving

Got it?

Now add A and C. Deduct the rent you'll collect, if any. The balance will be how much money you'll need for that sabbatical year.

Divide that amount by the number of pay periods between now and the beginning of the sabbatical. Round up and save just a little more each month.

Suppose it costs you $30,000 for your family's base expenses. And you expect to spend another $30,000 on travel and enter-tainment that year. Let's say you can rent the house out for ten months for $2,500 per month. You'll deduct $25,000 from $60,000 and only need to save $35,000.

Now, let's say that you want to take this time off seven years from now and you get paid twice per month, so you have 168 pay periods (7x12x2).

Divide $35,000 by 168 pay periods and that's only $208.33 per check. Save $225 per check and you'll have $37,800 when it's time to leave.

saving some more...

Six Months Off by Hope Dlugozima, James Scott, and David Sharp, is an excellent guide to planning a sabbatical. "Plan three months ahead for every one month you plan to take off," Hope told us. "So six months off would be eighteen months ahead." Then figure out how much you need, divide by the number of months before you leave, and set aside that much each month. "It comes down to a mathematical equation."

Yes, budgeting is fairly straight-forward—and kind of a snore. The good news is that the non-employed lifestyle costs less, so you'll be able to get by on fewer dollars than you usually spend. This begs the question: how much *do* you usually spend?

Start by journaling your expenses for a full month. Track every last dime you spend—on morning coffee, afternoon snacks, cab fares, movie tickets, non-network ATM fees, everything. Include your housing and utilities costs, and make sure you record those "invisible" debit card charges by saving your re-ceipts and tallying them up later. Save your credit card receipts too, and if you carry a revolving balance, budget for your minimum monthly credit card payments.

An Excel or Quicken spreadsheet can help show you where your money goes. You might also experiment with one of the free online financial calculators found at **Bankrate.com** (www.bankrate.com). Finally, even though it's a pain (and sometimes painful), remember to bal-ance your checkbook.

With your expenses laid out on the table, you should be able to figure out where you spend your money. The average household spends two-thirds of their income on housing, healthcare, utilities and transportation. The remaining third is where you most want to cut the flow of dollars from your wallet. If you're curious how you compare to average, check out these stats:

Spending Proportions of the Average American

Housing	28%
Groceries	16%
Healthcare	5%
Utilities	8%
Transportation	10%
Other	33%
TOTAL	100%

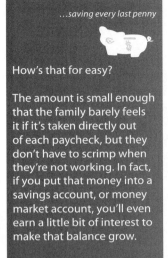

...saving every last penny

How's that for easy?

The amount is small enough that the family barely feels it if it's taken directly out of each paycheck, but they don't have to scrimp when they're not working. In fact, if you put that money into a savings account, or money market account, you'll even earn a little bit of interest to make that balance grow.

Note from Leisure Team
If seven years is just too darn far away, get even more frugal with our tips from *Finance 202* on how to cut back.

Separate the necessary expenses from the discretionary ones, which are usually the easiest to cut and make the biggest impact on your budget. But you can reduce even your fixed expenses, as we'll explain. Wouldn't you rather spend that money on entertainment? Make realistic decisions and then stick to your new non-work budget.

Easy to say, not always easy to do. "It's not like I left a six-figure job to start all over, but at times it has been frustrating," says Cheryl Beck, who decided she'd had enough of being in the wrong occupation and left an insurance job in Michigan with nothing lined up. She couldn't find the temp work she assumed she'd be able to, and didn't have a big nest egg either.

Still, she prefers the financial stress over the stress of being in the wrong job. "It's a different kind of stress worrying about money," Cheryl says, "but I'll take it any day over being where I was." Keeping your goal in mind will help too. "I usually find it hard to save money," Hope Dlugozima told us, "but when I was planning for my sabbatical, I found it really easy, because the reward was my freedom."

the roots of sabbaticals

The modern sabbatical has its roots in academia, where the concept of checking out of the classroom is common-place. Those madcap professors are at least smart enough to have figured out a way to regularly ditch work and keep their jobs!

• • •

The origin of the word itself refers to taking a year off from planting crops once every seven years, to give the ground a chance to lie fallow and regenerate itself. This was before the concept of crop rotation, clearly.

• • •

Although it's taking them a while to come around, corporate America is begin-ning to grant its blessing to the notion of taking an ex-tended break from the job. Consulting firm Accenture, for example, proposed a progressive sabbatical program called "FlexLeave." FlexLeave allowed certain employees to take up to 15 months off at 20% pay plus benefits, and guaranteed their jobs on return. While the program may have been created specifically as an alternative to layoffs, it represents the increasing flexibility employers are offering their employees.

All I Wanna Do...Is Have Some Fun!

You might be in a real financial crisis. It would be simple to say, "Cut all discre-tionary expenses," but here's the prob-lem: that's no fun.

Are you paying your mortgage with your credit card? Subsisting on rice and vegetables? Walking distances to rival Forrest Gump? If you don't see much humor in that, make sure you do find humor somewhere else. Now more than ever, you need a little fun.

"No doubt about it, you need leisure," says Cheryl Beck. "There were times we went out to eat and I thought, 'I could be using this money to pay a bill,' but I still had a sense of, 'There's more to life than saving for that next bill.' I've found other ways to do without."

Do not—repeat, *do not*—deprive yourself completely. Deprivation has a strange way of costing you extra in the long run. Budget a monthly amount, small though it might be, for entertain-ing yourself. The investment you make in keeping up your spirits will surely pay off by keeping you motivated for other tasks—like resolving the crisis!

Sabbaticals

All right, we won't be totally bohemian. Few would fault you for wanting to have income when you return from your time off adventure. If you have a job now and you'd like to keep it, con-sider negotiating for a sabbatical.

Gone are the days when the word "sabbatical" was used primarily to de-scribe the wacky university professor who needs a year overseas to research the mating habits of the Australian wombat. Many traditional companies now offer paid and unpaid sabbaticals to their employees. The Society for Human Resources Management's 2004 *Benefits Survey Report* found that of U.S. companies with 500 employees or more, 8% offered paid sabbatical programs while 28% offered unpaid leave. In certain high-burnout industries such as law, high-tech and consulting, the numbers are significantly higher.

If your company doesn't offer a formal program, consider negotiating some type of custom leave of absence. Collaborate with your employer to create a win-win OOTO* spree: work extra hours before you leave, arrange to job-share, accept reduced pay, or take an unpaid leave.

Hope Dlugozima recommends workers have all their ducks in a row before negotiating. "In almost every company, there's already an example where people take sabbaticals: they're called maternity/paternity leaves...the companies have learned how to lose even key employees for three months, and everything's fine. Use that as an example."

If you do get the green light, you can spend your time off in countless creative ways, from environmental volunteer programs in Antarctica to cooking schools in southern Italy. *Six Months Off* includes ample ideas on what to do during that cherished sabbatical.

*That's "out of the office," in case it's been a while.

FINANCE FUNDAMENTALS

Pay off as much debt as you can.
Build a cash reserve.
Line up several sources of credit,
in case you need emergency funds.

FINANCE 202

How To Cut Your Personal Burn Rate

Think of yourself as a company, with revenues and expenses as well as operating cash. When you stop working, your monthly revenue probably drops close to zero. You'll have to cut your expenses to make your operating cash last—which might sound strangely familiar to those of you who have worked at a struggling startup! This means reducing the cost of things you need, and cutting the expenses you don't.

"You need to reduce all the cost that you might have in the world going forward," Hope Dlugozima told us. "During that year [off], you can't be hitting your mortgage and your car payments, etcetera. It would be an unusual individual who could save so much money that they could live without salary for a year and also keep up the normal rigmarole, what you pay out."

Alas, since most perks will have to get the axe, start with the small conveniences. Do you really need a cell phone *and* a landline? With call-waiting on both lines? Could you brew your own coffee instead of paying to have it brewed for you? Your nearest library branch probably has your favorite magazines and newspapers, so freeze or cancel your subscriptions and spend some time amongst the stacks instead. Consider putting your gym membership on hold as well—get your exercise free by walking, biking, or running.

You get the idea. Each "convenience" charge may seem small on its own, but squandering two or three dollars here and there adds up over time. In fact, just add it up, literally. A cup of coffee and a bagel every day at $3.50 will cost you more than a thousand dollars over the course of a year. Wouldn't you rather have that cash for plane tickets and hotel rooms? "If I knocked out one $50 meal once a week," Hope said, "that equaled $2,600 at the end of the year. All those things had a way of accumulating—I mean $2,600, that pays for three months of living in Portugal."

Maria Prokop cut her expenses to a third of what she used to spend by going back to a paper calendar, ditching her cell phone, and switching to Internet dial-up. "Having no cell phone was a big thing," she told us, "but once I got rid of it, I would be somewhere where everyone has their cell phone and think wow, it's so nice not to have a cell phone! I'm not reachable by anybody.... I'm free!"

When you're feeling the pain of cutting back, call this truth to mind: every dollar of your savings that's spent on the luxury of convenience could be spent on extra time off instead. "Live like a monk," says Hope, "knowing like you're going to live like a vestal virgin during your time off."

TIME OFF TREASURE TIPS

Even if you've budgeted for three months off, you know you're going to run out of money at the end of Month Two. There's always something that bites you, like health insurance premiums. So while you're getting paid, open savings bonds that will mature at the same time you'll be off. Then you can take off and use them as a substitute paycheck. You can't defeat yourself because you can't make an early withdrawal no matter what.

At certain big banks, you can specify the date when your CD will mature. If you're going to be off from January through March, for example, buy CDs that mature every two weeks after you get back—April 15th, May 1st, May 15th and so on. You can also buy prepaid gas cards, prepaid grocery cards, even a prepaid Visa and stow them away in case you run out of money. Prepay for other bills before you go away. Pay everything times two. If you haven't already, set up online bill pay.

Be honest with yourself—if you have the cash, will you just go shopping? If yes, keep two bank accounts: one that you can access with a debit card but another that you can't get to unless you walk into the bank. Finally, open an account in the country where you're going to travel so that you'll have money when you get there.

COME TO TAXMAMA, TAKE TWO

Some cost-cutting measures go down easy. Others apply only in extreme emergencies—or to the crazier characters among us. Never fear, TaxMama is here to help us all. "I've guided people over the years toward being able to live on one income and stay home and raise their children, or how to eliminate their mortgage and one job—yet live at their present lifestyle or better," says Eva "TaxMama" Rosenberg. "I can even tell you how to be homeless and live well."

Here's her advice for another scenario, in her inimitable words:

You're single, renting and out of work. Before you do anything else, ensure a stream of income by immediately filing for unemployment insurance—or disability (if you're so traumatized that you're sick). Unemployment is taxable; disability isn't. You'd be surprised how many people think they're going to get a job right away and don't file for unemployment until months later. File first. Job hunt later.

Cut your housing costs immediately, too. Move out of your lodgings and in with family or friends in exchange for housekeeping and shopping chores or whatever other skills you might have. Or you can live in a van! Or van conversion. It's okay if it's slightly used, as long as it's in good condition. It's also okay if it's not too big, just so you're comfortable if you have to spend a lot of time in it. Use a long electric cord to plug into a different friend's electric lines each night. If you don't want to give up your home, get a roommate to pick up at least half of your housing costs. If you don't know someone, join a reputable roommate service or run an ad, and screen the person carefully. Usually the thing that really puts a person in financial *[bleep!]* is the rent or mortgage costs. The rest are manageable.

BATTEN DOWN THE HATCHES

Here's what else you do while you still have money and a credit card:

1. Buy an annual membership to a national spa or gym. Pay the extra cost to use it anywhere in the country, if need be. Now you always have a place to shower, clean up and blow-dry your hair. Cost: about $700.

2. Get a Costco or other major warehouse chain membership. The cheap one for the later entry is okay. After all, you're not working. What's your hurry? Cost: about $50.

   a. Now, if you've got nothing to eat, just show up here and haunt the sample ladies. You'll get lots of free food each day.

   b. As long as you have time anyway, you can arrange to do your friends' shopping for them—at a discount. You save them time and money by buying in bulk for two or three working people, and they buy your groceries.

3. Pay your auto insurance, paying extra for as much uninsured motorist coverage as you can get away with. That way, if someone else runs into you and they're under-insured, you still stand to get a lot of money. Besides, treat that car well, it may have to be your home for a while. Cost: about $1,000.

4. Buy an **Entertainment Book** (www.entertainment.com). Two meals for the price of one. Two shows for the price of one. Hotel/motel rooms, two nights for the price of one. Here's the deal: you go out with your friends to shows or meals and yours is free because of the coupons. There are enough good places that your friends will enjoy it and not feel like they've got to pick up your tab. Cost: about $25.

5. Dump your home phone. Get a good, cheap cell phone plan with voicemail. Who needs a landline anyway? Cost: about $600 per year.

   a. This way, if you have to leave your place quickly, everyone can still reach you. It would be great if it also had wi-fi so if you still have your computer, you could access the Web.

   b. If you can't maintain a computer and Internet costs while not working, that's not a problem. The public library will give you free access and a warm, dry place to stay during the day.

So, now your costs are under $2,400 for the year. You have TaxMama's Three Ss: sustenance, shelter, and shower—the three essentials of life. And of course, if you can't find a position in your industry of choice, have the good sense to take any job. To heck with your pride. You'll lose even more pride if you have to file bankruptcy. So, wash dishes or paint fences, but take a job until you can get back into your own career.

HOUSING

Running from one-quarter to one-half of the average American budget, housing is one area in which you can potentially save a bundle.

Reducing Rent

Are you a renter? If you've lived in your place for a while, get up-to-date on what market rents are in your area by checking comparable spaces in your paper or online. They tend to go down as residential vacancies go up.

In a renter's market, many landlords will reduce rents when asked—some even without being asked. If your landlord isn't one of them, consider moving, especially if your place isn't subject to rent control. With a large amount of vacant properties, you have a solid chance of finding one that's cheaper. Shaving even $100 off your $1,000/month rent could stretch your housing budget from nine months to ten. That's a full extra month of housing leisure!

Bunking up is another way to get creative with your housing. "I live in an incredible apartment, I have a roommate, I have three rooms to myself, and I only pay $750," says urban-dweller Maria Prokop. Check out **EasyRoommate** (www.easyroommate.com) if you're looking for a room or have one to rent, or the housing-friendly **Craigslist** (www.craigslist.org).

Lowering Your Mortgage Payment

If you're fortunate enough to own your home and you've yet to refinance in the last few years, run—do not walk—to a lender to find out about refinancing. Mortgage rates are just off their lowest levels since the 1960s, but they're not likely to stay down for long.

Talk to a lender to get an idea of whether or not refinancing will save you money. If you already have a reasonably low rate but your budget is still stretched, consider a variable rate. This type of refinancing might mean you

mortgage mulligans

If you can present them with proof that you can pick up where they left off, the Department of Social Services in your state might help you catch up with your mortgage and utility payments by making a one-time-only, lump sum payment to you or your lender (or utility company).

Government grants issued through local charities can do the same.

Each requires that you show you have no other funds available, including a second mortgage lender (if you own a home).

only break even in the long run but it can reduce your payments now, when you really need the extra cash. You might also consider a cash-out refinance (see **Finance 303** for more details).

Buying a House Without Income

On Day Two of home ownership, Maureen Brown bought her first piece of hardware—a socket cover for forty-two cents. She kept the receipt in case it was the wrong size. "I need the forty-two cents," she said.

Needless to say, with zero income, you'll probably need savings to be able to purchase a home, but it can be done. When the building Maureen was living in came up for sale, she joined forces with her neighbors and bought it. She had enough savings to put down 25% plus cover the points and all the closing costs for the entire tenancy-in-common (TIC) partnership.

"With enough down, the lenders don't seem to care if you're not making any money," Maureen told us. Although her mortgage payments now consume almost 80% of the pay from her interim job, her down payment—combined with a superb credit report and the stated income of her partners ("who are not what I would call filthy rich")—allowed the TIC to take advantage of their lender's best rates.

Moving Home With Mom and Dad

The drawbacks of moving back in with your parents are obvious: living under someone else's roof requires a sacrifice of a little independence and a lot of privacy. Still, it can save you a lot of money. "It doesn't mean you are automatically spineless and still a Mama's boy or girl," says Chinyan Wong, who moved to Hong Kong to live with her parents after graduating from college in Boston. "Mama's chicken broth—or insert comfort food of choice—might just be the booster you need for trying times."

> **there's no place like—mom & dad's?**
>
> When Mary Mangold realized that she was running out of savings, her bills were looming, and no jobs hovered on the horizon, she decided to move home. "I was back in my old room with that ugly carpet and the horrible drapes that haven't changed in fifteen years," she said at the time. "I kept thinking, 'It's only going to last a month,' so I kept all my stuff in storage, but it's been over a year now and still counting."
>
> The renter's market eventually rescued Mary; she's back in a one-bedroom apartment—at the same rent as she used to pay for a studio.

If you're heading back to the nest yourself, prepare for some "casual" yet prying questions from your parents, particularly after you've spent a night out. Beware too of regressing to childlike and dependent behavior. Is your mom doing your laundry again? Your dad paying your phone bill? As well-intentioned as they are, Mom and Dad can sap your drive to find work by making it too easy not to. You might want to keep track of any parental subsidies so you can pay them back later.

On the other hand, you might treasure the chance to spend quality time with your folks, especially if you've been living far away from them. "Moving back in was much to my mother's happiness," Mary Mangold said. "She never liked the idea of my moving away in the first place." Having someone to lean on financially might be just the break you need to stay afloat during your time off.

House Sitting

Picture all the empty houses lonely for their owners on vacation. Tugs on your heartstrings, doesn't it? Then make yourself known as a house sitter and console those companionless homes. "I put the word out that I was available," Eliza said, after quitting her dead-end job. "I called every homeowner I knew, and every friend of my family's. Now I'm at eight months going on nine, and living large in some extravagant homes."

JANTI'S HAPPY ISLAND

Think you have to be rich to have your own island? You need only as much as your imagination will afford. Janti loved his bar on Union Island in the Caribbean but had to admit it was a little too far from the yachts for the business to keep him afloat. Yet he refused to be sunk. As a member of the local tourist office's environmental team, he'd been asked to clear the unsightly mounds of empty conch shells littering the beach. Dirty beach...bar too far away... Putting two and two-thousand together, Janti decided to ship the shells—boatload by boatload—to a dead and shallow part of the outer reef. He stacked them up there, and voila! A new island, for only $1,500 and a bunch of old snail shells. With a little cement and a lot of work, Janti built a new bar on his new island and christened it Janti's Happy Island. Now dinghies pull up every night to sample his tasty and inexpensive rum punch. Some stay for a meal of barbecued lobster, served with a clear view all the way to Palm Island. It may be the smallest inhabitable island in the world, but it is also one of the most content—and comfortably profitable.

The **Caretaker Gazette** (www.caretaker.org) is a monthly newsletter that lists ski lodges, farms, resorts and other destinations that need house sitters and are willing to pay you to care for the dwelling, usually in the off-season. If you have a shareable place of your own, partake in the give and take of **GlobalFreeloaders** (www.global freeloaders.com). "I signed up for that," beach dweller Dane Larson told us, "and have been getting tons of inquiries to stay at my house from people in the U.S. and abroad. Pretty cool thing, actually. It's a great way to meet people from all over the world."

Find more on overseas house sitting gigs in **Chapter 4**.

FOOD
Definitely one of the necessities of life.

Cooking at Home

"Dining out—forget about it! That's like way expensive," says Hope Dlugozima. Indeed, cooking at home can save you a lot of money. If this is not a new idea to you or you're already on your way to becoming a celebrity chef in your own right, guess who's coming for dinner!

If you've had the inclination to cook but haven't had the time until now, this is the time to feed that desire (pun intended). At the extreme, someone who's used to having an expense account or in the habit of eating on the run might spend upward of $1,000 a month on food. Eating every meal out, buying a couple of coffee drinks each day, and chipping in for cocktails with your friends can add up to a per diem of $50+, which might easily be as much as or more than your rent.

Shopping for your own food and cooking it at home can trim the fat from your food bill. See if you can match Marlo "The Balinese Gigolo" Sarmiento, who spent only $25 a week on food when he was in law school. That's less than the tip you might leave for a single dinner at a Zagat Top Ten restaurant, a potential savings of $9,000+ a year. Now that's food for thought!

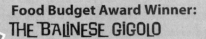

Food Budget Award Winner:

THE BALINESE GIGOLO

Marlo Sarmiento ate on $25 a week by buying multi-purpose ingredients and catching his own fish. "Hey, if the people from the Mediterranean have been thriving on anchovy and sardines for millennia, why can't we?" he asks, noting that no license is required to fish off many public piers.

Marlo's weekly grocery bill included a $3 bag of rice ("not the Uncle Ben stuff"), $4 on ground beef or tofu, $2 on dry pasta, a $1 can of whole beans (pinto or kidney), $3 on fruit, $3 on onions and garlic, $3 on canned and fresh tomatoes, $2 on tortillas, $3 on cheese, and a buck on miscellaneous spices and peppers.

With minimal investments in a crab net ($25), a rice cooker, a crock pot, and a cheap rod and reel set—Marlo enjoyed a varied diet of spaghetti with fresh seafood sauce, fish tacos and burritos, chili, and seafood stir fry. "Supplement with fresh fruit as needed," Marlo says.

Marlo recently spent three years living and working in Saipan, getting three eggs a day from his chickens (Humu-humu, Nuku-nuku, and Apua'a) and tending to his coconut, papaya, and mango trees. "Fresh fish—yellowfin, wahoo—all for two dollars a pound," he reported. "Life is grand."

Drop Marlo a line for his recipes: *balinesegigolo@hotmail.com*

Food Shopping

Even if you already cook at home, you can save more through judicious grocery shopping. Avoid the high-priced specialty grocers, shop with a list to curtail impulse purchases, and escape huge markups on cleaning products by making your own, or even by shopping at a discount at a janitorial supply company.

How about farmers markets? Meals were a group effort not so long ago, when households shared refrigerators and stoves, and communal food-buying is enjoying a renaissance today. Farmers markets offer fresh produce, open-air shopping and a casual place to socialize with your neighbors and the people who grow your food—not to mention the samples.

In the main search bar at **Recipe*zaar** (www.recipezaar.com), click on "Advanced," then select "Inexpensive" from the "Other" drop-down menu, and hit "Search" for more than 12,000 ways to make home-cooking even more affordable.

Budget Beveraging

Between mixed drinks, coffee drinks and bottled mystery waters, the beverages you consume can start consuming you, or at least your pocketbook. Save a few dollars through judicious imbibing.

It doesn't take heavy analysis to conclude that alcohol feeds you a lot of empty calories at a high expense. No need to teetotal—just partake a little less, or start your happy hour at home. When you're out, learn to nurse a single mixed drink all night or explore your affinity for warm, a.k.a. long-life, beer. Think of it as a survival skill that could come in handy if you return to a job that includes frequent office parties: while others become loose-lipped after too many cocktails, you'll be a model of decorum, and all ears for taking in intriguing inside information. If one drink per night is a little under your normal quota, let your employed friends pick up a couple of rounds—you can always even things out at a later date.

Are you addicted to caffeine? Do you spend $10 a day ($300 a month!) on coffee drinks? You'll have more energy, more money and probably better health if you drink water instead. Skip the energy water, electrolyte water and other fitness drinks. Carry a water bottle, and fill it up with purified water at the local market. Or drink straight from the tap if the quality is good. Filters for your sink transform tap water into something potable for a small one-time fee. That's something any budget beverager can be glad for.

Oh, okay, okay. Buy some beer or wine for drinking at home—as long as you shop wisely for it. **Trader Joe's** (www.traderjoes.com, 800-746-7857), the original home of Two Buck Chuck, has stores in twenty states and is growing fast. Stock up with some selections from their inventory of perfectly fine wines, then you won't have to stop by the pricier corner store on your way to a dinner party.

HEALTHCARE

Health Insurance

With healthcare costs on the rise and health insurance costs soaring even faster, it might be time to consider whether you need all the HMO bells and whistles. If you're lucky enough to be in good health, look into "major medical" plans offered by providers such as Blue Cross or Health Net. These plans come with a high deductible—up to $5,000 a year—and you'll have to pay for incidental checkups and prescriptions yourself, but you'll have the peace of mind that you will not have to deplete your own savings or bankrupt your family should some major accident befall you. Depending on your age, health and location, individual major medical plans can cost well under $100 a month for both medical and dental coverage.

COBRA

Continuing healthcare coverage through your former employer's plan falls at the other end of the cost spectrum. COBRA, or the Consolidated Omnibus Budget Reconciliation Act (simply rolls off the tongue, doesn't it?), is the federal law that allows you to stay insured through your former employer for up to 18 months. The bad news is that you'll have to pay the premiums yourself, and they're usually expensive. The good news is that you have 60 days to decide whether you want to enroll. Within that period, coverage is retroactive—if you get sick on day 59, you can activate COBRA and be covered that same day.

If you're confident that you'll have a new job and therefore new health benefits within two months, you might skip paying for COBRA. But if you're not so sure, or if you're going to be traveling out of the country (yeah!), don't wait. It's also not a good idea to wait if you have any preexisting conditions—a new insurer can refuse to cover treatment for that condition for up to a year if you can't prove that your coverage was continuous.

If you do elect for COBRA, you'll be legally entitled to health coverage through another company when your COBRA coverage expires, even if that same company refused to insure you before.

Community Health Clinics

Look for a clinic in your area. Most offer primary healthcare as well as specialties, and welcome everyone who walks through the door. While they can't treat emergencies like broken bones or severe bleeding, they can provide you with referrals and community resource information.

Staying Healthy

Various sources estimate that each dollar spent on prevention saves between three and seven dollars in treatment costs. Does that mean if you spent another $10 on prevention, you'd spend $20 to $60 less overall? That's how the math works, anyway. Yet prevention accounts for only three cents of each healthcare dollar spent in the United States. See if you can't save money by keeping yourself educated, preventing illness by clean living (yes, we mean flossing every day!), and staying in shape (see **Chapter 7**).

UTILITIES

Utility costs might not eat up a real big chunk of your budget but they can add up. So change a few grooves and save a few quid.

Shut off your cable subscription for a while and watch TV at a friend's instead, or offer to run a daytime errand for someone who's willing to tape your favorite show for you. Same goes for that new TiVo system. Save on your electricity bill by turning out the lights when you're not home. Turn off your computer when you're not using it. Avoid text messaging charges on your cell phone by sending emails instead.

Live without a cell phone for a while, or think about how to combine it with your landline to better advantage. Most major cell phone service providers offer plans that let you call long distance within their nationwide "network" at no extra charge. Make your long distance calls on the cell and all your local calls from home, or make long distance calls only when the rates are at their lowest. Or, if you're feeling crafty, call when you know your friends are out so the call-back will be on their dime.

The U.S. Department of Energy proposes countless energy and water saving tips at the site for their **Office of Energy Efficiency and Renewable Energy** (www.eere.energy.gov, click "Information for Consumers" and then choose the "Energy Savers Online Booklet"). It's pretty comprehensive, and full of choice persuasive suggestions; installing a low-flow showerhead, for example, saves enough to provide drinking water for one person for an entire year.

low income *is* low income...

If you're not generating much income (a strong probability when you're not working), you might qualify for reduced rate programs for phone, gas and garbage.

The income cutoff for these programs was $19,600 in 2003 and is adjusted each year to reflect changes in the average cost of living. If you qualify at the beginning of the year but end up earning more than the income cutoff, you'll owe the difference between the regular rate and what you already paid.

If you need one-time help to pay utilities, contact *The Salvation Army* (800-933-9677) and ask about their REACH program: Relief for Energy Assistance through Community Help. When you're back in the green, you can help your neighbor by making a tax-deductible donation.

Internet Access—Wired

There are any number of places to log on these days, which can help you stay in touch with email pals or apply for jobs online (but only if you have to!). You can pay by the hour via wired terminals provided in various cafés and hotels.

However, we prefer our rates a little cheaper, as in gratis; complimentary; on the house. Free wired access isn't prevalent but it does exist.

If 15-20 minutes will do ya, stop by a public library or look for a café that offers brief access with a purchase. If you get lucky and no one's waiting, your briefly-free minutes can go on indefinitely.

Many computer appliance stores, such as CompUSA and Apple stores, offer untimed, unrestricted, free wired access—just be prepared to wait in line behind the local high schoolers.

Internet Access—Wireless

Wireless access, on the other hand, is easier to obtain for free. Where it's not free, it's generally less expensive than wired—as low as $5 a day for drop-in usage or $20-$30 a month for a remote subscription plan. Beware though of locking yourself in for a year or more to get those rates.

Broadly speaking, wireless access is to Internet service what cell phones are to phone service—you're connected "over-the-air" versus over a physical line. To access it, your computer needs to be equipped with a wireless card, which you can procure for $50 or so (if it's not already built in). You can then either pay for your own wireless "receiver" and subscription plan, or you can access someone else's.

More and more cafés, bookstores and hotels share their wireless subscriptions with their customers at no charge, with new hot spots cropping up every day in heavily populated places such as airports, train stations, libraries, marinas, convention centers and hotels. Other venues do charge for the services provided by ISPs such as **Wayport** (www.wayport.com), **Deep Blue Wireless** (www.deepbluewireless.com), **Boingo** (www.boingo.com), or **T-Mobile** (at the ubiquitous Starbucks, www.tmobile.com).

Wi-FiHotSpotList.com (www.wi-fihotspotlist.com) charts zillions of cafés and hotels that offer wireless access—some free, some for a fee. The hot spots catalogued at **Wi-Fi Free Spot** (www.wififreespot.com) are all free, all around the world. The truly intrepid can scout for signals elsewhere with the right equipment, or even share a wireless subscription with neighbors. This might not be kosher with the Internet provider involved, mind you; we're just saying it's been done.

What's even cooler, and definitely legal, is remote printing via PrinterOn's **PrintSpots** (www.printeron.net). It's priced by minute of printer time. For printing short docs on the run, it sure beats the fees at the local copy shop!

TRANSPORTATION

In this category more than in others, saving money means spending time; the faster you want to get there, the more it'll cost. Slower-paced travel does offer advantages beyond saving money, though. You get to enjoy the fresh air and even get some exercise. You might help keep the sky a little cleaner, too.

Drive Less

Gas is expensive. Insurance is expensive. Parking tickets—we won't even go there. Add in car payments and maintenance, and it becomes clear that giving up a private car could fund many extra months of free time. If you're really dedicated to cutting every cost and you have a car, sell it.

Does the mere thought of being at home without wheels give you the jitters? Then check out car-share programs or talk to a friend or neighbor about sharing a car. With a little planning and good communication, you can create your own car-share plan. Or simply drive less. "I got more choosy about when and where I drove," says Cheryl, who spent her downtime in the country on the edge of Metro Detroit. "If I could consolidate errands, I might save five dollars—then I had five dollars to go out for an inexpensive something-or-other."

Perhaps you won't be sticking around town. You car might still need a home while you are away from yours. "Lend your car to a carless friend while you're gone," Hope Dlugozima suggests. "They pick up the car payments during those months."

DITCHING YOUR CAR

No, we're not talking about launching your old clunker off a cliff Dukes of Hazzard-style (not that that wouldn't be really cool), but donating your tired old vehicle to charity (see "Charitable Donations" p. 71). Zillions of non-profits will take it off your hands. Locate them or get assistance with the paperwork through *America's Car Donation Charities Center* (800-237-5714, www.donateacar.com).

Cab Less

Door-to-door service without the hassle of parking is hard to forego, especially when it's cold or after an evening out. But cabs are pricey. If you're not late for an appointment and you don't need a cab for safety, try another form of transport. When you are time-rich and money-poor, it doesn't matter so much if you get home a half-hour later by bus.

Use Public Transportation

In addition to individual transit providers, a couple of online resources tie together the seemingly fragmented public transit network. Although most are geared toward commuters, there's no reason excursionists can't also take advantage of their free commute consultation service. For really long-distance trips, call **Amtrak** (800-872-7245, www.amtrak.com) or **Greyhound** (800-231-2222, www.greyhound.com) and leave the driving to them.

Bike More

Since you've got more time on your hands (and feet), why not use them to ride a bike instead of driving? You'll save money on gas, and the extra exercise will help keep you fit. Look for official bicycle lanes and talk to regular bikers to discover the best local bike routes.

For longer journeys, you can combine a bike with other public transportation. Check with your local transit authorities to see which buses are equipped with bike racks. Cyclists should be prepared to load and unload their own rides. Many light-rail or train lines allow bikes too, on designated bike cars.

Walk More

Pick your town's most commercial streets to explore and you might find that you can get all your errands done without the hassle of looking for parking, instead enjoying the pleasure of strolling leisurely past storefronts. The fitness benefits are an added perk. Find ideas on all things related to getting around on your own two feet at **The Walking Site** (www.thewalkingsite.com).

OTHER

Not all of the expenses that fit into the "other" box are truly discretionary, but most dining and shopping expenses are. Adopting frugal habits when it comes to entertainment and purchases will save you from having to cut them out completely.

Replace Expensive Outings With Activities That Are Free

No doubt, eating out fits nicely into a busy schedule and can also be fun. You can meet up with friends, have a bottle of nice wine, talk about how the stalwart steakhouse that's been in your neighborhood for generations has real staying power in a world of fly-by-night Asian-Fusion-Americana-homestyle wanna-be's....

Or, if your life is now moving at a slower pace, you can entertain at home. Banish the image of chomping a bowl of cereal in the kitchen and morph that vision into a potluck dinner party with good friends, listening to music and drinking the bottle of fine wine that your guests have generously provided. Your friends will probably thank you for setting a low-cost trend. Plus, you'll have that much more incentive to keep your house clean.

As far as the music goes, see if you can't borrow the latest Moby CD from the library before you go out and buy it. Guess what? You can borrow cookbooks there too!

Throwing your own party is just one way to entertain yourself inexpensively. For evening events, look for house parties instead of bars. Skip expensive concerts in favor of free music in the town square or local parks.

Want *more* fun yet frugal action? Find plenty of ideas in **Chapter 4**.

Let Others Pay

Maureen Brown wasn't used to going on expensive outings after losing her job (especially after her savings were depleted to buy a house!) so when the bill came for a sushi dinner with an out-of-town friend, she told us she "looked at it and felt sick." Her friend offered to pay. "I said 'No, I'll pay,' but inside I was thinking, 'Oh god, yes, yes, please pay!'" He did.

Don't be afraid to skip the suspense when your friends offer to pay. Just say, "Thanks, I'd appreciate that," and make a mental note to return the favor when you can. Same with Mom and Dad—if they want to treat you once in a while, let them. If you're unemployed and asked out, we think it's perfectly acceptable to let your date pick up the tab, men and women alike. This is the new millennium, after all.

If you're married and your spouse agrees to support you, go with it. Mike Norman from Minnesota did—it was one of the best decisions he and his wife made after he lost his job. "Thankfully for us, my wife had developed a decorative interior painting business over the past three years on a part-time basis and it had been ramping up quickly prior to my being involuntarily separated from the company," Mike told us. "While I looked for work and collected unemployment benefits, she busted her tailbone to bring in money to cover the majority of the bills. I must say, she did a great job at that."

Spend Less On What You Do Buy

What's that you say—no discretionary funds? Don't deprive yourself completely just because your income isn't stable. And remember that shopping doesn't necessarily mean buying. Pick some lower priced items, such as music or books, and do a lot of looking before buying. Buy things on sale or secondhand. Go to garage sales (or sidewalk sales, or estate sales). Be aware of when you're shopping not for things but for instant gratification, and avoid major purchases for now—that's right, no plasma TV.

buy nothing day

You can try Spartan living on for size on the Friday after Thanksgiving, which was designated first by the British and then by the world as "Buy Nothing Day"—a day to either shop less and live more or to "conga against consumerism." www.buynothingday.co.uk

Patronize the retailers who offer the best values on items in the unemployed budget. If you do find yourself needing a major appliance (a vacuum cleaner, say), look for places that offer refurbished appliances, which often come with a limited warranty. They can cost less than half as much as new ones.

DEALING WITH DEBT

Unemployment isn't always fun and games, and pressing financial burdens can make it especially grim. You may be a careful shopper now, a master of frugal living, but your past money transgressions will come back to haunt you. Take them in stride, don't fall back into bad habits, and deal with them head on.

If you have debt but purchased unemployment protection insurance from your credit card carriers way back when, now would be a good time to file a claim. If your debt is still oppressive, you might find **Nolo** (www.nolo.com) a valuable resource. Nolo publishes Robin Leonard's *Money Troubles: Legal Strategies to Cope with Your Debts*, among other self-help legal titles, plus they are just good friendly people. Other organizations can help you alleviate financial strains or avoid financial crisis altogether (see below for some leads).

Avoiding Debt

The easiest way to get out of debt is, of course, not to get into it in the first place. As obvious as this may sound, most Americans spend 10% more than they make, and then spend 14% of what they make servicing their debts. Servicing debt without generating income can be a juggling act, especially if you weren't expecting to be out of work. If you're under a mountain of financial liabilities, you're definitely not alone.

But you can't afford to be average when you're not working, so first and foremost, control your credit cards. Adopt some simple habits—pay card balances in full each month, setting aside enough money in your prospective budget to cover each purchase.

If you must make a major purchase while you're unemployed, budget and save for it *before* you make it, not after. The **Consumer Credit Counseling Services** (800-873-2227, www.cccsintl.org) can help you with debt management and other financial matters via phone, the Internet, or at one of their free or low-cost workshops. **Debtors Anonymous** (www.debtorsanonymous.org) meets all over—to find out exactly where, click on "Find a DA Meeting."

Reducing Debt—Consolidation

Consolidate your debts if you can. A home equity loan can be a great way to go as it can come with the added benefit of a tax write-off. Another option is to transfer high-interest rate card balances to lower-rate cards. The average American's credit card debt is $8,500. Letting this big of a balance revolve can cost you a seven-course dinner every month, depending on your rate (and your taste in wine). This is lost money that could be paying down your debt (or financing your enjoyment of a succulent foie gras washed down with a '97 Cab).

To reduce debt most efficiently, focus on paying off the highest rate debt first. Make minimum payments on everything else until that entire loan is paid off. Then move to the next highest rate, and so on.

If you have good timing, you can float debt with teaser rates, transferring balances from card to card. Many credit card companies now offer 0% introductory rates for a set amount of time—consider transferring your balances to one of these cards, keeping in mind that the rate will jump up after the introductory period. Be forewarned, however: if you do this too often the card companies might catch on; plus, you can damage your credit rating by opening too many new accounts.

On the other hand, your credit rating might be the least of your concerns, in which case we'll just note that federal interest rates are near a 40-year low—which means that other interest rates are low too—and likely will be for a while.

Reducing Debt—Negotiation

Americans carry consumer debt like no others. In true American fashion, entrepreneurs have capitalized on this by creating companies and services to get people out of the very debt that other companies helped get them into.

Debt reduction service providers will negotiate with creditors on your behalf to try to reduce your debt to 55-60% of what you currently owe, but you'll have to give them a cut of what they save you. If you're a good negotiator, you might try calling your creditors directly and negotiating with them yourself.

Consumer credit counselors can also help you negotiate away some of your debt—but unlike debt reduction servicers, credit counselors generally work for your *creditors*, not for you. If you decide to go this route, look for a non-profit agency such as Consumer Credit Counseling Services (see previous page), which offers counseling for a sliding-scale fee.

Credit counseling has its pros and cons. Some lenders view it negatively and won't lend to people who've recently used it. Other lenders are neutral. Some even see it as a positive, figuring that you're at least taking a proactive approach instead of passively defaulting. The company that created the most widely used credit scoring formula ignores credit counseling, observing that consumers who use it pose the same risk of default as those who don't. Since bankruptcy (the more extreme alternative) is *universally* considered a negative, credit counseling is worth looking into.

Erasing Debt—Bankruptcy

You've probably heard that declaring bankruptcy can damage your credit rating—while you might solve some short-

the negotiator

Marina Sarmiento highly recommends trying to strike a deal when you can't pay what you owe.

"I've been out of work a bunch of times," says Marina. "At first, I couldn't pay my bills. Then I started negotiating with my creditors. I felt good about it. At least I was doing something."

Marina points out what the creditors know too: if they don't negotiate with you and you're forced to declare bankruptcy, they'll probably get just a small fraction of what you owe them. They also know that a collection lawsuit against you would be time-consuming and costly.

Faced with these realities, savvy creditors will entertain reasonable offers.

It's worth a shot!

term financial problems, future landlords and lenders will be able to see "bankruptcy" on your credit report for up to ten years. But do you know all of your bankruptcy options? The bankruptcy code's Chapter 7, the "liquidation bankruptcy," (not to be confused with **Chapter 7** of this book, which is about rediscovering yourself, and is a lot more interesting) allows debtors to walk away from their debts only after handing over all of their assets to a trustee, who will sell them and divide the proceeds among the creditors. The code's Chapter 13, however, the "wage earner plan," allows debtors to continue to own and operate a freelance consulting business. That could come in handy for the self-unemployed.

Find more free information online—from the free advice folks! **FreeAdvice** (www.freeadvice.com, select "Bankruptcy Law") answers such important questions as, "Can I go to jail for filing bankruptcy?" You want to check right now, don't you?

Consider your options carefully. If you need a lawyer, most state bar organizations can point you to certified referral services. Although they cannot themselves refer you to a lawyer, they can tell you whether the one you have found has the required bankruptcy specialty certification. Most local and county bar associations have lawyer referral programs. **Weblocator** (www.weblocator.com) can also help you locate attorneys, and even legal research in some areas.

TAXES

Below, we pass on selected general tax information (found on official websites or from the experts we consulted) that seems—to our novice eyes—to be specific to the unemployed, self-employed or self-*un*employed. We also point out a few national organizations that will gladly accept your charitable contributions, should making them be on your agenda. This information is certainly not exhaustive and it may have changed by the time you read this, so please confirm with the powers that be that you're doing everything right.

What's Taxable

You, like Odd Todd (read his story in **Finance 303**), might receive gifts or donations when you're unemployed, and you might be relieved to know that they are generally not taxable. Unemployment insurance payments are, however, and what's more, your state's employment development department will report them to the IRS. Most state unemployment offices will withhold federal taxes from your unemployment check, if you want, which can save you an unpleasant surprise at tax time. On the other hand, you can increase your cash flow now by planning to pay a lump sum later on.

Also taxable is all bartering "income" and self-employment income if you've earned more than $400 of it. Self-employment tax isn't easy to calculate—it's an "above the line" deduction and you'll owe higher-than-normal social security and Medicare taxes, but then you can deduct them as business expenses.... Good luck with it!

What's Deductible

"Attend tax planning seminar" might not top your to-do list but you might learn something worth your while. Some are even free! Mike, a Lake Tahoe real estate agent and "alpine specialist," came back wide-eyed from one such seminar saying, "Everything is deductible!" Not that the IRS needs to audit his returns to make sure.

IRS Publication 501 discusses whether you should itemize your deductions but we won't here. We'll just point out that if you do want to itemize, save your receipts. Also worth investigating is whether you're eligible to deduct student loan interest—an "above the line" deduction that can adjust your income even if you don't itemize other deductions.

Job Search Expenses. One tax attorney we consulted explains that if you're out of work and you're looking for new employment, you can deduct your job search expenses. For example, if you travel to New Orleans and apply for a job when you're there, you can deduct some of the meals, lodging, and travel expenses. The rules say you're supposed to divide your trip into two portions—the portion for pleasure and the portion for job hunting, and you can deduct the job portion.

Charitable Donations. Gifts to tax-exempt charitable and religious groups might be deductible. Straight from the horse's mouth (a.k.a. the IRS website) is the following guideline: "The tax benefit for charitable contributions is only available for taxpayers who itemize deductions—about one-third of all filers. Those who take a standard deduction receive no additional tax benefit for their contributions." You can include only those contributions actually made during the calendar year. Ask for a receipt—you'll need a written acknowledgement from the charity for any single gift of $250 or more.

Business Expenses. If you're self-employed or running your own business, you might be able to deduct certain business expenses, including a portion of what you spend to outfit a home office. Determining the right proportion can be tricky and you'll have to fill out an IRS Schedule C. If you travel and earn some money on your trip, you can deduct a portion of your travel expenses if you "actively" work (spend 500 hours/year or more) in the field that corresponds to your deduction. If you're a self-employed snowboarding instructor, for example, then you might be able to deduct snowboarding expenses from any money you earn as an instructor. Note that you can actively work in more than one field. If you're working as an independent contractor for someone else, you might be able to deduct certain non-reimbursed business expenses from your personal income.

SAY... "WRITEOFF!"

"If I wasn't self-employed, I'd tell my boss to 'shove it' and take a hearty rest," says 38-year-old photographer Adam Crowley (www.adamcrowley.com). "As it is, being a photog is basically leisure anyway, so I'm sure I won't get too much sympathy. I really like what I do. We get to do a lot of travel, as a family, and as long as I bring a camera, I'll write a lot of it off. Now if I can get a better tax break on my Sonics tix...." Good luck on that one, Adam!

Tax Credits

Whether or not you take deductions, you might be eligible for tax credits. While deductions can reduce your taxable income (which can in turn reduce your tax liability), credits reduce the amount of tax you owe dollar for dollar. In fact, some credits entitle you to a refund—even if you had no tax withheld and owe no tax. The Education Credit, the Earned Income Credit, and renter's credits all come to mind but there might be others you can use. The standing caveat applies here—please do your own research. The **IRS** website (www.irs.gov) is a good place to start.

Deferring Taxes

Want more time to file your return? You can get up to six more months by filing two different forms. IRS Form 4868 (Application for Automatic Extension of Time to File U.S. Individual Income Tax Return) extends the deadline from April 15 to August 15—no reason needed—and IRS Form 8809 (Request for Extension of Time to File Information Returns) extends it again, from August 15 to October 15. On this second form, you will need to state your reason, such as, "Additional time is needed to file a complete and accurate tax return."

The catch is that these are extensions to file, not extensions to pay. If you owe any taxes, the payment is still due by April 15. You'll have to estimate your tax liability reasonably well and pay a sufficient percentage (90% for federal) of what you actually end up owing to avoid penalties.

The Authorities

Both the **Internal Revenue Service** (IRS, 866-860-4259, www.irs.gov) and most state tax authorities will answer your tax-related questions over the phone. The IRS provides downloadable forms and instructions on its website and makes them available in hard copy at most post offices. As always, we recommend consulting professionals for individualized financial and legal advice.

War Story

A tax advisor who requests anonymity relates a tactic he's seen more than once—people deducting a portion of their expenses for every vacation they go on. As he tells it: "They just get a local paper from the city where they're vacationing and when they get home, they mail a resume to one of the employers who advertised in that paper. They choose a 'high profile' employer like GM so they're sure to get a rejection letter. That letter, they assume, would serve as proof to the IRS—in the event of an audit—that they were actually looking for a job in that city." We won't comment on this one.

Good Deeds That Are Also Good Deals

Year after year, you can donate to certain local charities and record your own assessed value on the blank receipt they provide. Worthy beneficiaries include **Goodwill** (www.goodwill.org) and **The Salvation Army** (www.salvationarmy.org or www.satruck.org), and other community-based stores that will give the non-profit of your choice a percentage of the proceeds from selling your donated items. Note that most thrift stores can't accept personal computers or software.

a traveler's run at fooling the California EDD

To be eligible for unemployment insurance benefits, you will need to be actively looking for work (read: not traveling). Unfortunately, this means that anytime you are on the road, you will disqualify yourself for that time period's benefits unless you can verify the purpose of your trip to the state's satisfaction.

James' layoff from his job as an architect coincided nicely with a pre-planned trip around the world. He successfully filed for unemployment insurance and decided to try to keep the ball rolling during his trip.

He had his address with the EDD changed to a friend's address, and had his friend forge his signature and send back the claim forms when they arrived. For bank deposits, he left deposit slips and addressed envelopes to his financial institution. The plan worked fine until the EDD randomly scheduled a phone interview to check on James' progress in "looking for work." As he wasn't available for the interview and unable to otherwise respond, his benefits were discontinued.

FINANCE 303

Stashing Some Cash

Whew! Budgets, bankruptcy, and taxes—if you're still with us, we salute you. Now it's time to get out of the red and into the black by bringing in some much-needed cash.

Unemployment Insurance

The joint federal-state Unemployment Insurance program, or UI for short, provides weekly payments to most unemployed workers who lose their job through no fault of their own. "Fault" is a subjective term, of course, but depending on your circumstances, you could be eligible for UI even if you quit your job or were fired.

You can't apply for benefits until you are actually unemployed, even if you know you're about to get laid off. You *can* apply if you're working part-time. While some part-time workers will be eligible for benefits, most self-employed workers will not.

For an individualized assessment, contact your state's employment development department. For a general overview, check out the information provided by the U.S. Department of Labor's **Employment & Training Administration** site (www.doleta.gov, "Other Topics" at the bottom of the right-hand nav bar, then choose "U" for "Unemployment Insurance"). Make sure you figure out how to file a claim, how to maintain eligibility, what your benefit amounts will be, and whether you are eligible for any special programs. You should also find out how your state feels about moonlighting—some states decree that even one hour of paid work constitutes "employment."

ODD TODD, ODD JOB

Check out an investigation of a guy you might have heard of: Todd M. Rosenberg, better known as "Odd Todd" of online fame.

Rosenberg made $9,000 in cybertips from his animated cartoon, *Laid Off: A Day in the Life* (*www.oddtodd.com*). The trouble was, Rosenberg was also receiving unemployment insurance benefits. The combination did not go over well with the New York State Department of Labor—at least initially.

The unemployed are generally not supposed to collect unemployment and earn money at the same time. They are supposed to be actively looking for work, not loafing on the sofa, drawing cartoons or appearing on television to talk about being unemployed. It's also true, however, that the unemployed are generally allowed to accept donations. Lucky for Rosenberg, New York put his tips in that category and agreed that he didn't have to repay any benefits.

Score one for the unemployed guy!   *Oddtodd.com*

The Bank of Mom & Dad

Without significant assets such as a house or stocks, you might find that a loan from the Bank of Mom & Dad is the easiest to obtain, and carries the best interest rate (0% financing, anyone?). But any family loan comes with its own unique costs, usually in the form of unsolicited opinions and parental "guidance."

Some of you will find those hidden costs prohibitive. Others will reject the familial borrowing notion straight away out of pride. Be wary of "pride," however; it often represents little more than a false sense of obligation based on societally-imposed expectations.

Leisure Loans

Depending on the circumstances, the concept of a "leisure loan" can be a good one: borrow money to fund more time off. Not that we're encouraging you to accumulate large amounts of debt, but if the timing is right to take some time to yourself and you don't have the cash reserves, a small loan to support your leisure may be just what the financial doctor ordered. Particularly in a low interest rate environment, borrowing money to fund leisure can be a savvy investment in your well-being.

Leisure loans can come in many forms, including personal loans from family or friends, a home equity loan if you're a homeowner, or even a margin loan if you maintain an equity portfolio. Unfortunately, we were unable to find any banks out there that offered loans specifically with the intent to "fund leisure." We therefore call upon our nation's financial institutions: offer leisure loans as an investment in the balance and health of the American worker!

Cash Out Mortgage

If you own a home and have built up some equity, refinancing might get you more than a lower rate or better terms. It might get you cash back—just like at the grocery store! With a "cash out" mortgage, you can pay off your existing first mortgage and have cash left over, up to the entire value of the equity in your home.

As appealing as that sounds, cash outs can be risky business. Around two-thirds of homeowners refinancing today are borrowing at least five percent more than they already owed, and using more than half of that cash to straighten out their bills, up from thirty percent just a couple of years ago.

In the words of one savvy home owner, "It's really attractive to think you can refi and put some cash in

home equity loans

If you own your digs, a home equity loan may be a secure way to borrow. As the name implies, these are loans against the value of your house. Home equity loans are usually available at lower rates than margin debt, and to the extent that homes are more stable in value than stocks, they are less risky assets to borrow against. As with any borrowing situation, weigh the debt to equity ratio—in this case, the amount of the loan to the total value of the house—and consider your total equity too. The last thing you need is to jeopardize your home simply for a little extra cash.

your pocket. For some people, this might be more than they make in, say, six months—so the unemployed might find this attractive. But you really do not affect your monthly payments much, and you do not pay off your house any quicker."

Margin Loans

If you own stocks, why would you borrow against them when you could sell?

For starters, if the markets are down, selling could net you a very poor price. You might be better off taking a short-term loan, then repaying it by selling when stock prices are higher. Brokerage houses make it very easy to borrow money; most offer checks that automatically draw on margined funds.

Neil Brown, a California-based CFA and financial services consultant, recommends that stockholding leisure seekers not borrow more than 20% of their total holdings, although the exact percentage would depend greatly on the composition of the portfolio. If you own only volatile equities such as small technology issues, for example, you probably shouldn't borrow against them at all.

Brown further cautions:

> Margin borrowing should never become an addictive panacea for the chronic leisure seeker. Essentially, you are borrowing against the future earnings of your portfolio. At some point you will need to pay off the margin debt you have incurred with capital gains from the sale of winning positions, dividends, and/or interest earned from your investment portfolio (or if your portfolio goes nowhere, then cash from other sources). The worst words an equity borrower could ever hear are "margin call."

Raiding Your Retirement Fund

Explore all your other options before you raid your nest egg. Look for more ways to cut expenses; reduce your debt as much as you can; even use a teaser-rate credit card to borrow money before you turn to your retirement fund.

If you're really in a bind, however, and you have an Individual Retirement Account (IRA), you can make an early withdrawal.

Beware: you'll be subject to a 10% tax penalty, plus lose the real tax benefits of a retirement account.

Are there ways to avoid the penalty? Yes, a couple. You can withdraw up to $10,000 to buy your first home, or withdraw any amount to pay for qualified higher education expenses. You'll owe ordinary income tax on these withdrawals, of course, but at least your tax hit will be in a year when your overall income is probably low.

If you have a 401(k), roll it over into an IRA, because you can't make an early withdrawal from a 401(k) without proving undue hardship, and that's unduly hard. According to one notorious tax attorney, "You have to write a letter to the IRS—it's not a form—and explain your situation—you're about to get evicted from your apartment, you can't afford to eat, and you can't find a job anywhere. If you can throw in some medical problems and/or starving kids, that would work even better." As if being unmonied weren't hardship enough!

Note, however, this small perk for the unemployed: the jobless can take money out of any qualified retirement plan, including an IRA, a 401(k), or 403(c), to pay for health insurance premiums.

lotsa daddies

Coming out of graduate school, Internet and television producer Erik Olsen scored a sweet scholarship through the Rotary Club of Seattle, allowing him to travel and "work" in Chile for an entire year.

His part of the bargain? Report back to the Rotaries on what he learned and tell them about his experiences—which, among other things, included meeting infamous Chilean dictator Augusto Pinochet.

SHOW ME THE MONEY

It's been said that free money is the best kind of money, although "free" is usually open to interpretation. Even as a gift, money rarely comes without strings attached. Still, you can find alternative sources of funding to finance time off.

Patronage

Explorers and artists of eras past were supported by the rich, powerful and royal. Famous sponsors flocked to Galileo, for example, and Shakespeare wrote some of his greatest plays and poems under the haven of patronage. Where are today's patrons?

Scholarships and grants are modern forms of patronage. Corporations are probably the single biggest patrons today, sponsoring such far-flung endeavors as science, athletics, and travel. How do you think the America's Cup yachting race with its multimillion-dollar high-tech boats fills its sails? It may be a competition famous for its billionaire boys' club, but the America's Cup rakes in hundreds of millions of sponsorship dollars from corporations as well.

The time-honored yet controversial concept of having a "sugar daddy" or "sugar momma" to fund your leisure won't appeal to some, but its attractions have certainly withstood the test of time. Many a grand project has been funded through the "sweetness" of such sugar over the years. We're not here to pass judgment, only to present another option.

GREAT MOMENTS IN UNEMPLOYMENT

LANDING A LEISURE PATRON

It seems Karl Marx was the prototypical "slacker"—or so say those who report that he never did hold a real job. Rather, he found a wealthy benefactor, Friedrich Engels, who doled out a generous allowance while Marx maintained a lifestyle akin to today's perpetual graduate student. Marx did, however, manage to create a lifetime's worth of philosophical and political works in his leisure time, and—oh yeah— come up with the concept for that little thing called Communism. Score one for the proletariat slacker!

Explain to your relatives or wealthy friends the concept of patronage. Enlighten them as to how many great artists and philosophers have made world-changing contributions this way! Your modern leisure patron may come in the form of a rich uncle, a corporation, or perhaps even a government grant.

Marlo Sarmiento found an old housemate to be a good sport. "I am a lawyer and so is she," Marlo told us, "so she was more than sympathetic when I told her I really wanted to be a photographer." Marlo left the law to spend four rent-free months under his old housemate's new roof so he could focus on photography. The patronage paid off when he won a photography competition sponsored by *Smithsonian Magazine* that he entered during his mini-sabbatical. Now let's hope the prize money will be enough to start paying some rent!

Regardless of where you find your funds, remember to share the leisure!

TaxMama on Patronage

"I was lucky enough to date a homeless guy," Eva Rosenberg told us. "He was gorgeous and had the most engaging smile. And he hung out with millionaires." We were all ears! She continued:

He'd lost all his money when the price of silver tanked. But he and his brother had built an airplane and they had a motor home. So, they lived in the motor home and parked in front of friends homes. They gave friends rides in the plane in exchange for fuel money and having them pick up meal or entertainment tabs, or even providing lodging when they went traveling. They were invited everywhere—lots of great parties—because they were such good company. And they used to shower and work out at the Marina Club. Hanging out with him, I met Stella Stevens, Connie Francis, Billy Barty, Edd Byrnes, Zsa Zsa Gabor, Ruth Buzzi, and a bunch of other people. So, knowing Hans, I starting thinking about just how little you could get away with, and still retain a pleasant standard of living. Thinking about him still brings a big smile to my face.

Who *is* TaxMama? You should meet her!
Give her a call at 800-594-9829.

Grants and Scholarships

Scholarship and grant money is usually geared toward funding education—but not always. Numerous programs fund other goals in areas such as business, healthcare, or the delightfully nebulous "personal" category. (We like! We like!)

An entire industry, not all of it ethical, exists to help you locate this money. Beware of get-rich-quick spins and advance-fee Internet offers unless you can verify the integrity of the organization.

Your first stop should be the thorough **Catalog of Federal Domestic Assistance** (www.cfda.gov), available online. For finding grant money, this might be the most useful stop on the Web you'll ever make. If you'd rather get it in writing, see the book *Finding Funding: The Comprehensive Guide to Grant Writing* by Daniel M. Barber, which is, in fact, a comprehensive guide to finding grant money. You might also have luck with *I'll Grant You That* by authors and teachers Jim Burke and Carol Ann Prater.

Judi Margolin, vice president for Public Services at **The Foundation Center** (www.fdncenter.org) and author of numerous books on grantseeking, recommends that individuals align with a non-profit to increase their options. "Making an affiliation with a non-profit, typically accomplished by means of fiscal sponsorship, can dramatically increase one's chances of securing funding," she told us, "since only about 6,200 out of more than 75,000 foundations make grants directly to individuals."

---

dream money

Live the dream on some-one else's dime with these choice charities:

Rockefeller Foundation's Bellagio Study and Conference Center
(www.rockfound.org)
Nestled in a small town on the shores of Lago di Como in Northern Italy, the Bellagio Center provides a tranquil setting to create alongside other artists and scholars.

Rotary International Ambassadorial Scholarship
(www.rotary.org)
Let Rotary International appoint you cultural ambassador to the world. All you have to do is make a report on what you learned.

Fulbright Scholarship
(www.fulbrightonline.org)
The Fulbright is for any U.S. citizen with an undergrad degree and a desire to study, teach, or conduct business or research abroad.

Professional Development Fellowship
(www.iie.org)
This fellowship funds three to seven months of study and research in Eastern Europe or the former Soviet Union. A monthly living stipend in addition to travel and study costs makes this a prized program.

Headquartered in New York, The Foundation Center is a national organization with chapters throughout the country. You'll be impressed with the breadth of their data! They catalogue countless regional grants, which can be peculiarly specific. Little-known, focused grants like these could be just your ticket.

eddie's super sale of mass deduction

Not your typical sidewalk sale, Eddie Foronda's "Super Sale of Mass Deduction" is all about efficiency and high-tech advertising. He's got it down to a science, from "deciding the objectives of the sale" to "tying in the title to something relevant" (in this case, the U.S. Iraq conflict), to putting something new on there, "like a sealed USB printer."

"On there" means Eddie's own website, where he posts meticulously arranged photographs of every item to be sold (even the small stuff), along with item specs ("specs are very important") so that buyers will know exactly what to expect.

Eddie thinks that even Colin Powell would agree: "Who needs proof with those low prices?"

SELLING YOUR STUFF

Offline

One of the smartest ways to shop isn't shopping at all. It's more like *reverse* shopping—not the five-finger discount, but trading or selling your used records, books and clothes for cash or store credit. Buy-sell-trade stores will turn them over at a fair price, just as fair as the prices you'll pay for any used goods you buy there.

Fair...fair...how about a street fair? "I've done things like take all my good used stuff—jewelry, clothes never worn with tags still attached—and participated in street fairs," says Gina Clark. "On the day of the fair, I approach someone with a booth and offer a few bucks to use a small portion of one of the tables. Then, I spend the day hawking the stuff and walk away with a considerable amount of cash."

Online

The Internet has become a grand virtual marketplace for buying and selling. This represents a boon to the leisure seeker because it offers a way to raise cash quickly by simply selling your junk. "People love junk," says Eddie Foronda, an experienced seller. "You can quote me on that." Thanks Eddie—we just did.

eBay (www.ebay.com), and the culture that has emerged from it, is at the center of this magnificent bazaar, where everything is for sale. The portion of the 40-million-plus registered users who make a living just by trading on eBay defies all the conventional wisdom bantered just a few short years ago. Professional eBay traders now number in the hundreds of thousands.

Choose some non-essential items—furniture, sporting goods, and electronics are in particularly high demand—and put them up for auction to see what you can get for them. You'll have to arrange for payment and shipping of course, but this is pretty straightforward. Be honest, or buyers will use eBay's feedback system to ding you. "At first it doesn't seem like feedback is a big deal, but it's the biggest thing ever," Eddie says. "Even if you have a thousand transactions and only one negative, people will look at the negative to see what it says."

To support your local cybermarket, the site to see is **Craigslist** (www.craigslist.org) and its sale/wanted section. "I think Craigslist is one of the greatest things ever invented," says Maria Prokop. "You learn how to get furniture for free and then resell it."

Garage Sales, Flea Markets, Swap Meets

Garage or moving sales, if they're well advertised, can pay off not only in money (no matter what the state of your finances), but also in reclaimed space in your closets and cupboards. Other people actually want your cast-offs—imagine that!

In addition to the typical places to list your garage sale, try posting flyers at a local college, especially in late summer. Don't forget your favorite café or pub, and sending a mass email to your friends wouldn't hurt either. The point is, get the word out. Also important is not to advertise too early. For a Saturday sale, post to Craigslist ("no need to advertise in the paper if Craigslist covers your town," says sale maven Eddie) on Thursday, and don't let anyone show up early except your friends. On the other hand, be prepared to get bought out before your sale begins. "Some people just want the whole shebang, to see what they can get," Eddie has found. If you get an early request like this, entertain it. Be ready for business on time, with your wares tagged, plenty of change available, and some peppy music playing. Finally, sell cheap.

Flea markets and swap meets present a more consolidated market. First-timers should arrive early with their "mystery truckloads."

Bartering

If you have a useful talent or skill, consider bartering your services to others (no, we're not talking about anything sleazy!). If you're a photographer, for example, offer your work for trade-in-kind. You could get more in trade than you would in cash, and end up with a needed product or service.

If you're operating on a limited budget, perhaps bartering for a nice dinner out is just the ticket to spark your taste buds as well as your social life. So go on, make a deal!

brainstorm

Just to jolt your brain cells, consider these job titles:

• tutor ($27-80 an hour) • substitute teacher • personal assistant (to anyone who's always so busy!) • junior college professor (if you happen to have a master's degree) • child sitter • pet sitter (same thing? $20-$36 per night) • day trader • Amway Mary Kay Tupperware representative • house painter • handyman • launderer • tour guide (create a tour of your own!) • balloon maker • day laborer • sperm or egg donor • blood donor • focus group participant • lecturer for the University of Phoenix • cigarette & candy girl • medical research subject • professional organizer • dogwalker •

ODD JOBS

You can find your own odd job in the classifieds (some of those listings are serious McJobs), or register with a temporary placement agency, such as **Manpower** (www.manpower.com), **Coit Staffing** (www.coitstaffing.com, under "Services" click "Contract/Temp") or **Net-Temps** (www.net-temps.com).

Chinyan temped at a consulting company where a buddy worked, and found the pay was excellent for what she calls "relatively brainless work"—doing telephone follow-up.

Maria Prokop took a break from engineering to work in catering at a luxury hotel. "I got to experience what it's like to be a blue collar worker," she told us. "It was an experience. At the beginning it was really hard, to put on a uniform and have people bark at you all the time, but at the end I really missed it. I actually made more money there per hour than I did when I was working full-time at my consulting job in Fresno."

Surely you have an unusual skill or two, even if your name isn't Shirley. Let people know that you're available for

SUBBING

If you're after the big bucks and don't have nerves of steel, forget about substitute teaching, advises full-time classroom teacher Alayne Brand. "The sub jobs range anywhere from a highly enjoyable experience to possibly being the worst day in your whole life," she says.

But if you can live with an erratic schedule, love working with youth and want to be more visible in the school setting, go ahead and launch the (sometimes many-month) process of testing and documentation. Requirements vary by state.

Becoming liked and well-known at a couple of schools is the best way to get consistent, steady work. "A good, reliable sub is a gold mine," Alayne says. "You will be called almost daily if teachers like you and the students get their work done when you are in the classroom."

Although you won't receive employment benefits, you can earn up to $200 per day subbing, depending on where you live, and sometimes more for long-term positions. But if you'd prefer higher pay, consider attending the year of school you'll need for full-time work. Alayne did, and has found the intangible rewards amazing. "I have never for a moment regretted going into teaching," she says. "And it gets better each year."

services like small business bookkeeping, freelance photography, bodywork, whatever. Put on your marketing hat and get creative! Better still, look around, see what people need, then figure out how to get it to them. Services like tutoring, yard work, house sitting, and housecleaning (we like "Spouses Do Houses") are always in demand.

Bartending and waiting tables might be reliable standbys. Actors and extras earn $100-500 per day. The "coolest jobs on earth" are found at **JobMonkey.com** (www.jobmonkey.com). And don't forget—there's always consulting!

PART TWO

THE UNEMPLOYED ODYSSEY

CHAPTER 4
LOCAL LEISURE

There is no need to go to India or anywhere else to find peace.
You will find that deep place of silence right in your room,
your garden or even your bathtub.

~ Elisabeth Kübler-Ross

IF YOU don't have the budget or time for a long-term adventure, why not find leisure at home?

Leisure doesn't have to be expensive or complicated. You can find fun things to do for little or no money right around town, just take your everyday agenda to a new level. Plain old eating becomes "budget banqueting." Clothes shopping becomes *reverse* shopping—walking *in* with the goods and walking *out* with some money. Your regular nine-to-five day becomes a blank slate on which to schedule colorful outings such as movie viewings, movie appearances (as an extra), court appearances (in the peanut gallery), trips to the museum, afternoons at the bookstore, and visits to the public library.

Learn more about your community, your neighbors—your country! If you get motivated to take action, go for it. Civic participation is one of the greatest casualties of overwork.

No need to rush into things. Start slow. Sleep in. But take advantage of the fact that you can now enjoy your "weekend" on a weekday, when the service is better, the crowds are smaller, and the sun shines just a little bit brighter. Do all the things you've been wanting to do around town if you only had the time, because now you do. Become a tourist in your own hometown!

THE PERFECTLY NON - EMPLOYED DAY

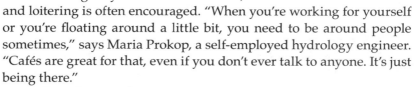

Home Base: The Café

The café is the unofficial home of the non-working set. It offers a connection point to your community (or at a minimum gets you out of the house) and loitering is often encouraged. "When you're working for yourself or you're floating around a little bit, you need to be around people sometimes," says Maria Prokop, a self-employed hydrology engineer. "Cafés are great for that, even if you don't ever talk to anyone. It's just being there."

"I still go down to the Sugar Bowl," says Ernie Zelinski of his regular coffee stop. "I fell into the habit of not getting up till noon, and I joke with my friends that rather than get up at the crack of dawn, I get up at the crack of noon." No need to rub it in, Ernie, but we've shared that guilty pleasure of watching others scramble to work while we relax over a croissant and latte.

Find one coffeehouse you like and make it your regular hangout, or create your own distinctive tour by picking a different one each week. Exceptional coffee and nibbles are a must, as is a neighborhood focus. Beyond that, look for friendliness toward loitering, conduciveness to doing personal and creative work (a.k.a. the "laptop factor"), and an overall pleasant and funky atmosphere. Consider the café your anchor, your office, your home away from home—even if it's just down the block.

Exploring The Neighborhoods

And just what *is* down the block? You might be surprised at what's new in your 'hood since you last poked around. Anna, an independent filmmaker, took a different route home from a friend's place and was shocked to find a snazzy café where she had last seen a laundromat. "I felt like I was in a different town for a minute," she told us. And she was—her own town seen through fresh eyes.

"Take time to stroll around places where you've never been able to go to when you were employed, because you were too busy," advises Chinyan Wong, a recent college grad who didn't go straight onto anyone's payroll. "Instead of taking the freeway, take the back streets once in a while." We like! Try also a bus on a route you've never traveled before. Ride it to the end of the line and check out the outskirts of your city. Explore a neighborhood you thought you knew, or choose a new spot and poke around.

"I try to dodge traffic when I drive," said Cal, a programmer, when asked about the advantages of work-free weekdays. "If I go into the City, it's going at 1pm and coming back at 8pm. That leaves me more time to check a new area once I get there." Chinyan told us, "I started a thing two days ago—I'm aiming to find a new route to get home on foot every day. It'll let me see places that I pass in a car but never pay attention to."

Are there historical landmarks where you live? Places with a story to tell? If not, how about in the closest big city? There's nothing that makes you feel more a part of your town than having a few bits of trivia up your sleeve. "There's a historic fort an hour south of downtown," said Cheryl Beck, a Detroit-area denizen who recently emancipated herself from a job that didn't fit. "It was closed but you could give yourself a free self-guided tour just by reading the signs. Another day we went to the beach at the Great Lakes. We planned enough money for dinner, went to the beach, and just walked around."

Look around for guided walking tours as well, available in most big cities—sometimes for free!

Nature, Parks & Beaches

One thing conspicuously absent from most work environments is nature, so get outside and get some sunshine while you can. You don't need more than a brisk walk to reconnect with your environment.

"I go to parks when I'm in town," said Jared, a computer programmer who takes a leave from work every year, "especially when the weather is sunny. I will get a lunch, take a portable chair and spread out."

Perhaps there's a state park, marshland, wildlife sanctuary or zoo in the vicinity. Aquariums are downright luxurious when you're in no hurry to leave. Remember, what seemed too far to drive to when you were at the mercy of work can now be an easy afternoon's outing.

You don't need animals to enjoy the open air, of course. How about a hike on a community trail? If you're lucky enough to have a beach where you live, go to it. Take off your shoes and squish in the sand. Loll around the lake, rent a paddleboat, go fly a kite! If you *do* have a pooch, lavish it with love by taking it for an off-leash outing.

NAPPING, RAYS AND READING

Well, you've been up for an hour or two by now. Must be time to take a nap! All you need is a big beach towel and a flat place to lay it out. Bring a magazine or a book (may we suggest *The Art of Napping* by William Anthony?), set yourself up in a comfortable spot, stretch out under the sun, and…*(zzzzzzzzzzzz…)*.

People Watching

People are animals. Watch them and you'll see!

Females can be observed in their own native habitat: the shopping mall. Human athleticism, competition and aggression are all on display during the Nordstrom Half-Yearly Sale. Doh! We *meant* to say in amateur sports and games.

Males, on the other hand, congregate around the watering hole (read: the nearest sports bar) starting in the early afternoon.

Be it at airports, malls, public squares or bars, your study of human behavior will come in handy once you're back in the workforce. How do you think Machiavelli got so good at politics? Observing humans in action is free entertainment that can give you valuable insight into your future boss or co-worker—even if that boss turns out to be yourself.

Go one step further and strike up a conversation. Paul Heller, founder of **The Big Blue Marble** (www.thebigbluemarble.com), a comprehensive site on how to travel like a local, recommends learning how to say, "Hello, how are you?" in a number of different languages. "Even obscure ones," he says, "so you can use it when you come across someone from China or Croatia or wherever. It'll open doors."

TOURIST IN YOUR OWN TOWN

Travel like a local? Hey, you *are* a local! But it's easy to take a familiar environment for granted. "I've lived in New York for fifteen years," says florist Patricia, "and I've never been to Staten Island."

But what if you were seeing your surroundings for the first time? If you were a tourist with a camera, what would you photograph? All towns have some innate appeal. What's the draw in yours? Is it the views? The history? The people? Make it your duty to stay up-to-date on your town—or at least as up-to-date as the tourists are. You're already out of your daily routine. Might as well go the whole nine yards and pretend you're on vacation.

Start at the local visitors center to find out what's available to sightseers, and keep an eye out for tourist brochures. "You would be amazed at the amount of fascinating things I found within two hours of the city, all because one day I was bored and decided to check out some brochures at a hotel while I waited for a friend to come down," says urban barkeep J. J. Dillon. "The car rental places have some of the best. I found out about spelunking from a brochure at the car rental place."

After you've scouted out the discounts, hop on a city bus tour of your own town or the nearest big city. It might sound a bit hokey, but you'll not only learn about the place you call home, you'll get to meet visitors from all over—maybe even become a part of their tour. "Look, honey, it's a local!"

Many cities have products, routes, tours and events specifically designed to appeal to residents. St. Louis, for example, makes sure that residents feel just as welcome as the out-of-towners (see their **Be A Tourist** site, www.beatourist.com) by offering them the same discounted admission and ticket deals, as well as hotel packages for in-town getaways. Cincinnati, too, has coaxed residents to downtown hotels by offering extra discounts. Lansing, Michigan, pitches special passports to 34 different attractions during the summer, along with 50-cent bus fare, meaning that a family of four can see everything in the city for less than the price of one movie ticket. In fact, having run more than ten annual "Be a Tourist in Your Own Town" campaigns, the staff at Lansing's Convention and Visitors Bureau are resident experts on residents specials, and have advised locales as far-flung as Holland on how to grab the hometown crowds.

annual happenings

Most visitor centers keep thorough calendars of annual and special events. If you're wondering what to do in any given month, ask about upcoming fairs-n-fests, such as:

★ street fairs ★ ethnic festivals ★ carnivals ★ film festivals ★ parades ★ crafts fairs ★ art festivals ★ music festivals ★ holiday parties ★ trade shows ★ conventions ★ sports events ★ car and boat exhibitions ★ rodeos ★ garden shows ★ the circus ★ book fairs ★ dragon boat races ★ comedy day

Many other communities across the U.S. hold a "Be a Tourist in Your Own Home Town" promotion each year during the first week of May in conjunction with national tourism week. Some of these festivities don't require local residency so look for similar deals wherever you might travel.

For more hometown touring ideas, check out the section "Traveling in Your Own Backyard" in *Travel Like a Local*, a new book from Paul Heller. Rack up enough knowledge and soon you can be the tour guide—volunteer for an organization like New York City's **Big Apple Greeter** (www.bigapplegreeter.org), a great way to meet people from other lands.

THE FINE ARTS

Ah yes, culture. We could all use a healthy dose of it, *n'est-ce pas?*

If it's been a while since you've seen an original work of art, find out which days the nearest museum opens its doors for free. Most do at least once a month. While you won't be the only one there on discount days, you can add people-watching to your agenda. A museum outing makes for an impressive date, and you don't need to spend a lot of money. No excuses!

We think fine art and fine wine make a great combination and so do many art galleries. Search out those that host evening receptions with free hors d'oeuvres. For something even more hip, cajole your way into an artist's open studio, where you'll find offbeat entertainment at little or no cost, and you won't need to tip the maitre d' or spring for a pricey round of drinks. "We like art glass and there were three galleries that were free to go in and look around," said Cheryl about the day that she and her boyfriend played hooky. "The third one was in a couple's home. They showed us around their home and studio."

There's a reason people think of the theater as a rich person's activity—a trip to the theater usually isn't cheap. Hurray for half-price tickets!

Big city box offices usually sell same-day tickets at a substantial discount starting sometime after noon, for a performance that same night only. You have to line up in person to buy. In New York City, **TKTS** (www.tkts.com) is the place. It's **BosTix** for Boston (find more info at www.artsboston.org, click on "What's Available Today?"), and **Hot Tix** for Chicago (see the "Hot Tix" link at www.chicagoplays.com). Search online for discounts too. Manhattan gets connected with **Entertainment-Link** (www.entertainment-link.com). The **Audience Extras** program (www.audienceextras.com) provides another entrée to Broadway. Search for shows and tickets in other cities at **Theater Mania.com** (www.theatermania.com).

If you prefer the ballet, opera or symphony, volunteer to usher. Wear white on the top and black on the bottom, and you're nearly there. Once your job is done, you can relax and enjoy the show for free.

Many arts organizations allow a limited audience for a dress rehearsal, occasionally advertising an "open" rehearsal. If you're interested in a particular show, don't be shy. Call and ask. If the director balks, explain that exploring the arts is a big part of your Unemployed Odyssey. Only a curmudgeon can turn down a true fan.

Failing all of the above, go ahead and pony up full price once in a while. This is your precious free time we're talking about, after all. "I've gone to the opera on a weekday and stood in the back but that's very tiring," says Cal. "It's depressing if you're too frugal!" We agree. Figure out how to make the dollars work and treat yourself now and then.

FOOD, GLORIOUS FOOD

All that sightseeing can sure work up an appetite! Time to try that diner you'd been driving by every day on your way to the office—or, not to plant any seeds or anything, but maybe it's time to grow your own food in your back yard or down at the neighborhood pea patch.

Eating Out

Eat, drink, and be merry, right? Well, right—but if you're on a furlough fiesta, watch your budget, connect with your community, and keep it real.

Everyone has a favorite cheap-eats joint. The problem is, you want something good, not just cheap. So when thinking about breaking bread, consider the following four criteria: quality for the money, connection with the community, uniqueness or "funkiness factor," and positive vibes.

If this sounds like an inexact science, it is. The bottom line is that culling choice chow is all about value, which doesn't necessarily mean bargains. You'll discover nuggets in a variety of price ranges and places, whether you're operating on $30 a day or $300 a day, a tattoo artist or a yuppie. "I am re-learning Hong Kong," says Chinyan, "for example, how to live here on a shoestring—finding budget places for lunch." Just so long as you're living *on* a shoestring, not living *off* of them!

Staples of the Non-Employed

Sometimes there's no denying the value of a good burrito, slice of pizza, or all-you-can-eat buffet. Can you eat all your meals like this? Not likely, but that depends on your metabolism. Quantity and quality come together as one in these staple foods.

The Burrito

Atop the budgetary food chain, so to speak, the "little burro" has a fascinating history. Its origins can be traced to our friends the Aztecs who, when the Spaniards first arrived in Mexico in the 1500s, were already pounding out corn tortillas of various sizes and filling them up with meat and beans. It wasn't until the Europeans brought the gift of wheat that the flour tortilla was added to the mix, enabling the more modern, gut-busting versions so prevalent today. The modern burrito was further internationalized with the "wrap" phenomenon of the mid-1990s. Burrito blasphemy to some, wraps use international ingredients and a variety of flavored tortillas to achieve a healthier result.

Why should you care about all this? Well, other than squirreling away random tidbits of burrito trivia for that opportune moment at your next dinner party, it's nice to know a little about our culinary influences, *comprende*?

The Slice

Pizza wars. New York style, Chicago style, thin crust, thick crust. It's a little disingenuous to take sides in this debate until you've tried all varieties, isn't it? So what are you waiting for?

Be sure to bone up on your history of pie before you start to sample. Keep in mind, for example, that an Italian named Raffaele Esposito baked the first pizza for visiting royalty in the late 1800s. Legend has it that the patriotic baker created a dish with the colors of Italy: flat bread topped with red tomato, white cheese and green herbs. King Umberto and Queen Margherita were quite impressed! Word got around, and soon the masses were concocting pizza pies of their own. See **AboutPizza.com** (www.aboutpizza.com) for all things pizza. The **Slice** has a lot to say too (www.sliceny.com), and **pizzatherapy.com** (www.pizzatherapy.com) counsels you on how to bake your own.

The All-You-Can-Eat Buffet

Always a way to pack in value, buffets offer the hungry diner quantity for the money. Just don't expect to take home a doggy bag! Then again, stranger things have happened.

Bring your appetite and a friend or two and serve yourself at the buffet bars of places like **Fresh Choice** (www.freshchoice.com). Yes, it's a chain, so no local quirks, but hey—it's fresh, and you have a choice, so quit your griping. Or use that festering energy to search out the buffet trays nearest you. After all, part of rediscovering your community is discovering the local retailers who make it unique.

Indian food restaurants have cornered the ethnic buffet market; there's nary an Indian joint that doesn't serve some sort of all-you-can-eat fare. So don't just sit there—look up your neighborhood Taj Mahal and get in line!

history of hot dogs and hamburgers

The Greeks called it *oyra* and the Romans called it *salsus*, but we just call it a hot dog. Okay, sometimes a sausage. Would you believe that officials in Rome tried to ban sausages? Not once, but several times. The little puppies were so popular on the black market that the bans were repealed faster than you can say "hot links."

Sausages evolved into frankfurters and made their way, like many other immigrants, to New York, where they become popular pushcart fare.

The hamburger, on the other hand, derives its name from the German city. It made its way to New York as well—winding up at the Delmonico Restaurant (in steak form, of course).

By the turn of the 20th century, hamburger had evolved to twice-ground meat mixed with onion and pepper, much closer to the hamburger we know and love today.

On average, each American consumes three hamburgers a week—and one hot dog.

Slow Food

You might be too young to remember a time when families ate a home-cooked dinner while sitting at a table, together, with no television set in sight. They talked, told jokes, caught up on each other's days and made plans. If this sounds foreign to you, try it—you'll like it!

Slow Food (www.slowfood.com) was founded in—where else?—Italy in 1986 and now boasts more than 80,000 members in over 100 countries. Although not quite old enough to be of legal drinking age in the U.S., the Slow Food movement seeks to revive communal dining and the pleasures of the table, develop taste education, conserve agricultural bio-diversity and protect transitional foods at risk of extinction. Advocates organize food and wine events, and support local food artisans. Localized clusters of food enthusiasts create their own *convivia*, forming a centerpiece to the movement as alluring as flowers on the table. Indeed, sharing the joys of food with others is key to the movement's appeal.

Find the slow foodies near you via the **Slow Food USA** (www.slowfoodusa.org) list of "Local Convivia" or contact their national office for help with starting a *convivium* of your own. If you acquire a taste for membership, current fees run $60 per person ($30 for those under 26) and $75 for a couple. You'll receive four issues of *Slow: The International Herald of Tastes,* and discounts on certain Slow Food books, merchandise and events. But wait—there's more! Act now and you'll be among the first to read the next issue of the U.S. newsletter, *The Snail.*

Take It Slow With Tea

Ever done tea? It's hipper than coffee and better for your breath. Black, green, white or herbal, its languorous imbibing rituals make tea the beverage of choice for those who take life at a slower pace.

Tea lounges (emphasis on the "lounge" part) host entire evenings dedicated to exploring tea's history, culture, and traditional drinking methods, offering a welcome respite from your usual quick jolt before work. One lounge regaled guests with a Yerba Mate ceremony, complete with lecture and slide show. Yerba Mate (pronounced yerba matay), an ancient medicinal tea introduced to the world by the Guarani Indians of South America, was served in traditional gourds with *bombilla mate* straws, along with scrumptious Paraguayan treats.

eat american

★ San Francisco Sourdough ★
★ Boston Clam Chowder ★
★ Vermont Cheddar ★
★ New York Steak ★
★ Tex Mex ★
★ Idaho Potato ★
★ Baked Alaska ★
★ Georgia Peach ★
★ Washington Apple ★
★ Florida Orange Juice ★

Hosts in many cultures invite guests to sip tea with family, friends and co-workers, as this simple ritual provides the ideal opportunity for social interaction. People take the time to visit, share ideas, and get to know each other over their cups.

Delicious and healthy, many varieties of green teas and herbal infusions are also known for their invigorating effects, such as reducing stress, obesity, headaches, and arthritis. Find out where to partake in the ceremony of tea by using the zip code locator at **Tea Map** (www.teamap.com).

Markets & Co-Ops

If you have the storage space, stock up on staples at a big-box store. **Costco** (www.costco.com) is great for bulk purchases; your savings should more than cover the $45 annual membership fee, especially if you split the membership with a "spouse." An alternative to the big box are food cooperatives, which buy their food in bulk and pass on the savings to members who take turns with food pickups, deliveries and other tasks. To fully experience local products, visit a **Farmers Market** (see www.ams.usda.gov and click on "Farmers Markets" for a directory by state). Leave some room in your pantry for the 20-lb. bag of rice available from most Asian grocers.

Grow Your Own

Even if you live in a yardless apartment, you can grow herbs in a window box. Buy one at a garage sale, improvise with pots or build one yourself. But if you *are* lucky enough to have a yard, take an afternoon or two to plant a garden and look forward to grazing on fresh homegrown tomatoes and lettuce.

Growing your own gives you the bonus of learning the meditative art of cultivation. If you're a novice or would like some company while you pull those weeds and hunt down slugs, join a community garden—a place where neighbors and friends get together to make use of even the smallest patch of vacant land. Anyone can start a community garden, sometimes known as a "pea patch." Check with the **American Community Gardening Association** (www.communitygarden.org) for advice.

THE UNEMPLOYED SHOPPING GUIDE

Sipping your coffee and surfing the Net at your café base, you may think your free time should be planned around "quality" outings or survival basics. But let's face it, shopping is a staple too. Leisure shopping is not just a stop gap until you bring in another paycheck. It's a lifestyle change—a way to be selective, consume less, and enjoy shopping more.

"It's amazing, the shopping experience you have when there are no other shoppers in the store," says Jeannette Watkins, who lives outside of Seattle and works only four days a week. "I walk out of there feeling good and energetic, not like when you are in Wal-Mart on a Saturday and there are millions of people."

As small as your war chest might be, trading a few bucks for some choice goods is still a wise move. Books, music, and clothes to carouse in are all key ingredients of quality free time.

True, the more often you pay full price, the shorter your leisure, but by the same token, you don't have to buy something just because it's on sale. Avoid "bargain binging" on yet another souvenir T-shirt when you didn't need the other ten in the first place.

This shopping guide will help your dollars go the distance at a time when you need them to stretch. It's a primer on how to swap your tired old things for what you really want, co-opt the secrets of veteran garage sale shoppers and cutting-edge online auctioneers, savor the window-shopping experience, and transform plain old shopping into an educational adventure.

No need to bust the piggy bank or surrender to impulse when you're shopping. Be selective. Keep a higher purpose in mind— lengthy leisure time—and you will resist the forces urging you to overspend. Plus, if you veer away from trends and choose classic items with staying power, shopping becomes investing. A new skill for your resume!

Plan ahead while you are enjoying your bagel. Browse the local paper for garage sales, consignment shops, or any other venue that might peddle what you're in the market for, then go scout it out.

Buy, Sell, Trade

Some of the best places to buy are also places where you can sell or trade items you're ready to part with. Music, book and clothing stores top this list.

A word of warning: it can be humbling indeed to have some 16-year-old sprite pass harsh judgment on your clothing, or reject every single one of your used CDs—not that this has ever happened to us. For best results, tailor your wares to the venue, and present them clean, pressed, and on hangers (no, not the CDs). With a little scouting, you can find the retailers who buy sports equipment or furniture too. Just don't buy back your own stuff!

Used Music

Music is vital to the non-working soul. Treat yourself to some fresh tunes now and again, especially if you can acquire them by trading in old tunes for new grooves. Dealers for recycled records and CDs set prices based on the title and condition of your submission—with the biggest bucks paid for what's rare, popular and in mint condition. You will generally receive 20% more in trade than in cash, so swap instead of sell unless you're in serious need of *dinero*.

You can easily kill an afternoon perusing the stacks. Listening stations will come to a venue near you soon enough; meanwhile, stay tuned to news of free in-store performances.

Duds Traders

Let's face it, you're not going to wear those legwarmers again. Put them in the hands (or on the legs) of a teenager who will revel in their retro-ness.

Sell or swap at stores like **Buffalo Exchange** (www.buffaloexchange .com). You'll earn around 40% of retail when you sell, and more when you trade. For your fancier, dry-clean-only type duds, your retired office suits or expensive evening wear, ask used clothing stores if they work on consignment, if that's the kind of transaction you'd prefer.

Read It Again, Sam

Those versed in the art of leisure have been known to read, read, then read some more, and when they're done, donate the books to a library (tax write-off!) or trade in the tomes for something new.

Instant Replay

One national chain of individually-owned stores will buy your "gently used" sporting goods and pay on the spot. They'll let you trade up, too, or price your goods for consignment. *Play It Again Sports* (www.playitagainsports.com) makes a strong pitch to parents of rapidly-growing kids, but hey, there's a kid in all of us, especially those of us with time on our hands.

Even if you don't have anything to trade or sell, buying used equipment is a great way to try out a new sport without making a big investment. "The place rocks," says Dane Larson. "I bought my golf clubs there. They happen to have a great selection of lefty clubs, very rare for even new sporting goods stores."

And how's the quality? Excellent, according to Dane. "Most used sporting goods stores carry a lot of crap," he says, "but Play It Again stocks only equipment in good condition, and generally not very old."

Batter up!

Trading Online

Spot a garage sale item that's peanuts to you but would be a treasure to someone else? Don't be afraid to buy it now and then sell it online for a tidy profit.

Shop for or sell new and used goods using online auction and community sites like **Craigslist** (www.craigslist.org), one of the most efficient ways to buy or sell just about anything you need. The larger **eBay** (www.ebay.com) is a good place to shop for bargains as well as auction off your goods. eBay's "half" sister, **half.com** (www.half.com), markets others' used goods to you at substantial discounts.

Auctioning Fleas In The Garage?

With time on your side, you can afford to wait for the weekend retailers in garages and along sidewalks. "There's a whole science to it," says shopper Eileen Sendrey, who bought a perfectly good laser printer at a garage sale for $10. "You're looking for people who really do want to clear out their closets. Every now and then you'll hit a total jackpot."

After you check the "garage & moving sales" section of **Craigslist**, track down the freebie paper *Classified Flea Market* or scour the classifieds under "garage sales" to plan your route. When the weekend arrives, scout out the signs on the streets. "I've learned to judge the quality of a sale by the quality of the sign," says Eileen. "If it's just a cardboard sign with an arrow, chances are it's a junky sale. If it's an estate sale, however, you don't want to miss it."

tricks of the traders

To get the best pickings of a flea market or sidewalk sale, forget about breakfast. Most early birds hit an 8am garage sale closer to 7am, and some of the best flea market loot doesn't even make it off the flatbed. Take the opposite approach if your definition of success means getting the lowest price. Most sellers don't want a shred of that stuff going back into their house, so they slash prices or even give things away at the end of the day.

More tips from the experts:

★ Plan a route if you want to hit more than one sale.

★ Be polite and reasonable, but don't be afraid to offer a price lower than what's marked.

★ Carry money in small bills. Garage sellers will love you for it, plus it'll be a lot easier to use the "I've only got five dollars" tactic if you don't yank a 20-spot out of your pocket.

★ Ask to plug in anything electronic to confirm that it works before you pay for it.

★ If you buy something large, make sure you have the means to lug it home.

If flea markets are more your circus, check out your options at the **FleaMarketGuide** (www.fleamarketguide.com).

How about auctions? The mailing list of **A1 Auction Service** (www.a1auctionservice.com) announces live auctions. The site itself gives instructions on how to hold your own auction—you can even sample the vocal skill peculiar to auctioneers: chanting.

Outlets, Off-Price & Used

Manufacturers' outlet stores can't advertise what they sell, but here's a hint: it's the same garb as at their retail stores, only it costs less. Some goods are new but slightly damaged, others are overstock or discontinued, but all of your time off needs will be covered and then some.

Expect an odd cornucopia at awesome prices, although shopping fan Kelli Elliott advises, "It helps to know comparison pricing ahead of time." Outlet guides and publications such as *Where* and *Quickguide* are available at most major hotels, offering coupons and discounts on retail goods as well as entertainment.

Vintage, pre-owned and pre-antiqued clothes can be bought by the pound—or the bagful. One shopper saw another stuff two wedding dresses in a bag and tote them home to her bride-to-be daughter. Her cost? A mere four dollars. Sure, both could end up as inventory for her own garage sale, but at that price, she'd probably turn a profit!

THE CAMPER'S CORNER

"If shopping for a polar expedition, the following doesn't apply," advises veteran camper Kelli Elliott, "but most of the time, **Target** *(www.target.com)* is hard to beat for basic outdoor gear. They usually have great prices and a good selection of inflatable mattresses, ice chests, tents, lanterns, folding chairs, camp grills, and insect repellent. I was surprised and impressed by their sleeping bag selection last season."

To rent instead of buy, try **Campmor.com** (www.campmor.com). Search there for specialty items too—the requisite sunshower for your first Burning Man expedition, perhaps?

SECONDHAND PRIZE PURCHASES

#1 Shopper

Jane shopped a garage sale and found a clean, intact and nearly-new 9'x12' area rug for only ten dollars. The worktable that Serafina bought at a going-out-of-business sale cost only five dollars. Foronda shopped at Goodwill and found a bag for his new laptop for a tenth of what he would have paid at even a discount office supplies store. It was a perfect fit!

More Retail Alternatives

Unemployed Discounts

Think the unemployed deserve a price break? Many businesses agree. Gyms, newspapers, car rental agencies, even markets have been known to offer discounts to those who bring in an unemployment insurance check stub. We even heard about one guitar teacher who strums at reduced rates for those out of work. It never hurts to ask.

D-I-Y

Feeling the urge to create? Project stores where you can create your own oil painting or glaze away on a ceramics masterpiece are good places to wile away some hours and leave with a functional piece of art, in proportion to your skill level, of course.

The do-it-yourself theme can apply to clothes as well if you've got the knack and a workable sewing machine. Start with something simple if you need a refresher, like curtains or a duvet cover. Heck, sew two sheets together and get your duvet cover that way!

If your goal is to get a necklace for less, you probably won't save much money by beading it yourself, but if you size it up in terms of entertainment, you'll see that it's a much better value per hour than most movies. Six hours spent beading can be a valuable lesson in delayed gratification— and you'll wind up with something personalized, to boot.

Skip The Buying Part

There's no reason to put your cultural education on freeze frame just because you don't have a lot of disposable income.

"Your radar gets attuned to free things even more than before," said Cheryl, describing what it was like to be suddenly free on weekdays. "Sometimes we'd just go to a city and window-shop." The alternatives to making purchases (no, we're not talking about the five-finger discount) will keep your fingers snappin' and your head buzzin' with the most up-to-date music and literature, and let you suss out your goods before paying full retail price.

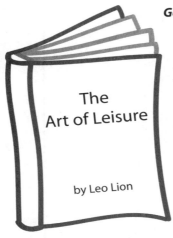

Go To The Library

Still an American institution, today's public libraries are worth a second look. They're not your parents' libraries any more—they're hipper, revamped with the latest technology, and frequently renovated into architectural wonders. "Shopping" for books, magazines, video or audio at the library can offer you choices you never knew existed. Dive into the stacks, or head over to the audio section for free DVD and video rentals.

The range of events at the library also spans the gamut of needs for discount leisure. Today's library hosts readings, lectures, films and classes—from Internet training to children's story times—and many are free. Ask for a calendar of events at the information desk.

Sample Music For Free

Couldn't find the tunes you were looking for at the library? A wealth of music is still available for download off the Internet, despite the Napster meltdown.

Check the websites of your favorite artists, as many offer a taste of their newest album for your listening pleasure. There are also an ever growing number of MP3 blogs out there, compiling these free and (mostly) legal downloads for your perusal. The **MP3Blogs Aggregator** (www.mp3blogs.org) is an excellent source for this untapped gold mine of music.

Human resources coordinator Dave Casuto suggests checking out new tunes at the listening stations at stores like **Virgin Megastore** (see their store locator at www.virginmegamagazine.com). "It's really rewarding, and it's free!"

Borrow Your Sports Gear

Borrow gear from friends before you buy gear of your own, particularly if you're trying a new sport. You'll get a much better idea of what to look for if you do decide to buy. And who knows? You might decide that you don't even like the sport that much. Or your friends could decide that they don't really need the gear...

Shop While You Sip

The truly frugal can "shop" for books by becoming a regular at a café with a well-stocked bookshelf. Drop in, stock up on the herbal tea, and pick up right where you left off.

NINE TO FIVE

Nine to five? No, we're not talking about work (or the Dolly Parton movie), but about creative ways to occupy yourself during standard business hours, while others are in the office but you're not. You won't be able to enjoy these activities after you go back to work—at least not very easily—so don't waste your hours watching daytime dramas. Go out and make one of your own!

window-shopping

For particularly tasty eye candy, stroll down a busy commercial street to take in the fine art of window display. Especially during the Christmas season, the art of selling rises a notch above crass commercialism into—well, less crass commercialism. Notable window displays for Neiman Marcus stores and others are archived online back to the year 1997 at *Fashion Windows* (www.fashionwindows.com).

But don't feel you can't actually *enter* the stores. Go ahead, walk in and enjoy the ambience.

Antiques make for pleasant perusing. Mingle with the browsers and buyers at antique shows, sample sales and design centers, and you'll compile a mental list of what to buy when you're back in income mode. Bath and body shops make particularly good choices as well, with scents as fragrant as an aromatherapy massage, plus plenty of in-store samples.

Drop by an herb or candle store. Stay awhile and breathe in the aroma. Think of it as window-shopping for your nose!

get political

Who has the energy to get political? You do. Whatever issue you're passionate about—campaign finance reform, genetic engineering, the death penalty—the time is ripe to get involved.

Nelson Hyde Chick is taking a year off. "I write lots of letters to the editor now," he reports. City Hall is another ready venue for voicing your opinion: lobby to fix a broken traffic signal, or apply to sit on the grand jury.

Perhaps you savor the taste of battle? Assist with a mayoral, or even national, campaign. One politically active soul we know quit his job to help run a presidential campaign for about six months in Pennsylvania. Another dropped out of college to campaign for President H.W. Bush and ended up spending four years in the White House.

Organized political protests require another level of civic dedication. Some folks will protest anything. Others pick and choose where they picket.

If you're going to get political, be sure you're registered to vote first. Contact your state Department of Elections to get yourself squared away.

Ride-Alongs

Ever hankered to jump on the back of a screaming red fire engine? Catch a ride with the fire department. Although they reserve the right to limit the activities depending on the dangers involved, many fire departments have formal ride-along programs. Others accept informal requests case-by-case. Or, hitch a ride with local law enforcement—it's an eye-opener! You may spend more time drinking coffee than chasing bad guys but no matter. Cops 'n' coffee have come a long way since the days of Columbo—it's nothing but gourmet lattes for today's men and women in blue.

Brain Candy

Miss the intellectual stimulation of office life? Never fear. You can absorb career-worthy information by dropping in on an industry conference. Most are free for non-exhibitors. Walk the floor, visit with vendors, people watch, and learn a ton—about what, of course, depends on the convention.

We'll See You In Court

Step inside a courtroom and see justice in action. Some trials are downright fascinating! If you get a doozy, hey, it's not jury duty—step out at any time, or join the jury member who nods off during closing arguments.

If you choose small claims court, remember that no lawyers are allowed, which makes for some juicy if not always well-reasoned debates. Then again, lawyers aren't always the most logical creatures themselves....

U.S. VITAL STATISTICS QUIZ

Sometimes you just need a dose of good old-fashioned American baseball. Lighten up the mood with this test of how well you know your home (or neighbor) country.

Q: Who made it into the National Baseball Hall of Fame first, Babe Ruth or Ty Cobb?

A: Neither. They were both inducted in the same year, 1936, along with Walter Johnson, Christy Mathewson and Honus Wagner, who together comprised the first five Hall of Fame inductees.

Q: Where is Old Faithful and why is it the most photographed geyser in the world?

A: Yellowstone Park, Wyoming. It erupts at irregular intervals but more frequently than most bigger, hotter and more predictable geysers, with an average time between bursts of 78 minutes—but don't set your watch by it!

Q: What made Bill "Bojangles" Robinson different from most other tap dancers?

A: While most tap dancers wear taps made of aluminum, Bo's were made of wood.

Q: What happened to the Liberty Bell the first time it was rung?

A: It cracked.

Q: Who invented fireworks?

A: The pyrotechnical delights used by Americans to celebrate our national independence day were invented by the Chinese in the 9th century.

Q: In which hand is the Statue of Liberty's torch?

A: Her right hand, all 17 feet, 3 inches of it.

Q: Why is the White House painted white?

A: The British set fire to it in 1814. When it was repainted to cover up the smoke and soot damage, they chose white to make it even more brilliant.

Q: Why did Malcolm X go to prison?

A: He was convicted of burglary when he was 21. He joined the Nation of Islam while he was serving his sentence.

Q: Where is Mt. Rushmore and which four presidents are sculpted into it? Bonus points if you can name the sculptor.

A: Black Hills, South Dakota. George Washington, Thomas Jefferson, Theodore Roosevelt, Abraham Lincoln. Gutzon Borglum sculpted from 1927 until he died in 1941.

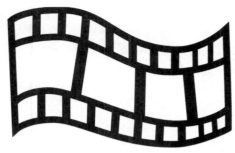

MATINEE MADNESS

Last but not least, we arrive at the movies. There's nothing quite like that aura of mystery as the lights dim, you await what's about to unfold, and the voice of the Chatty Cathy (who *always* sits right behind you) somehow fades away—along with the rest of the real world. Movies are magic whether you're in a sixteen-screen complex or at home on your couch. And now for our feature presentation.

Going To The Cinema

The classic, single-screen theater projects character in addition to first-rate movies. If you're lucky, a few such indies are hanging on within driving distance. No matter if it is the multiplex though; surround sound, 70mm projection and cushy seats mesh quite nicely with certain Hollywood blockbusters.

Most theaters offer discounts for the first showing of the day, and sometimes any pre-5pm screening will qualify. A few even set mid-week matinees, which presents the best odds for catching a movie with no one else in the house. It might sound lonely but seeing a movie in an empty cinema is something to experience. You'll feel like a director watching the dailies!

To promote upcoming flicks, movie companies typically give away tickets via a local business—if it's a thriller set in the Italian Alps, there may be some free tickets at the local rock climbing gym. Sometimes you just have to answer silly quiz questions and send a self-addressed stamped envelope, and free tickets will arrive right at your door.

The movie section of most free weekly papers will list what previews are coming up, and **Rotten Tomatoes** (www.rottentomatoes.com) can give you a list of current releases playing near you.

Home Movies

As cool as the silver screen is, it can't compete on a rainy day when you feel like just kickin' it at the crib. Rent a quirky documentary (we like *Road Scholar* by Andrei Codrescu) or a mega-blockbuster (like *The Lord of the Rings*), or choose your own faves for a custom-tailored movie marathon.

Don't feel you have to restrict yourself to the best, though. "Coming up with a top ten list is tough," engineer Shane said when we asked for his choices. "Some days, I'd say *Animal House* and *Repo Man* were up there. In other moods, I might choose a thinking movie like…well, I'd have to think about it."

While Shane is busy processing (it could take awhile), think about what would suit your fancy. If you're feeling retro, **The 80s Movies Rewind** (www.fast-rewind.com) catalogs all things Matt Dillon and Molly Ringwald. **Garner's Movie Classics** (www.garnersclassics.com) points out some solid comedy, action and sci-fi. For classics, try **Classic Movies** (www.thegoldenyears.org).

With the power of pre-paid envelopes and rentals beginning at around ten dollars per month, **Netflix** (www.netflix.com) brings current hits and oldies to your mailbox—several at a time with no late fees—and when you're done, just mail them back for free. **Blockbuster** (www.blockbuster.com) has gotten in on the mailing act as well. And don't forget about cable! Surely there is something good on one of those 500 channels….

On-demand video and TV is shooting through a broadband cable, satellite or Internet connection near you, and is an economical way to pay for only what you want to watch. If your cable or satellite operator doesn't already offer video-on-demand, they will soon. Online, catch movie stalwart **Movielink** (www.movielink.com) for downloadable flicks.

Lights, Camera, Action!

Looking for an opportunity to claim your fifteen minutes of fame? Or just interested in blowing off an afternoon and meeting some stars? Movies and television programs always need extras, hangers-on, groupies, or whatever you'd care to label yourself. You just need to know where to find them. The nearest film commission (usually a division of city government) will be able to tell you if any movies are being filmed in your area currently. It pays to be extra nice to them on the phone.

During a break between high-tech jobs, movie buff Joe Parente worked as an extra on the film *Bedazzled*. Although he calls the film itself "very forgettable," he thoroughly enjoyed the experience. "In addition to a couple of crowd scenes," Joe told us, "I was also chosen to play a policeman in full uniform. I met Brendan Fraser, and I think—*think*—Elizabeth Hurley actually checked me out when I was in my uniform." Joe could've sold his story to the tabloids, he says, but he chose instead to respect Liz's privacy. He received $71 for eleven hours of work. Woo-hoo! Drinks on Joe!

Finding work as an extra isn't hard. You don't have to be an actor or a member of the Screen Actors Guild, just look like a "real person" (we know, this is difficult for some of us), answer a film company's "open call" or go through a casting company. Keep in mind that the work isn't glamorous—the hours are long, there's a lot of sitting around, and you have to take orders all day. That said, getting behind the scenes can be a lot of fun, and it's work that few people (except you!) have the time to be able to do.

OURS GO TO ELEVEN

So you've read all the latest literary smashes, found the best bargain Thai food, and managed to land a few bit parts in forgettable movies. Still, you find yourself explaining at parties that you're between films right now—you might weigh your options if that next role doesn't come along. Admit it: you're unemployed. What better time to turn it up another notch?

Road trip, anyone?

CHAPTER 5
HIT THE ROAD

*The world is a book,
and those who do not travel read only a page.*

~ Saint Augustine

THERE'S no denying the genuine wonder and excitement of a jaunt overseas. If you're already a seasoned traveler with extra pages in your passport, this is hardly breaking news. Yet surprisingly few people take the opportunity, beyond a couple of weeks' vacation, to explore our world for an extended period.

Meaningful travel, in our opinion, educates you and expands your consciousness. It takes many forms, but two major factors unquestionably affect the depth of your trip: the duration of the journey, and how comfortable and familiar the surroundings are.

Here's a depressing statistic: numbers from the U.S. Department of State suggest that only about twenty percent of Americans have valid passports. Is it any wonder that we as a nation are sometimes baffled by other countries' views of the United States, when just one in five of us are crossing our borders to see what's out there? Our national ignorance of the world's affairs can have dangerous effects on international politics and policy. Consider this: the United States is routinely outvoted at the United Nations *one-hundred-forty* to *five*. And according to a University of Maryland poll in September 2004, thirty of our thirty-five closest allies oppose U.S. policies.

This leads us to our second premise: not only is travel extremely beneficial for your personal growth and exploration, but it also serves a higher purpose—increased cultural understanding, tolerance, and goodwill. As Mark Twain so keenly observed, "Travel is fatal to prejudice, bigotry, and narrow-mindedness, and many of our people need it sorely on these accounts. Broad, wholesome, charitable views of men and things cannot be acquired by vegetating in one little corner of the earth all one's lifetime." So think of travel as a significant responsibility—to yourself and those around you.

We strongly believe that travel changes your perspective on life, and many we spoke to agreed. Ariella Quatra, a film and television producer from San Francisco, shifted her outlook during her recent journey to Southeast Asia. "After eight months in Thailand, Laos and Cambodia, my perspective on what 'the good life' is has changed," she said. "I've learned that the value of mindful practice, everyday appreciation and gratitude is my personal key to leading a fulfilling and enriching life." We can only nod in agreement.

How long should your trip be? Only you can decide, but keep in mind that many before you have gone away a year or more and survived (and thrived) to tell the tale. Just take a look at the Aussies, known to go on walkabout for years at a time, if you need inspiration. Worried about marring your resume? Don't be. Savvy employers understand now more than ever that people need breaks from their day-to-day work. Think you're too old to travel, or have too many commitments at home? You're not, and you don't. Couples and families grow closer through their travel experiences. Homes can be sold or rented, bills can be paid in advance, pets cared for, children shipped off to boarding school (okay, we're kidding here). The point is, you'll always find excuses for not going, but how will these excuses sound ten or twenty years from now?

This chapter doesn't purport to be a comprehensive travel guide; we merely make some humble suggestions to get you started based on our own experiences and those of many other travelers. If none of them rev your engine, by all means—set your own itinerary. The important point is this: if you're fortunate enough to have the opportunity, take off and go!

DOMESTIC TRAVEL

As enticing as international travel may be, we often overlook great travel possibilities right in our own backyards. Considering that the United States is one of the top tourist destinations in the world, and that domestic travel is generally less expensive, you might try exploring down the street before you journey to the far side of the world.

Road Trips

Finally, you're free! And you have piles of time on your hands—but maybe not piles of loot. Enter the good old American road trip, an economical way to spark the wandering spirit. With the right car, it's a cheap alternative to air travel that can relieve stress, clear your head and rejuvenate your spirit.

Matt Green, a former software executive, found his post-work road trips to the desert rather soothing, to put it mildly. "Staying in a rat-shit hotel," he said, "I slept better than I did in those $350-a-night first-class hotels I stayed at when I was working."

America is one vast network of open roads, so the routes we suggest are only a starting point. And if your starting point isn't your hometown? Fly out to your ground zero and then buy or rent a car; invite friends who live near your launching point and use their car; or use a vehicle transportation company.

Wherever you begin and whatever method you choose to get there, don't forget to make a few wrong turns. You never know where they might lead you.

---

leisure lesson #1: stretch your road trip dollar

Look up old friends. Surely they'll invite you to stay if you promise to do the dishes!

Consider bed & breakfasts. *BedandBreakfast.com* (www.bedandbreakfast.com) lists over 27,000 B&Bs; see also *Bed and Breakfast Inns of North America* (www.inntravels.com).

Arrange a homestay using *GlobalFreeloaders.com* (www.globalfreeloaders.com). The catch? You have to be willing to host from time to time as well.

Contemplate camping. There are more than 100,000 campsites in the U.S. alone. Bring a sun shower to freshen up in the morning, and you'll smell ahead of the game. See *Reserve America* for help (www.reserveamerica.com).

Load up the cooler! It'll shrink your food costs. Besides, where else are you going to keep your cold ones for the end of a long day's drive?

Sing songs in the car. Will it save you money? No, but everyone likes a sing-a-long, and it's one way to keep the driver awake!

IN SEARCH OF A HOMESTEAD

Think the days of homesteading in the Wild West are over? Think again. The stakes may have risen a bit, but the search continues, at least for those with an adventurous spirit.

Mike and Angela Sarmiento had always dreamed of building their own cabin in the woods, someplace "with a stream nearby filled with trout." They knew they'd have to raise some capital for their dream, so they bought an old home at below market price, restored it, then sold it when the market was hot. They squirreled away most of their profit for their dream property-to-be, but used a small portion to buy a sweet camper trailer that they could tow with their SUV.

Along with their beloved golden retriever, Kenzie, they spent several months driving through California, Nevada, Wyoming, Montana, Idaho, British Columbia, Washington and Oregon in search of the perfect homestead. Because the trailer was fully self-contained, they were able to prepare their own food and sleep in the trailer each night, regardless of where they went.

"The night we got engaged we were soaking in a tub, drawing out the plans for our cabin on a paper napkin," said Angela. "Two hours later the napkin was full of drawings and getting a little ragged from splashes of water.... Now we've been driving around looking for our homestead, but an architect friend of ours was kind enough to replace our tattered napkin with some real floor plans."

At last check, the couple was still merrily on the road in their quest. When they do find their dream property, they intend to sell the trailer and start building their cabin.

Of course, maybe they'll try to hang onto the trailer to keep the road close at hand!

General Tips for the Road

A little bit of planning will drive you a long way on the open highway. Tom Williams, professional tour guide and road trip expert, recommends cribbing from organized tour companies for free itinerary ideas. **TrekAmerica** (800-221-0596, www.trekamerica.com), a company he's worked for, is one of his faves. After 30 years of running road tours across North America, they may have learned a thing or two.

Better yet, says Tom, consider going on one of the treks yourself. "They are hidden gems for people in the U.S. The company markets primarily to international tourists, but the trips are a great way for Americans to see their own country and to meet people from all over the world at the same time."

Tom also recommends the off-season to avoid crowds, save money and (sometimes) score better weather.

"Avoid hotels if at all possible," says U.S. tour guide Greg Blaug. "Beaches, campgrounds and hostels are always cheaper, and much more exciting."

Greg also strongly advises travelers keep an open mind. "No matter how well worked out your travel plans are, it's always nice to be able to change them when something else comes along."

The West Coast Trail

Total Distance: 1,400 miles
Drive Time: 3 days (one way)
Start / End: Vancouver / San Diego

Pack up your vehicle and head out on the Pacific Coast Highway for a spectacular West Coast tour.

If you head south to San Diego from Seattle or even Vancouver, the climate will improve as you go. Take advantage of the many excellent coastal campsites along the way, and don't miss Mt. Rainier, Mt. St. Helens, Hood River, Humboldt, Santa Barbara, or La Jolla.

westys @ the wal-mart

Autumn and Joe Ervin drove from Northern Illinois to Key Largo (that's 1,600 miles!) in their trusty "Westy," a 1984 VW Vanagon Westfalia camper. They lived on $20 a day, plus whatever gas their economical ride consumed (19 mpg). Instead of burning their cash on hotels, they cooked and slept in the Westy each night (which comes complete with a foldout queen-sized bed)—with a little twist.

On a tip from friends, they scouted out all the Wal-Mart Superstores along their route, and camped each night in the store parking lots. They weren't alone. Open 24x7, with clean bathrooms and supplies to end all supplies, Wal-Marts have become de facto pit stops for mobile campers. And if you wake up with a craving for a late-night snack, well, then, you're covered. No showers, so the Ervins "improvised."

"Owning a Westfalia means instant membership into the 'Westy Club,'" the couple told us. "In the mornings, we often found ourselves encompassed by other Westy travelers who would come and chat." The Ervins rewarded themselves with an $80 snorkeling trip when they arrived in Key Largo. We hope it doubled as a shower!

The Right Coast
Total Distance: *1,600 miles*
Drive Time: *3 days (one way)*
Start / End: *Portland, ME / Miami, FL*

Traipsing the eastern seaboard may seem at first glance to be a bland trip through miles and miles of urban wasteland. But look again, and you'll find a journey through American history, filled with quirky beach towns and fishing villages, and mixed with provincial charm and tradition. Beginning with some fresh Maine lobster, you can crawl your way down through the urban centers of Boston, Providence and New York, then ease your way into the quieter shores of Virginia, the Carolinas, and Georgia, and finish with a flourish in Florida.

Get Your Kicks...
Total Distance: *2,100 miles*
Drive Time: *4 days (one way)*
Start / End: *Los Angeles / Chicago*

Get hip to this timely tip: although it's no longer "The Mother Road" John Steinbeck described in *The Grapes of Wrath*, Route 66 is still the iconic U.S. road trip, showcasing Americana at its finest. Immortalized in song and TV, "Historic Route 66" has connected Chicago to Los Angeles for almost 80 years. Put on some Nat King Cole and do what the man says—get your kicks.

You can travel this time warp in either direction. For the best views and the full historical experience, take a convertible—or even a motorcycle! To get yourself tuned up, motor on over to **Route66.com** (www.route66.com). To hook up with a phat Harley hog, see **Route 66 Riders** (www.route66riders.com).

PARK IT FOR AWHILE

Steve Yung turned misfortune into opportunity when he was laid off. "Sometimes you just need to look for the opportunities when life hands you something unexpected," he told us. "When I was laid off, I was worried for a while, but then I saw it as a chance to do something that I had always thought about, but didn't think I would ever get the time to do—visit the National Parks." The road trip reinforced an old travel adage for Steve. "The journey was truly as important as the destination," he said. "To be able to not live by a schedule and literally stop off at the side of the road to smell the roses was a great feeling.... I came back refreshed and in the best shape of my life."

National Park Loop
Total Distance: *variable*
Drive Time: *10-28 days, depending on route and number of stops*

There's a reason people come from around the world to see our national parks—they're the best on the planet. Tour the parks of the west to finally understand the meaning of purple mountain majesties!

Kick off a giant loop along the north coast of California at Redwood National Park, home to some of the world's tallest trees. Continue along the Oregon coast and into Washington, where Mt. St. Helens (now a National Volcanic Monument), Mt. Rainier, Olympic, and North Cascades National Parks await you. Then cut across to Montana's Glacier National Park, and finally down to Wyoming for Jellystone—er, Yellowstone—the granddaddy of them all. The dazzling Grand Tetons beckon a short distance to the south. When you reach southern Utah, break out the mountain bike and take your pick of parks, which include Arches, Canyonlands, Glen Canyon, Bryce Canyon, Capitol Reef, and Zion. The Grand Canyon lies across Arizona and it is, despite the crowds, undeniably spectacular. If you're feeling lucky when you reach Vegas, slap your money on black. If not, avoid the magnetic pull and point yourself southwest to California's Death Valley, with its fantastic desert ecosystems. Continue north through Sequoia and Kings Canyon, and finish your journey in Yosemite, the crown jewel of the national park system.

parks prep

Can't wait to gas up the ol' family truckster? Make sure the time is right.

Professional tour director Tom Williams advises visiting in the fall. "The summer crowds are gone, the students are all back in school, and you get the great fall colors with cooler temperatures in the southwest." Avoid July and August, he says, unless you like it really hot.

Tom recommends a National Parks Pass ($50) with a Golden Eagle hologram ($15 extra) for entrance to any national park or land managed by U.S. government agencies.

To buy one or research your journey, see the *National Park Service ParkNet* *(www.nps.gov).*

holy toledo!

Cross-country road trips are indeed grand, but sometimes you don't need grand, you just need to get out and enjoy a nearby escape. A weekend (or midweek) getaway to someplace new can often be just as adventurous, and much easier on the pocketbook.

Cheryl Beck of Detroit, Michigan, who quit her insurance job of ten years to pursue her passion of writing and journalism, took short road trips to nearby destinations with her boyfriend, who wasn't working either, at the time.

"We took one day to go to Toledo, ninety minutes away, and it was like a mini-vacation," she told us. "We had an inexpensive lunch at Tony Paco's, the restaurant where Klinger from M*A*S*H always ate when he was in Toledo. The art museum was free.... We filled up the entire day with free stuff."

Pull the map out of your glovebox to plot your own would-be Toledo trek.

The Coast-to-Coaster
Total Distance: 3,000 miles
Drive Time: 4-6 days (one way)
Start / End: Newport, OR / Boston, MA (US-20); Oakland, CA / Ocean City, MD (US-50)

Everyone should drive across the U.S. at least once. Think of it as a rite of passage! For a speed run (set that radar detector), use the major interstates funded during the Eisenhower administration, such as I-70, I-80, or I-90. For a more leisurely trip, take the roads less traveled, such as "The Loneliest Road" (US-50) or "The Oregon Trail" (US-20). The Oregon Trail follows paths taken by early American settlers from the the sandy, highly refined shores of Cape Cod to the rugged crunchiness of the Oregon coastline, with a little bit of everything in between. Don't rent any barrels at Niagara Falls but say hey to Yogi as you pass Wyoming's Yellowstone National Park. The two-lane US-50 is less dramatic, but will steer you through a fine and dandy sampling of small town America on your way from San Francisco to coastal Maryland.

Southern Man
Total Distance: 2,400 miles
Drive Time: 4 days (one way)
Start / End: San Diego, CA / Tybee, GA

The southern states boast some of America's most distinctive cultures, from Texan to Creole to Old South genteel. US-80 (not to be confused with the larger Interstate-80), stretches from southern California to Georgia, and passes through just about every southern state in between. You'll traverse the great plains of New Mexico and Texas, then find the true heart of

the ultimate road trip

Bret Livingston and Patty Segar thought they'd unwind with a quick drive after they quit their jobs—across the North and South American continents. So they took a year, and hit the road.

The two outrigged their Toyota truck with a camper shell, complete with sleeping quarters, a propane stove, camping supplies, food, water, surfboards, snowboards and various other sundries they thought might come in handy on a leisurely one-year drive. They gassed up in northern Alaska and cruised the entire length of the Pacific coastline. Along the way, they encountered crazy bush pilots, plane crashes, gun-yielding banditos, over-sexed field workers, defective roof racks, extorting border agents, ornery customs officials, stomach-churning ferry rides and dubious characters of questionable legal standing.

Despite its challenges, the trip was the adventure of their lives and they wouldn't change it for anything. What's more, it didn't cost them a dime career-wise—they each went back to the same company that they'd worked for before they left. Let that be a lesson for the worrywart in us all!

"Travel and celebrate your free time while you got it," say Bret and Patty, who are proud new parents back in the States, "because it's sure to change when you have a kid!"

the green tortoise: an alternative to driving

The Green Tortoise has been running adventure travel buses since 1974, and "adventure" is truly the operative word. The trips are known for their communal atmosphere, with custom sleeper coaches, activities and group meals. "This is not gonna be one of those vacations where all you did was sit by the pool in the daytime and drink beer at night, only to forget all about it a few years later," says Greg "Bernie" Blaug. "If you're ready for fantastic scenery, beautiful people, quality homemade food and a memorable experience, we're ready for you." He should know—he became a driver and trip leader after falling in love with the trips as a passenger.

Based in San Francisco, where they also own and operate a youth hostel, the Green Tortoise steers regional, national, and international journeys. This ain't your average Greyhound, so be prepared to have some fun on "the only trip of its kind."

Green Tortoise Adventure Travel
800-867-8647
www.greentortoise.com

Dixie, from the Mississippi Delta through the Appalachian Mountains, finishing near Savannah, Georgia.

Hank, a California native, recalls fondly his detours in southern Texas, "floating down the Rio Grande on inner tubes, and sneaking across the border into Mexico to drink at local cantinas." Time your trip right, and you can swing through New Orleans for Mardi Gras. Don't forget your banjo!

Road Trip Resources
Planning

The book *Road Trip USA* by Jamie Jensen can help drive your planning (check www.roadtripusa.com) but for more extensive resources and support, consider joining an auto club. You generally pay an annual fee, but will more than make it back with benefits such as maps, insurance, travel planning, and emergency roadside assistance for that inevitable breakdown on a lonesome highway.

AAA (www.aaa.com) has long been the preeminent auto club, with chapters in each state or region. But there's a new kid on the engine block: **Better World Club** (www.betterworldclub.com). Better World prides itself on being the nation's first environmentally aware auto club, offering eco-friendly services such as hybrid car rentals, eco-travel, and an innovative bicycle roadside assistance program, in addition to benefits similar to AAA's.

Car Buying

Spare your own car the dings and dents by buying (and later selling) a used one. For deals on used cars, try **Autobytel** (www.autobytel.com), **Craigslist** (www.craigslist.org), **PoliceAuctions.com** (www.police auctions.com), or the old-fashioned classified ads in your local paper. The **Kelley Blue Book** (www.kbb.com) will tell you how much to pay—and it's free (the site, not the cars). Look for a reliable make such as a Toyota or Honda, or something easy to repair (anything old and American).

Driveaway Into The Wild Blue Yonder

If it was good enough for Jack Kerouac, it might work for you: drive someone else's car for a vehicle transportation company, sometimes referred to as a "driveaway."

It's pretty basic: you put down a security deposit (normally $300 cash) refundable upon "successful" arrival, and take one of their cars from point A to point B. They'll even pick up the first tank of gas. After that, you need only pay for gas and stick to a pre-determined time and mileage schedule, roughly 400 miles per day—which unfortunately won't get you to Mexico. Leisure Legend Tim drove from Denver to San Diego. "I scored a brand-new Mustang convertible," he said. "It was so sweet!"

Auto Driveaway Co. (800-346-2277, www.autodriveaway.com) is the biggest and best-known company, with offices throughout the U.S. and even a few in Canada.

Skipping The Road Altogether

Okay, so you can't drive forever. Eventually, you might tire of the wind in your hair, not to mention the bugs in your teeth. Time to spread your wings and fly!

Does a jumbo jet mean a jumbo fare? Not any more. In fact, you can proudly release your inner miser when it comes to airfares these days. Gregg Brockway, a co-founder of **Hotwire** (www.hotwire.com), says, "Americans are putting more of an emphasis on saving money. 'Cheap' isn't a dirty word anymore. These days, cheap is like a badge of honor—people will talk endlessly about how they saved twenty dollars on a hotel room or fifty dollars on airfare. They like to feel smart that they paid less than the next person." So go ahead, feel smart. Make our day!

Indeed, Hotwire is *the* central resource for finding deals on domestic airfare. As for the domestic airlines themselves, the smart money (not to mention the value) is on the young guns **Southwest Airlines** (www.southwest.com) and **JetBlue Airways** (www.jetblue.com). They've both managed to come up with a novel concept: flying people around the U.S. for cheap.

GREAT MOMENTS IN UNEMPLOYMENT

John Steinbeck
(1902–1968)
Not only did the Salinas-born writer John Steinbeck spend years of his life unemployed, partially-employed, or points in between, but woven throughout his most famous novels are persistent themes of unemployment, struggling workers, and the common man. *The Grapes of Wrath*, probably his most famous novel about labor, profiled the plight of dispossessed farmers during the Great Depression. · · · Steinbeck knew when to take a break. Fresh on the heels of *Grapes'* successful release in the spring of 1940, he sought refuge in Baja with close friend and marine biologist Ed Ricketts. The pair chronicled their adventures on the wild peninsula in *Sea of Cortez*, a literary voyage of natural beauty, exploration, and science.

INTERNATIONAL TRAVEL

"Through travel I first became aware of the outside world; it was through travel that I found my own introspective way into becoming a part of it," wrote American author Eudora Welty. International travel can teach us as much about ourselves as it can the world around us. If you have the ways and means, the world is out there waiting for you. We highly encourage taking off for several months or longer if you can, but even a week abroad is better than none.

All of our travel ideas would fill another book; below are just a few uniquely suited for the leisure seeker or non-employed wanderer—inexpensive travel, a sophisticated travelers' infrastructure, or opportunities for volunteering, work or study.

As you travel, remember that you are both a pilgrim and an ambassador of leisure. Take some time to learn about your destination before you go. You can start your schooling on the **U.S. Department of State** website (www.state.gov, search for "Country Background Notes" under "Travel and Living Abroad").

And take some time, period. Most of the world doesn't operate at the pace of the American office drone. Everything takes longer, especially when you don't speak the language. You're on a journey, and you're on your own clock. Enjoy it.

Getting Started

A trip of a thousand miles begins with one step—to the library. Avoid the bookstores and the plethora of high-priced budget travel guides if you'd rather spend your hard-earned cash on that gilded Balinese headdress or another week at a hostel set in the rarified air of the Andes. Please, make your mother proud and return the books to the library when you're done.

The best book to start with, hands down, is *Consumer Reports Travel Well for Less*. With the objectivity they are famous for, Consumer Reports reviews and rates popular travel guides, websites, airlines, tour operators, rental car companies and the like. You can also check out the travel section of **ConsumerReports.org** (www.consumer reports.org) but note that subscriptions to the site currently run $4.95 per month or $26 per year.

Should you still have a hankering, after reading the book, to dog-ear your own travel guide, get one used at **Amazon.com** (www.amazon.com).

The Power of the Internet

There was a time when booking travel on the Internet promised huge savings over booking through the traditional travel agents or airline carriers. While deals do still exist online, a certain amount of price parity has emerged between traditional travel agents and online retailers and wholesalers.

The good news, however, is that the online travel world has quickly evolved into a virtual cornucopia of valuable info. "Sometimes you can save some money by booking with Orbitz or a Euro consolidator like Mobissimo, but I find the Net is much more useful for other benefits," says Michael Shapiro, travel writer and author of *Internet Travel Planner: How to Plan Trips and Save Money Online.* "I use online resources to discover and learn about destinations, to connect with people there before I go, and to learn about current political, economic and environmental conditions—by reading their local newspapers online, for example."

Lonely Planet (www.lonelyplanet.com) hosts a particularly good online travel forum called **The Thorn Tree** (see "Thorn Tree Forum" off their homepage), where thousands of travelers from around the world chime in on the latest and greatest destination in virtually every region of the world.

Travel For Free

If a lack of funds has held you back from journeying to exotic locales, think beyond cash. Believe it or not, there are ways to travel and stay for free, or at least at significantly reduced expense.

What's the catch? Well, for one, it may require some work on your part. But with a bit of ingenuity and a willingness to exchange some elbow grease, ultra-cheap travel is absolutely within reach. A word of caution: beware of unscrupulous websites that purport to find you, for a fee, free accommodations and travel deals. Trust your instincts—if the website doesn't disclose how many members they have or the frequency with which they post new listings—stay away! Also, do remember that "free" does not necessarily mean scot-free. Items may cost you zero in the dollar sense, but you very well might pay up in a different way, be it through barter or hosting or just plain inconvenience.

Your bible in the free department (which is itself not free, except at the library) is *Pay Nothing to Travel Anywhere You Like*, written by the king of freebies, Eric W. Gershman. Gershman breaks down all that is attainable for zero bucks in the travel biz. While some of the tips aren't for everyone (creating an "over 62" fake ID to get senior discounts, for example), it is nonetheless a helpful resource for all.

WORK iT

*Work your way around the world with
the following travel-friendly gigs:*

Scuba Instructor

Become a certified Scuba instructor or divemaster and work at the world's most beautiful tropical locations. Dive into your research at two watery sites: **PADI** *(www.padi.com, go to "PADI Pros")* and **NAUI Online** *(www.naui.com)*.

Club Med Staffer

You've seen it in the movies, now you can experience it for yourself. Get hired on as an infamous **Club Med** "G.O." (*Gentil Organisateur* in French), working in one of the many Club Med villages scattered throughout the world. Flexibility is key—you won't know where you'll be based until after you get hired but hey, that's part of the fun! Read up on all at *www.clubmedjobs.com*.

Cruise Ship Employee

Ahoy, all you Julie McCoy's! You social types can cruise your way around the globe. For general information to get started, sail on over to **Cruise Ship Jobs** *(www.shipjobs.com)*. Of course, if you want to get specifics, you'll have to purchase their book and CD for a couple dozen bucks or so. We know, we know—we'll take the matter up with Captain Stubing.

Deckhand

Thousands of boats out there await your sturdy seamanship as a deckhand on a private yacht. Surprisingly, experience is not always required, as many captains don't mind training young sailing protégés. Just make sure it's not Captain Ahab—a boat on the open seas becomes very small indeed (not to mention dangerous). Connect with boats through **Find a Crew Online** *(www.findacrew.com)*, where searching is free but contacting members directly will cost you a premium membership: currently $39 for sixty days.

An exemplary reference for seeing the world for the cost of sweat equity is now in its 11th edition: *Work Your Way Around the World* by Susan Griffith. Written from a British perspective, it is nonetheless thorough and informative for Americans. Consider yourself warned: this is one of those books that's liable to launch a thousand fantasies.

Stay, Sit and Swap

No, we're not talking about anything kinky (see **Chapter 6** for kink) but about alternative accommodation. Bypass cramped hostels and impersonal hotels by staying in someone else's digs.

Are you a born freeloader? It's not as bad as it sounds. Get free accommodation in exchange for your promise to host like-minded guests. **GlobalFreeloaders.com** (www.globalfreeloaders.com) happens to be loaded with good stuff on arranging homestays, both foreign and domestic. They charge no fees, serving only as a meeting ground for guests and hosts to make their own private arrangements for stays.

Similarly, albeit more altruistically, **US Servas** (www.usservas.org) promotes cross-cultural understanding through cross-hosting. They enable people to host guests from all over the world in their homes, and provide listings for those looking for a hospitable place to stay. The fee is $85 per adult for unlimited home stays during a twelve-month period, plus a $25 deposit for host lists. For domestic travel, the fee is $50 for a twelve-month period plus a $15 deposit for host lists. Ask about their student and other discounted rates.

Do you fancy someone else's castle? **The Caretaker Gazette** (www.caretaker.org) publishes a bi-monthly newsletter containing ads for homeowners near and far who require the services of a willing and responsible housesitter (hey, that's you!). The subscription costs $29.95 a year and includes email alerts for positions requiring an immediate filling.

If you own your own home, consider trading spaces with other homeowners. Paul Heller, travel expert and founder of **The Big Blue Marble** (www.thebigbluemarble.com, a wonderful site full of tips on how to "travel like a local"), puts it bluntly: "It saves you a hell of a lot of money, and it's a lot more comfortable." You'll need to have a desirable home in order to attract a swap but if so, the benefits stand to be significant. "The quality of the accommodations can be amazing," Paul says. "I know people who've exchanged homes for multimillion-dollar mansions in Puerto Vallarta that overlooked the sea."

As with any situation involving strangers, use common sense and verify as much information as you can about your guests (or hosts) before they show up at your door (or you at theirs). If you're the guest, choose reliable references such as former hosts, employers and persons who have observed you functioning in a position of

trust. If you do arrange a stay at someone else's house, mind your manners—you were not raised in a barn so keep their home clean and follow their rules.

Transitions Abroad (www.transitionsabroad.com) maintains a comprehensive listing of homestays, home exchanges, and plenty of other good stuff. Go to their "Family Travel" section linked from the homepage. Homeowners can also check out **Global Home Exchange** (www.4homex.com) for travel trades; annual membership costs $49 Canadian.

BE A RUNNER

Air couriers are the insiders' source for remarkably cheap international flights, provided you have flexibility. These companies offer extreme discounts to someone (you, hopefully!) who will "courier" a shipment to its destination.

This isn't *Midnight Express*; passengers don't ever handle the shipment. They simply go through an extra administrative step with the air courier's agent upon departure and arrival. The courier must usually sacrifice any checked luggage and bring only a carry-on. Round-trip travel typically requires you to complete your trip within a given time period, ranging anywhere from seven days to six months.

In general, the closer to departure you purchase a courier flight ticket, the cheaper it is. According to travel experts, John F. Kennedy in New York is the best U.S. airport to launch from for trips to Europe, followed by San Francisco International for the Pacific Rim. One traveler we spoke with recently flew from San Francisco to Hong Kong round-trip for $150, and another made it to Sydney and back for $200!

Listings with the ***International Association of Air Travel Couriers*** *(www.courier.org)* require a $45-per-year membership for U.S. residents ($50 per year for non-U.S. residents) to peruse courier opportunities; browse the site first to decide if it suits your travel needs.

How to Save Money by Traveling Overseas

No place will deplete your savings faster than the good old U.S. of A. So it may seem a paradox, but you can actually *save* money by traveling. The dollar goes much farther in places like Southeast Asia, Latin America, or Eastern Europe. Says Paul Heller: "I often wonder why people retire in the U.S. at all. If you have a modest amount of money, I don't really know why people wouldn't go to Mexico or some other place where the cost of living is much lower."

If you're a renter, consider subletting your place while you're gone or giving up your lease and storing your furniture. If you own your home, think about renting it out. The money you save (or make) on rent could cover months of roaming abroad. You can also save significant money on the day-to-day expense of food and lodging in areas where the cost of living is low. Presumably, you won't be spending nearly as much money on items like clothing, gas and utilities—or burning through cash at fancy restaurants or bars—so even after subtracting the cost of getting there, you still come out ahead. Cha-ching!

TRAVEL WON'T DETRACT FROM YOUR CAREER

Don't let your friends tell you that an extended hiatus will derail your career. Travel did exactly the opposite for Dennis, a financial services executive. His 14-month solo journey around the world enhanced his standing in the eyes of more than one potential employer, and ultimately helped him land a slot with a major bank.

"I was pretty concerned about [the gap] when I first got back," he told us. "I was making up all these excuses, trying to hide it on my resume. But it became apparent pretty quickly that the trip I took was perceived as an asset, not a liability. Employers kept wanting to talk to me about it!" Dennis was courted by several large financial firms before accepting an offer from his favorite. "Keep in mind that these were banks and investment houses," he added, "not exactly the most progressive firms in the world, so that says a lot."

A travel sabbatical worked for Dana Magenau, too. He scored a plum job as director of The GRAMMY Foundation in Los Angeles after more than a year spent climbing the world's biggest mountains. "I think they just figured if I could do something like that, then surely I could handle running a foundation," he joked.

INTERNATIONAL ITINERARIES

Although no corner of the planet should be considered out of the question, we hope the following ideas will set some wheels in motion.

Southeast Asia

Sample Budgets—

> *Vietnam:* $1,000 per month
> *Laos:* $500 per month (includes elephant rides)
> *Malaysia:* $750 per month (bicycle not included)
> *Thailand:* $750 - $1,000 per month (date with Leonardo DiCaprio costs extra)

Major Access Points: Bangkok, Hong Kong, Jakarta, Manila, Singapore

Any seasoned traveler will tell you that Southeast Asia is one of the world's most fascinating and affordable destinations. Tom "Mr. Travel" Williams sums it up: "The variety in Southeast Asia is just incredible. I can hike a volcano in Indonesia, stay in a two dollar hut on the beach in southern Thailand, and eat extraordinary food in a Singapore street stall for one dollar. And as far as crowds go, there's always that next island out there that's still unspoiled."

Right now is a prime time to visit the region. Vast areas remain accessible, despite the damage and unfathomable loss of life caused by the Indian Ocean tsunami, and whatever you spend will help to soften the blow dealt to these tourist-dependent economies.

If you're used to the fast pace of Western life, it may take you a little while to slow things down in a region that's not in a hurry. "It actually took quite some time to learn to relax with a book in a hammock without feeling that nagging need to 'maximize productivity' or fill each moment with tourist activities," said traveler Ariella Quatra. "Eventually though, I was living like the local villagers in Laos—sleeping when tired, only eating when hungry, and telling time by the sunlight."

Many parts of Southeast Asia, particularly Thailand and Malaysia, have an excellent travelers' infrastructure of inexpensive accommodations and transportation—perfect for stretching an unemployed budget. Bangkok, although noisy, polluted and altogether chaotic, is a backpacker's haven for cheap plane tickets and other transport. It's also a superb place to connect with other like-minded travelers—it won't be difficult to find your non-working brethren here! A good southern launch point is Singapore, well-served by major airlines.

For more information:

Lonely Planet Southeast Asia on a Shoestring. Nicknamed the "Yellow Bible," this was Lonely Planet's very first guidebook, originally released back in 1973.

China

Sample Budgets—

Western China: *$1,000 per month*
Eastern China: *$2,000–3,000 per month*

Major Access Points: Hong Kong, Shanghai, Taipei

China demands its own mention, separate from the rest of Asia. More than just a country, it's an entire world in and of itself. From its urban industrial wastelands to its ancient imperial ruins, China is a land of contrasts. Beijing and Shanghai are fascinating cities, but let's not forget about Hong Kong, handed back to the Chinese in 1997, which still maintains the busiest port in the world. "Hong Kong sports the world's longest elevator," reports frequent flyer Chris O'Reilly. "And there's the ferry to the mainland. Does seventy-five cents fit a non-working budget?" Add to that the island of Taiwan and a country full of spectacular mountains, rivers and culture, and travel in China could fill up more than a year's itinerary (if you could manage to extend a visa for that long).

For more information:

ChinaTravel.com *(www.chinatravel.com)* makes for a good starting point. *Lonely Planet China* by Damian Harper and Steve Fallon will get you the rest of the way.

India/Nepal/Tibet

Sample Budgets—

> **Tibet:** *$500 per month (prayer flags are free)*
> **Nepal:** *$500 per month (Everest will cost a bit more)*
> **India:** *$1,000 per month (includes all the naan you can eat)*

Major Access Points: Mumbai (Bombay), Delhi, Kathmandu, Lhasa

Of all the places in the universe to visit, this part of Central Asia may offer a Western traveler the most consciousness-altering experience. If exploring spirituality is one of your leisure goals, this region might reincarnate your spirit of self-discovery. Ross Taggart, now working for the U.S. Department of State on human rights issues, took a year off from teaching to live, study and teach at a Tibetan monastery in Dharmsala, a city in northern India. "The whole experience was very intense," he says. "It changed my view on life forever."

India won't be easy. The country has tested the mettle of even the most hardened travelers. But it has also provided rewarding revelations. The region's mix of Buddhist and Hindu religions adds to the rich experience.

The mountains of Nepal have long been a destination for international mountaineers and are home to some of the best trekking on the planet.

Tibet, for its part, has persisted in relative isolation. You'll need to secure a permit from China to visit this tiny country.

For more information:

Incredible India *(www.incredibleindia.org)*. Produced by India's Ministry of Tourism, this site delivers a useful overview of travel in India, with some handy trip-planning tools.

VisitNepal.com *(www.visitnepal.com)*. With an eye towards the adventurous, VisitNepal.com provides solid background information on Nepal, along with a booking portal for almost any outdoor activity imaginable.

Africa

Sample Budgets—

> *Tanzania:* $1,000 per month; $3,000–$6,000 per month on safari
> *South Africa:* $500 per month (feral living)
> $1,000–$1,500 (standard)

Major Access Points: Johannesburg, Nairobi, you name it

Africa is not a single destination but a giant continent of countries to explore. One would do best to focus on just a handful. South Africa's beautiful coastline and world-famous game parks summon the leisurely wanderer in the post-Apartheid era. Ted Witt, an operations director from California, spent one month in South Africa during a recent six-month journey. He tells us, "As long as all you're doing is surfing and hanging out, you can easily live like a king on a thousand bucks a month. You could pull it off even cheaper if you live more economically. Ostrich meat is really cheap, and low in fat!"

Tanzania and Kenya also offer adventure in abundance, be it surveying the Serengeti, climbing Kilimanjaro, or overlanding through some of the world's best game preserves. The exotic Zanzibar Archipelago, just 25 miles off the coast, offers pristine white sand beaches, and exceptional diving and snorkeling. Dana Magenau, who spent several months in Africa during a recent one-year sabbatical, says Tanzania was easily his favorite of the four African countries he visited. "The people, places and wildlife make Tanzania one of the most diverse countries I've ever visited. Where else could you safari in the Serengeti, climb one of the Seven Summits and dive in crystal clear waters near Zanzibar in just two weeks?" Other choice countries include mystic Morocco in the northwest; wildlife-rich Botswana in the south, or enigmatic Mozambique on the southeastern Indian coast. With so many choices, you may have to pick straws to make a final decision where to go (or where not to go)!

For more information:

GORP *(www.gorp.com, go to "Destinations" then "Africa")*. One of the best resources on the Web for outdoor adventure travel, GORP is part of The Away Network, which also includes *OutsideOnline* magazine.

ENSURE YOU'RE INSURED

Chances are that your current health plan doesn't cover you on foreign soil. If you're leaving the country, you'll likely need a policy tailored specifically to traveling or living abroad. One broker specializing in travel-related insurance, **InsureMyTrip.com** (www.insuremytrip.com), provides exactly that.

Peter Evans, their executive vice president, recommends figuring out your needs before evaluating plans. "People need to realize that travel medical plans are not major medical policies, but are designed more for emergencies," he says. "The more expensive programs, 'travel major medicals,' are designed more for expats."

Some plans cover accidental death (just in case), medical evacuations (just in case), and travel baggage, which is insurance for (no, not your spouse!) that iPod and other stuff.

Find useful tools to compare different plans on the InsureMyTrip site.

South Pacific

Sample Budgets—

> *Tahiti:* $3,000 per month (consider camping)
> *Fiji:* $1,000 – $2,000 per month (not including inter-island travel)
> *Australia:* $1,500 per month base ($3,000 per month including beer)
> *New Zealand:* $1,000 per month (bungee jumping, sky diving, rock climbing,
>   life insurance, all extra)

Major Access Points: Auckland, Nadi, Pape'ete, Sydney

Ay mate, is there anything more leisurely than island-hopping through the South Pacific? Well, if your name is Captain Cook, the answer is probably yes. Otherwise, the Society Islands (a.k.a. Tahiti), the Fijian island chain, the Cook Islands, and the islands in between all offer life at a most leisurely pace, with tall, swaying palms and gregarious, ultra-friendly locals. Dane Larson, a marketing consultant, surfed and lazed away several months in the Society Islands after a two-year stint of full-time work and says, "Life there was so slow, I almost got bored. *Almost.*"

Do yourself a favor while you're all the way down under, and continue to New Zealand, a land of vast, unspoiled nature. The country is an outdoor adventurer's dream. And, what the heck, since you already spent the 16 hours on a plane to get to the other side of the planet, you might as well throw in Australia as well, seeing as how it's one of the greatest destinations ever! You could spend a year there without skipping a beat. We wouldn't blame you if you up and emigrated!

In both Australia and New Zealand, the fully developed economy and English-speaking citizenry ease the task of securing an odd job, although acquiring a legal working visa is extremely difficult for Americans. Farming skills are particularly useful in New Zealand, where travelers can regularly trade farmhand chores for food and lodging.

Peruse **Destination Downunder** (www.destinationdownunder.com, "working in nz") for more information.

For more information:

The "Mooneys" have the upper hand in the South Pacific. Start with their web-based **South Pacific Organizer** *(www.southpacific.org)* and graduate to any of their excellent guidebooks on the region, including *South Pacific Handbook* by David Stanley.

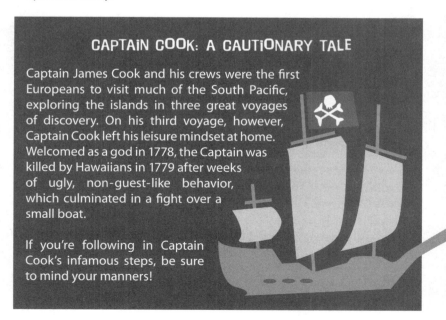

CAPTAIN COOK: A CAUTIONARY TALE

Captain James Cook and his crews were the first Europeans to visit much of the South Pacific, exploring the islands in three great voyages of discovery. On his third voyage, however, Captain Cook left his leisure mindset at home. Welcomed as a god in 1778, the Captain was killed by Hawaiians in 1779 after weeks of ugly, non-guest-like behavior, which culminated in a fight over a small boat.

If you're following in Captain Cook's infamous steps, be sure to mind your manners!

Western Europe

Sample Budgets—

France: *$2,500 per month (Champagne and Camembert extra)*
Spain: *$1,500 per month (includes flamenco lessons)*
Sweden: *$3,000 per month (consider camping for free in the woods)*

Major Access Points: London, Paris, Stockholm, the list goes on and on...

Western Europe, while more conventional than the other destinations we list, still emanates an irresistible aura of history and culture. One can hardly deny the allure of sipping wine on a sunny afternoon at a sidewalk Parisian café or savoring the sumptuous cuisine of Sicily. The north offers the unflappable refinement of Scandinavia; the south, the hot, Latin rhythms of Spain and Portugal; and the middle, the canals and the seat of European government.

The budget can be tricky here, especially as the U.S. dollar slides further into an exchange rate abyss. In general, prices fall with latitude: Greece, Turkey, Italy, Spain, and Portugal are going to be your cheapest bets, while Scandinavia is one of the world's most expensive regions. Unless you've got unlimited funds, you'd better plan to make friends up north who can double as hosts! Still, Western Europe's extensive hostel network and efficient train system have long made it a budget traveler's haven. The fact that English is widely spoken (much to the chagrin of the French) also makes travel relatively easy.

Western Europe may also be the region for you if you're interested in pursuing that studious sabbatical—say, in art, language, or cooking. The combination of English-speaking schools and "old world" expertise in certain specialty fields can make for a rewarding educational experience. For more information on European schools, see *The Back Door Guide to Short-Term Job Adventures* by Michael Landes, a book full of ideas for taking time off.

For more information:

Rick Steves' Europe Through the Back Door 2005. While not a comprehensive guidebook, *Back Door* serves as the quintessential trip planner for budget travel in Western Europe.

Rough Guide to Europe. An alternative to the ubiquitous *Let's Go* series, *Rough Guides* will keep you off the American college fraternity path and guide you into some real underground treats.

Eastern Europe

Sample Budgets—

Czech Republic: *$1,000 per month*
Croatia: *$1,000 per month*
Latvia: *$1,000 per month*

Major Access Points: Budapest, Prague, Warsaw, Zagreb, and so on

From the well-traveled Czech Republic, Poland, or Hungary, to the more obscure Slovakia, Serbia, or Croatia, Eastern European nations have plenty to offer the adventurous traveler. No one can deny the elegance and intrigue of such sophisticated cities as Prague or Budapest, but less-charted locales, like Slovenia, Albania, or the Baltic States of Estonia, Lithuania, and Latvia, all hide glorious treasures.

These days, the lines between Eastern Europe and Russia have blurred. Russia's still-volatile mix of the Old World, Eastern bloc-style culture combined with a deregulated economy can be both fascinating and dangerous—cultural treasures interspersed with crime and corruption. The Baltic States are a prime example, where Russian *mafiya* chat on cell phones in front of beautiful medieval churches.

Andis Blukis, an engineer and writer, lived overseas in Riga, Latvia. After jumping ship from a fast-sinking corporate vessel, he sought refuge in the small country of his ancestors. Originally planning a summer break, Andis remained in Riga a full year, working periodically as a software engineer for a Latvian phone company. "I worked with and learned from engineers who were rebuilding an unbelievably large and complex yet archaic phone call tracking system into Oracle as it simultaneously continued recording phone calls—the equivalent of rebuilding the engine of a 747 on the way across the Atlantic. Yet these same engineers also chose to haggle with an old bearded lady over the price of tomatoes, cream, and stinky cheese at the local medieval marketplace rather than go to a modern supermarket." He lived well in Latvia on approximately $1,000 per month.

For more information:

Lonely Planet Eastern Europe by Tom Masters, Lisa Dunford, and Mark Elliott. LP covers it all in this hip, up-to-date guidebook for this rapidly changing region.

Latin America

Sample Budgets—

Argentina: *$1,500 per month (living well)*
Costa Rica: *$1,000 per month (even in the rain forest)*
Mexico: *$750 per month (sombreros extra)*
Peru: *$1,000 per month (including Machu Picchu)*

Major Access Points: *Mexico City, Guatemala City, Lima, Saõ Paulo, Santiago*

"Latin America" is a broad term used to blanket a region of dozens of unique countries and cultures. From a travel standpoint, however, Latin America can be fairly divided into two primary areas: Mexico and Central America, for one, and South America, for the other.

The first region is almost as accessible by land as by air: Panama City is no farther from San Francisco than is New York, as the crow flies—or drives! Bring your water gear; two major oceans grace its shores and either side of the isthmus offers wonderful coastline to explore.

South America is more culturally diverse, with indigenous as well as European colonial influences on language, customs and architecture. From the sophistication of Buenos Aires to the raw, colorful communities of the Bolivian highlands, the continent begs to be explored. Bargains are not hard to find either. Argentina, with its economic woes, is particularly well-priced these days.

Melissa Manwaring and Bryan Jadot recently enjoyed four-course meals for two (including a nice Argentine wine) in Buenos Aires for just one $20 bill, and center orchestra seats at the symphony for only a fraction of that ($5). "Your dollar [in Argentina] now buys four or five times what it did a few years ago," Melissa told us, "so considering that Buenos Aires was once as expensive to visit as New York City, in many ways there's never been a better time to go. Plus, the Malbec is delicious!"

For more information:

South American Explorers *(www.saexplorers.org)*. A top-notch organization that publishes an extremely current quarterly magazine and maintains clubhouses in Ecuador (Quito) and in Peru (Lima and Cusco)

TRAVEL RESOURCES

BEFORE YOU GO
for research, maps, books, foreign-language dictionaries and more
- **your local public library** *(www.publiclibraries.com)*
- **Hostelling International USA** *(www.hiayh.org)*
- **GORP** *(www.gorp.com)*
- **Rand McNally** *(www.randmcnally.com)*

GUIDEBOOKS
- *Lonely Planet* *(www.lonelyplanet.com)*
- *Rough Guides* *(U.K.-based, www.roughguides.com)*
- *Time Out* *(www.timeout.com)*
- *Internet Travel Planner* by Michael Shapiro

BOOKING YOUR TRIP
- **Airtreks** *(877-247-8735, www.airtreks.com)* —an airline consolidator specializing in multi-stop, round-the-world tickets. Check out their online TripPlanner application for travel planning and pricing.
- **Air Brokers International** *(800-883-3273, www.airbrokers.com)* —an airline consolidator for cheap wholesale airline tickets.
- **Adventure Center** *(800-228-8747, www.adventurecenter.com)* —a wholesaler for international adventures. Good for group travel and ideas.
- **Southwest Airlines** *(800-435-9792, www.southwest.com)*
- **JetBlue Airways** *(800-538-2583, www.jetblue.com)*
- **International Association of Air Travel Couriers** *(www.courier.org)*
- **SmarterTravel.com** *(www.smartertravel.com)*
- **CheapTickets** *(www.cheaptickets.com)*
- **SideStep** *(www.sidestep.com)*
- **Orbitz** *(www.orbitz.com)*
- **Priceline** *(www.priceline.com)*
- **TripAdvisor, Inc.** *(www.tripadvisor.com)*

ROAD TRIPS
- **AAA** *(www.aaa.com)*
- **Auto Driveaway Co.** *(www.autodriveaway.com)*
- **Better World Club** *(866-238-1137, www.betterworldclub.com)*

OVERLAND TOUR COMPANIES
- **TrekAmerica** *(800-221-0596, www.trekamerica.com)*
- **Green Tortoise Adventure Travel** *(800-867-8647, www.greentortoise.com)*

INTERNATIONAL JOBS
- **JobMonkey.com** *(www.jobmonkey.com)*
- **International Academy** *(www.international-academy.com)*
- **PADI** *(www.padi.com)*
- **NAUI Online** *(www.naui.com)*
- **Club Med** *(www.clubmedjobs.com)*
- **Cruise Ship Jobs** *(www.shipjobs.com)*
- **Find a Crew Online** *(www.findacrew.com)*
- ***Work Your Way Around the World*** by Susan Griffith

ACCOMODATIONS & CAMPING
- **BedandBreakfast.com** *(www.bedandbreakfast.com)*
- **Bed and Breakfast Inns of North America** *(www.inntravels.com)*
- **ReserveAmerica** *(www.reserveamerica.com)*
- **National Park Service ParkNet** *(www.nps.gov)*

HOUSE SITTING, HOMESTAYS, & HOME EXCHANGES
- **GlobalFreeloaders.com** *(www.globalfreeloaders.com)*
- **US Servas** *(www.usservas.org)*
- **The Caretaker Gazette** *(www.caretaker.org)*
- **The Big Blue Marble** *(www.thebigbluemarble.com)*
- **Transitions Abroad** *(www.transitionsabroad.com)*
- **Global Home Exchange** *(www.4homex.com)*

LANGUAGE STUDY & TEACHING
- **GoAbroad.com** *(www.goabroad.com)*
- **Languages Abroad** *(800-219-9924, www.languagesabroad.com)*
- **Berlitz** *(www.berlitz.us)*
- **The Chronicle of Higher Education** *(www.chronicle.com)*
- **Dave's ESL Cafe** *(www.eslcafe.com)*

INTERNATIONAL VOLUNTEERING
- **Peace Corps** *(800-424-8580, www.peacecorps.gov)*
- **I-to-I** *(800-985-4864, www.i-to-i.com)*
- **Sierra Club** *(www.sierraclub.org/outings)*
- **Cross-Cultural Solutions** *(800-380-4777, www.crossculturalsolutions.org)*
- **The Center for INTERIM Programs** *(www.interimprograms.com)*
- **World-Wide Opportunities on Organic Farms** *(www.wwoof.org)*

MISCELLANEOUS
- **InsureMyTrip.com** *(www.insuremytrip.com)*
- ***Pay Nothing to Travel Anywhere You Like*** by Eric W. Gershman
- **South American Explorers** *(www.saexplorers.org)*
- **U.S. Department of State** *(www.state.gov)*
- **World Affairs Councils of America** *(www.worldaffairscouncils.org)*

TRAVEL WITH A PURPOSE

Ever ponder how Sir Francis Drake was able to complete his miraculous voyage circumnavigating the globe? Looking for a way to immerse yourself into a foreign community and hold normal conversations with the locals?

Add some pizzazz to your travels by choosing a theme or a purpose for your journey. Theme-based travel gives you a vehicle for seeing the planet while granting you a fulfilling educational, cultural, physical (perhaps even metaphysical) experience. Your travels might revolve around a particular activity like mountaineering or surfing, or they could include studying language or history at a local university. You could even take a food or wine tour, and eat your way across Europe!

"Meaningful travel doesn't have to mean going to a developing country and doing backbreaking labor for weeks, or serving in the Peace Corps," says Michael Shapiro, author of *A Sense of Place* as well as the *Internet Travel Planner*. "All that is great, but you can do little things on routine trips that make travel meaningful. You can convey a package from someone in Cuba to a relative in the U.S. You can listen to someone's story. You can stay at a family-run guesthouse rather than in a chain hotel."

Study the Local Language

Nothing will ingratiate you to a foreign community like speaking the local language. The fastest way to ramp up your language skills is to immerse yourself in the dialect with in-country study. The learning process itself will be a terrific way to get to know people, and a heck of a lot of fun.

Some areas, such as Paris or Shanghai, are known for their language schools, but you should be able to find some form of instruction virtually anywhere you look—including truly virtual instruction online.

Start your research with **GoAbroad.com** (www.goabroad.com), which covers everything from learning languages overseas, to teaching English, to interning and volunteering abroad. **Languages Abroad** (800-219-9924, www.languagesabroad.com) is another useful resource that focuses exclusively on language immersion.

For information on specific foreign language classes, try language stalwart **Berlitz** (in the U.S. www.berlitz.us) and their Berlitz Study Abroad programs. They also offer plenty of courses in the U.S. as well as online.

Learning Vacations

Language may be an obvious study, but you can take it a step further and study some local flavor as well. Dance, cook, sing, or paint your way through a unique in-country learning experience. Heck, you could even improve your snowboarding form. Almost any learning endeavor that you tie into your travels will have you looking forward to examinations.

"I spent a month in Buenos Aires studying Tango—it was a great, great month, and very cheap," says Paul Heller. "When you're going to school every day, you really feel like you're part of the community. You're taking classes from a local, you're living with a local, you're meeting other foreigners and locals who are interested in a subject."

The 411 on learning vacations tends to be spread throughout several resources. **Transitions Abroad** (www.transitions abroad.com) touts a keen "Adult Education" section linked from their homepage that's sure to tickle your fancy, if not your tootsies.

Teach English Overseas

Teaching English can be a groovy way to both make money while you travel and interact with locals. Raquel Rodriguez, a teacher from New York, is a self-described serial ESL (English as a Second Language) teacher abroad. "I love to learn languages and experience new cultures," she says. "The job market for college level ESL instructors is also pretty dismal in the States. Back home, I always

language study in latin america? ¡que bueno!

Seeking to dramatically improve her Spanish, Heidi Wells went directly to the source. For three months, she lived in Xela (a.k.a. Quetzaltenango), Guatemala, where she enrolled in one-on-one Spanish classes, five hours per day, five days a week.

"My instructor, Victor, doubled as my local tour guide," Heidi told us. "We'd go anywhere I could think of, from grocery shopping to trips to the pig farm. Everywhere we went, Victor grilled me on my Spanish and taught me new words." Her Spanish went from basic to keen in a Latin heartbeat.

Back stateside, Heidi kept the lessons going by tapping into the Guatemalan community in her hometown—over *cervezas* at the neighborhood cantina.

¿Porqué no?

get by with piecing together several adjunct positions. Abroad, I can always find good full-time work." Indeed, Raquel is currently overseas on assignment in the United Arab Emirates.

Raquel advises lining up gigs prior to landing in the destination country, for potentially better wages and benefits. For jobs at the university level, she highly recommends **The Chronicle of Higher Education** (www.chronicle.com), the definitive job resource for work at universities around the world.

There are a plethora of sources and schools dedicated exclusively to ESL or EFL (English as a Foreign Language). In addition to GoAbroad.com and Berlitz, peruse the informative, home-grown website **Dave's ESL Cafe** (www.eslcafe.com). The coffee may be lacking, but the information certainly percolates and you can connect with ESL teachers from around the world.

Sports, Music, and Other Hobbies

If you're a rock climbing or river kayaking fanatic, you probably don't need much persuading to pack your gear and seek out foreign climbs and rivers. But even if you're not an expert, choosing an activity outside of your own country will show you altogether different sights and experiences.

Music, for example, is a fabulous way to bridge cultural chasms. If you play an instrument, strap it to the pack for jam sessions with local musicians.

"When I travel I always bring my half-sized travel guitar," says veteran wanderer Ted Witt. "Music is a universal language, and musicians are part of a tribe that spans the globe—so anywhere around the world you can communicate on a very direct level with the locals through music. I can think of some real breakthrough cultural exchanges—an all night bossa nova jam session in Brazil, a campfire drum circle in Madagascar, a Guinness-soaked jig in Belfast—all spontaneous moments where I became an active participant in the community, rather than just a passive observer touring a foreign land."

We spoke with several people who toted their bikes along and cycled across countries as diverse as Europe, Cuba, and New Zealand. Breathing in the culture, meeting residents, and even sharing portions of the trip with local cyclists more than made up for the challenges (harsh weather, breakdowns, and accidents, to name a few) they reported. "New Zealand was a great place to bike," said Travis, an IT manager from Portland. "The roads were good, without much car traffic, and the scenery was amazing. And if I ever got tired of biking in the rain, I would just pull off and stay at one of the thousands of guesthouses."

Volunteer Vacations

"Volunteer vacations" are quickly rising in popularity, and organizations now specialize in arranging them. Programs run the gamut from remote environmental projects to inner-city teaching, and can range from two weeks to a year or more. The good news is there are a surprising number of ways to incorporate work and volunteering into your travels. "It's a wonderful way to meet people, learn about other cultures, and it's a great way to feel like you've had an opportunity to make a difference in someone's life," says travel guru Paul Heller.

PEACE

Long before volunteer travel programs became hip and trendy, the Peace Corps was doling out serious doses of life-changing experiences through two-year placements in developing nations around the world. Formed in 1961 under the leadership of President John F. Kennedy, the Peace Corps was founded as a way for Americans to serve their country in the interest of world peace. Volunteers get paid a local living allowance plus funds at the end of their service to help with the transition back to life in the U.S.

The granddaddy of all volunteer vacations is the **Peace Corps** (800-424-8580, www.peacecorps.gov). One need not sacrifice two full years, however, to do some good whilst traveling. Numerous organizations offer shorter stints, some as brief as a week or less. U.K.-based **I-to-I** (800-985-4864, www.i-to-i.com) caters to the more adventurous volunteer, offering "meaningful travel" ventures, from teaching computer skills to youth in Tanzania, to assisting with shark research in South Africa.

For the environmentally conscious, the **Sierra Club** (www.sierraclub.org/outings) offers what they call "service trips" in the U.S. and U.S. territories. The trips focus on outdoor volunteering (no surprise) and can range from maintaining turtle nesting grounds on the island of Culebra, Puerto Rico, to tracking mountain lions in western Arizona.

Cross-Cultural Solutions (800-380-4777, www.crosscultural solutions.org) offers what they call Intern Abroad, a two- to twelve-week program immersing volunteers into a variety of local cultures within the fields of education, healthcare, or social services. The **Center for INTERIM Programs** (www.interimprograms.com) seems to have been created for the specific purpose of helping people do something cool with their time off, or their "time on" as they like to call it. Their tagline ("If you could wave a magic wand, what would you do?") sums up their philosophy quite nicely, and their wish list (possibly yours, as well) includes programs as varied as surfing and studying Spanish in Central America to conducting whale research off the coast of Hawaii. Cool? You bet.

For more on Volunteer Vacations, see **Chapter 9** under "Volunteer Abroad."

Create Your Own Theme

If a pre-fabricated program is too confining for you, get creative and devise your own premise for a journey. Browse the annals of history for a topic that interests you, and design an itinerary around it. Your trip through Latin America could trace the conquests of Hernán Cortés, for example, or your South Pacific voyage could follow Captain Cook's—but be more courteous than he was! We heard of one couple who quit their jobs, flew to Italy, bought a Volvo and drove all over the Mediterranean following a map of the ancient Roman conquest. "We could always tell the Romans had been there," they said, "because the first thing they always did was build baths and roads."

go organic, dude

A network of organic farms around the world awaits the manual labor of those who like a more organic approach to volunteer travel. In exchange for work on their farms, many growers will offer up free room and board.

World-Wide Opportunities on Organic Farms, or *WWOOF* (www.wwoof.org) maintains a list of international organic farms that accept volunteer labor. The farm stays can be a rewarding way to tap into the local culture, as well as an opportunity to see some beautiful, rural areas.

Another tried and true source of inspiration is literature: let Michener, Hemingway or Theroux steer you through new and exotic lands. Hemingway fans beware—more than a few have already made the pilgrimage to Pamplona.

DRESS FOR SUCCESS (-FUL TRAVEL)

Lots of people suffer from the inability to pack well. We put it off until the last minute and just throw stuff from our closets and bathrooms into a bag (or three). But there *is* help!

Check out Barbara DesChamps' book *It's In the Bag: The Complete Guide to Lightweight Travel (www.chateaupublishing.com)*, where Barbara supplies decades' worth of packing advice, including how to buy the right luggage, breeze through baggage inspection, and build a travel wardrobe. Another great source of advice on how to travel light is Lani Teshima's *www.travelite.org*. Wondering where to find travel-size items? If you can't find it at your local drug store, you may find what you need at *www.minimus.biz*. If you need packing aids, look at **Magellan's Travel Supplies** *(www.magellans.com)*. They also carry alarm clocks, steamers, water and air purifiers, talking translators, and picnic gear (and more!).

Unless you love to stand around the baggage carousel praying your luggage will find you again, learn to pack only what fits in a carryon. Think about the location's weather, your planned activities, whether or not to bring clothes that look like a wad of used tissue paper even after careful packing…. You may have to purchase apparel that is more wrinkle-resistant, comfortable, and versatile than your regular wardrobe. **L.L.Bean** *(www.llbean.com)* sells travel apparel—even fishing shirts that repel insects—from their site's Luggage & Travel section. **TravelSmith** *(www.travelsmith.com)* specializes in travel apparel and lightweight accessories. If you're going on an outdoor adventure, **REI** *(www.rei.com)* is *the* place to shop.

If you like to shop when you travel, you'll want to leave a little extra luggage space. Or, bring some clothes that you're on the verge of getting rid of. Hang onto the favorite-but-needing-to-be-fixed pair of shoes, though, and find a cobbler en route.

Travel Without Leaving

Perhaps you don't have the budget for a big trip overseas, yet still would like to explore a new area or culture. Not to worry. With the level of ethnic and cultural diversity found in the United States, you are sure to find a palette of exotic colors and flavors right here at home.

Language, for example, doesn't need to be studied in a foreign country. You can do it right in your own hometown, and it's a great way to introduce yourself to a new region. Shake your international booty to some world music, and learn a thing or two about a regional dance in the process. Globally orient yourself with seminars, events, and talks on a topic or region of interest; they take place all the time in urban centers throughout the country.

A healthy starting point would be the **World Affairs Councils of America** (www.worldaffairscouncils.org). Reach out and connect with a council near you; they are sprinkled throughout the U.S. A journey of the mind can help satisfy and whet your appetite for travel at the same time—minus the jetlag and Aztec two-step of course.

A FINAL NOTE

Travel can be enormously fulfilling, even life-changing. Unfortunately, in this modern era it also can be hazardous, particularly for Americans. The status and safety of different international regions is constantly changing. Use your best judgment when choosing a destination and take appropriate precautions when traveling to "hot spots." Be sure to consult the latest travel advisories from the U.S. Department of State when considering international travel.

CHAPTER 6
UNEMPLOYMENT ON THE EDGE

Temptation rarely comes in working hours.
It is in their leisure time that men are made or marred.

~ W.N. Taylor

TRAVEL can open your eyes, and introspection can open the windows to your soul, but nothing takes you farther from the office than living day-to-day with pure abandon. Wanna rock and roll all night? Run amok with the spring break crowd in Fort Lauderdale? Go ahead, toss out your alarm clock. Let your hair down and dye it purple. Take a walk on the wild side. You're free at last!

Sometimes legal, sometimes not, life on the edge can be as innocent as nude sunbathing or as risqué as watching a peep show—or starring in one. One thing's for sure: if you open yourself to new experiences, you will find doors opening for you in return.

Just make sure the doors are ones you want to go through. Getting arrested, blowing your budget or losing the respect of friends or family would be anything but liberating. Remember that freedom is as much about charting new ground as it is about learning your limits. If you don't know your limits, take this opportunity to find out. Only you know how far you can safely push the envelope.

ante up

Poker's meteoric popularity can be attributed in part to ESPN's regular broadcasting of poker's premier event, the World Series of Poker, held at the Horseshoe Casino in Las Vegas. From its heyday in 1970, the WSOP has sported champions from cowboys to a Vietnamese immigrant, demonstrating the accessibility to the glamour, drama and big money of this card game.

In 2002, the World Series total prize money reached almost $20 million, and in 2003, the championship attracted viewership from more than one million households. The winner of the 2003 series, Chris Moneymaker (with that name, who could lose?), an accountant from Tennessee, worked his way to the fabled final table by starting with $39 in an online tournament. Last year's champion, Greg "Fossilman" Raymer, a patent attorney from Connecticut, also parlayed his online entry into a grand prize of $5 million, the largest ever winner's pot in a poker tournament.

Moneymaker's and Raymer's routes to success have spawned wannabes around the world.

FUN & GAMING

Gambling interests rake in nearly $400 billion a year, more than all other types of entertainment. Those who study these things put games into the category of casual leisure, as opposed to "productive" leisure like hobbies or competitive sports. But that depends on whose productivity you're talking about. "The House" has created a variety of methods for parting you from your money. Get tips from "Daddy" at **Il Dado** (www.ildado.com). Remember: never bet more than you can afford to lose.

Riverboat Gambling

Iowa legalized riverboat gambling in 1989—slots and tables, baby! Other riverside states soon followed suit. So if casinos are what float your boat, steer yourself down the Mississippi, Ohio or Missouri rivers. Actually, land-based casinos are permitted in New Orleans, even though casinos elsewhere in Louisiana must be on a fully operational riverboat with the appropriate historical paddleboat look (remember, this is cultural *history* we're talking about). Riverboat casinos in Mississippi are legal only if they're on a stationary barge. Indeed, Mississippi now ranks second in the world in terms of casino space, with a big gambling center in Biloxi.

Poker

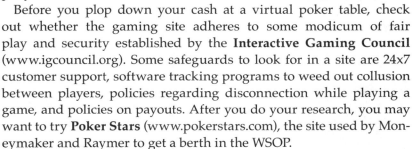

Poker on TV. Reality poker. Celebrity poker. Back-room poker. It's trendier than cigars, and the company is even racier.

Before you plop down your cash at a virtual poker table, check out whether the gaming site adheres to some modicum of fair play and security established by the **Interactive Gaming Council** (www.igcouncil.org). Some safeguards to look for in a site are 24x7 customer support, software tracking programs to weed out collusion between players, policies regarding disconnection while playing a game, and policies on payouts. After you do your research, you may want to try **Poker Stars** (www.pokerstars.com), the site used by Moneymaker and Raymer to get a berth in the WSOP.

You can get real table experience by taking a poker seminar. Dylan Simpson, co-founder of **The Poker Camp** (www.thepokercamp.com), offers two-day trainings in Reno, Tahoe, and Vegas that let you pit your skills against other newbies, enthusiasts and even pros. The seminar's graduation involves one tournament feeding the top players into a satellite tournament that feeds into an even larger tournament. Simpson created the seminar to provide opportunities to mingle with poker's elite. "If you are a golfer, you will never have a chance to play Tiger Woods," Simpson points out, but with poker you have a chance to play against the big names, such as Antonio "The Magician" Esfandiari, who teaches at the seminars and has been ranked in the top twenty players of the world. You may even have a chance to mingle with movie stars. Ben Affleck outplayed seasoned pros and won over $350,000 at the 2004 California State Poker Championship.

And don't think that playing high-stakes poker is limited to men—Annie Duke, a mother of four, beat out a field of men to win the $2 million top prize in the 2004 ESPN World Series of Poker Tournament of Champions.

Who said it's just a card game?

TALK THE TALK

For a refresher on your gambling jargon, visit *The Good Gambling Guide* (www.thegoodgamblingguide.co.uk) and click on "Glossary." Whether you prefer a carpet joint or a goulash joint, just stop before you're down to the felt—and whatever you do, don't be a fish!

Pai Gow Poker

Pony up to play Pai Gow Poker, one of the fastest growing games in gambling. The card game is a combination of traditional Chinese dominoes ("Pai Gow") and American poker, and was first introduced in 1986 to the card rooms of California. Nevada and other states quickly followed. As with traditional poker, it's considered a game of skill and is legal wherever poker is legal. In California card houses, games of skill are legal, as long as it's not considered a percentage game, where the house takes a percentage of the earnings. Games considered "gambling" (like blackjack) are banned.

You don't have to hold a hand of cards to play. Even passersby can bet. Full of superstition and showmanship, Pai Gow Poker and traditional Pai Gow games are now a fixture at Las Vegas casinos. Learn the basics of Pai Gow Poker from **LasVegas.com** (www.lasvegas.com, click on "Gambling," then "Games," then "Pai Gow Poker").

Tribal Land Casinos

No reservations required—Indian gaming casinos are likely in or coming to a town near you. The casinos have been allowed on qualifying tribal lands since Congress passed the Indian Gaming Regulatory Act in 1988. Of 557 federally recognized reservations, about a third have commercial gaming, and another third want to. The successful casinos constitute virtually the only business win the reservations can boast. As controversial as they may be, tribal casinos pull in far less than even state-run lotteries.

States are now considering allowing American Indian casinos on non-tribal land. Wherever they are, should they pay regular taxes? If Governor "Ah-nold" has anything to do with it, the casinos in California will be muscled into paying perhaps more than their fair share, which will likely tip the scales in favor of locational migration. Too bad Jesse "The Body" Ventura no longer reigns in Minnesota; he and The Gubernator could arm wrestle to resolve the controversy.

The **National Indian Gaming Association** (www.indiangaming.org) catalogs tribal casinos. Click on "Indian Gaming Visitors Guide" to find a casino near you.

Betting On Sports

Gone are the days when you needed to ring up a bookie named Vinny who threatened to break your legs if you didn't pay up (sigh...the memories). In-person at a casino or online, betting on sports is accessible and easy. There are literally thousands of options available: fantasy football, Superbowl pools, college sports, whether the beer tastes great or is less filling—you get the picture.

Online gambling is geared especially for those who want to ruin their established credit, with approximately one gajillion websites standing by to take custody of your money. Start at **Sportsbook Review** (www.sportsbookreview.com) for reviews and comparisons of different online sportsbooks, and **Online Casino Reports** (www.onlinecasinoreports.com) for reviews of online casinos. Odds are you'll find a site to your liking.

Know When To Fold 'Em

Gambling in excess can lead to financial catastrophe and dash your hopes for a long sabbatical. If you find yourself wagering on the neighbors' dogs racing in the street, you might be due for a reality-check. A 1999 federal commission on gambling estimated that there were two-and-a-half million pathological gamblers and three million problem gamblers in the United States.

More popular than golf but not as popular as gardening, gambling is most attractive to those who can least afford it. Know when to take your winnings and split!

award winners

Gambling on the Academy Awards isn't going too far—is it?

Cinema fan and leisure connoisseur Dane Larson bets every year on the Oscars, and every year he wins. In 2005 he won four out of five bets. "Unfortunately, my one loss was on Best Director (Scorcese was robbed!) where I bet pretty big, significantly cutting down my winnings," Dane said. "But [Million Dollar] Baby came through in the clutch, even with underdog odds [7-5].

"That's what's so good about betting on the awards shows," he added. "Big upsets are rare, and there's always some anomalies in the odds that you can take advantage of."

A nomination for Best Gamble of the year? We'll take those odds.

GREAT MOMENTS IN MIS-EMPLOYMENT

Stephen King was teaching high school English for slave wages when he was offered a position to coach the debate team, which would have meant a considerable boost to his salary. His wife Tabatha told him to turn it down when she learned it would cut into his writing time. Billions of book sales and gazillions of dollars later, turns out she gave him good advice. That's one horror story with a happy ending!

PARTY CITIES

Time to fold your hand and throw a party instead! Perhaps in a city where you're best advised to check your inhibitions at the door. Atlantic City springs to mind (spring breaks to mind?), along with the once-sleepy-fishing-village of Cancun, now bedecked with miles of white sand, honeymooners and scuba divers. And don't forget Rio, home of the *caipirinha*, samba dancing, and the world's most famous Carnaval. Yet, two U.S. cities simply scream for non-disclosure. If you're looking for life on the edge, they are the two you don't want to miss. That's right—Vegas and New Orleans.

Vegas

Stuck in the middle of nowhere, Las Vegas is so over-the-top phony that you gotta love it. From the 20,000-gallon saltwater aquarium behind the registration desk of the Mirage Hotel to indoor skydiving in a modified wind-tunnel to a $60 fifteen-minute helicopter ride, Vegas is the mecca of the man-made attractions, the land of the constant hard sell.

> **finding that loving feeling**
>
> Scott and his gal came to Vegas once. "After buying the plane tickets and paying for the hotel room, we had twenty-five dollars left to spend," he told us. "It was the best trip I've ever had."
>
> Scott travels with a lot more money now but he's still trying to capture the magic of that twenty-five dollar trip.
>
> "This trip I'm up twenty-five dollars," he says. "I'm happy." Maybe he should pocket that cash and buy another lover's retreat!

But so long as you can avoid the allure of the gambling tables, it can also be a low-cost paradise.

Look for half-price tickets on shows and the many two-for-one coupons in city guides like *24x7 Magazine* if you have only a few tokens to spare. Ride the monorail across town for just $3 each way. If you have even less than nothing once you've booked your cheap travel package, hang onto your money and enjoy the amenities, because you could easily fill a three-day weekend with nothing but free attractions.

Vegas, baby. Even if you're unemployed, you can live like royalty.

If you're considering a move to Sin City, remember that it still retains the edge of a Wild West town. Rachel Karagounis drove straight from Orange County one day, armed with only several hundred

FEELIN' FREE

Here is just a partial list of what you can enjoy for free in Las Vegas:

- the Mirage Volcano, erupting 100 feet high every fifteen minutes from 8pm to midnight
- the Bellagio Hotel's Conservatory and Botanical Gardens, changing every season
- the fountains in front of Bellagio, rocking out in synch with top pop songs
- the Fall of Atlantis Fountain Show
- the Big Top Show at Circus Circus all day long
- an indoor rainstorm at Desert Passage at the Aladdin Hotel
- belly dancers, contortionists, acrobats and musicians, also at the Aladdin
- free pedi-cab tours *(but tip your cabbie!)*
- the Ethel M. Chocolate Factory Tour
- a botanical cactus garden
- a medieval court jester's stage with jugglers, puppetry and musicians
- a flamingo wildlife habitat
- a lion habitat at the MGM Grand
- a white tiger habitat at the Mirage *(it's all about being captive)*
- the Hawaiian Marketplace show with fireknife dancing, hula and Polynesian drumming
- the Rio Masquerade Show In The Sky parade
- the Azure Mermaid show at the Silverton

dollars and the encouragement of family and friends. "I was going to make it my town," she told us. "I learned a hard lesson: don't tell anyone you just moved here! Vegas is a city where you definitely need to watch out."

But you certainly won't starve. Rachel regularly took advantage of the $6.95 to-go specials at any number of Vegas buffets, famous for their lavishness and reasonable prices. "I'd load up, take it home, eat half, then the next day I had enough for another meal," she told us. All the better for fueling the all-night party! Or is it daylight out? No matter. Just remember that what happens in Vegas, stays in Vegas.

seeking fun?

True masters of fun can take their merriment to a whole new level by perusing a copy of *The Fun Seeker's North America* by Alan Davis. This travel tome is painstakingly researched, and takes its fun quite seriously.

"I went to the Running of the Bulls in Pamplona, Spain," says Alan on how he came up with the idea for the book series. "I couldn't find any useful resources for the trip. By luck, I caught the most thrilling moment—the opening of the Fiesta. The whole event was the greatest party I'd ever seen. I decided to find all of the other great events and produce a guidebook that would be about being in the right place at the right time."

In addition to profiling and ranking events throughout North America, *Fun Seeker's* includes a Gold List of the best parties and party cities in the world. Las Vegas and New Orleans top the elite five-star city list (no surprise), while Burning Man and Mardi Gras nab top entertainment honors. Looking to hook up? Scan the "Mating Rating" in the back, which categorizes fiestas by level of nookie potential: "Viagra" *(there's Hope),* "Prozac" *(Slight Chance)* and "Hemlock" *(No Chance).*

New Orleans

Good at so many times of year—for Jazz Fest, for conventions, and of course for Fat Tuesday (otherwise known as *Mardi Gras* to you Frenchies)—N'Awluhns is a can't-miss kinda town. Amble down Bourbon Street any day of the year and, with all the crowds milling about, you would swear it's Carnaval. Keep an eye out (or maybe some other part of your anatomy) for the free beads on the street, and offer the largest, shiniest, wackiest beads around for your own sneak peek. Note: Christmas ornaments strung together work really well.

Oh, you were looking for some *cultural* action? Take a cemetery tour. If you're lucky, your guide will let you try on an above-ground crypt for size.

Perhaps that's a bit bleak. How about feeding your face with oysters instead? The **Acme Oyster House** (www.acmeoyster.com) in the French Quarter serves up a dozen for a price so reasonable that you might want two platefuls. The staff shucks them for you right at the bar. Take Cool Hand Luke as your inspiration and see just how many you can squeeze into your belly. You'll have to power down forty-two-and-a-half dozen—that's 510 oysters, to be clear—to knock the current champion off his throne. The fifteen-dozen club might be more your speed. Monitor your competition through Acme's OysterCam (hit the main website and then "OysterCam").

Last but not least: the music. The swingin' sounds of Uptown will lift you up, the rousing jams at **House of Blues** (www.hob.com) will stir your soul, and the smooth jazz of Frenchmen Street will soothe you back down. Find out what's happening with the local music scene when you're in town at **Satchmo.com** (www.satchmo.com), a site built in honor of the father of jazz, Louis Armstrong.

For more on New Orleans in general, check out **CrescentCity.com** and **NewOrleans.com**.

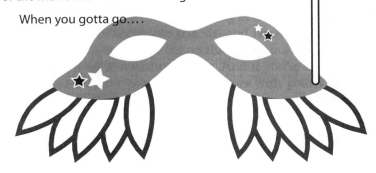

NO HOLDING BACK

One problem that the Crescent City guidebooks won't mention is the shortage of toilets for all the drunken revelers. You'll be lucky to find a porta-potty. The bars and restaurants won't let you use their bathrooms unless you plop down some patron cash and even then, the wait could be an hour. Ouch! Peeing in the open is ill-advised unless you're willing to risk the police cutting your stream short, socking you with a fine and dragging your tush to impound, depending on your attitude.

Mark X and his buddies devised a way to get around the police and the long lines at bathrooms: a large plastic cup held strategically under an oversized jacket...and when you're done with your business, dump it into a drain. Just remember which cup your beer is in and which one has already been processed. This technique won't work as well for women so may we suggest just cutting in line for the men's bathroom and using a stall there?

When you gotta go....

BURNING MAN: A RELIGIOUS EXPERIENCE?

What began in 1986 as a small Summer Solstice celebration on Baker Beach in San Francisco has become a worldwide movement: **Burning Man** (*www.burningman.com*), an annual event that welcomed more than 30,000 participants in 2004. Every year during the week prior to and including Labor Day weekend, attendees make the annual pilgrimage to Black Rock Desert in Nevada. What transpires can be adequately understood only by those who experience the phenomenon in person. Suffice it to say, the event could qualify in any number of categories within this very chapter: drugs, sex, extreme activities, and yes, even religion.

At its core, Burning Man is a celebration of creativity, community, and self-expression. There's only one rule: participate, don't spectate. If you go, strap on your safety helmet—you're in for a wild ride! The event culminates with the burning of a wooden sculpture cum artpiece, lighting the desert skies and casting shadows on the hordes of faces shifting and radiating in concentric pulses from the center.

DRINKING & DRUGS
A Night on the Drink

With your days wide open for riding out a hangover, non-employment beckons you to tie one on. We're not *promoting* alcohol use, mind you; just saying that if there ever was a time to indulge a bit, now's probably it. A few basics will enhance any night of drinking. Not that you need any guidance in this area....

One, don't drink alone—get yourself some drinking buddies. Girls or guys, it doesn't matter, but no one should be drinking solo. Two, don't drive—take cabs, public transit, or a limo, or designate a reliable driver, no exceptions. There's absolutely no reason to get behind the wheel after a night of drinking. You can be past the legal limit even if you don't feel drunk and the consequences of getting busted are not at all fun. Three, expand your horizons. Venture beyond your standby taverns and get a dose of diversity.

Think there's no place like home? Save some money and host your own cocktail party. Stock up with proper cocktail gear: low and highball glasses, martini glasses, essential mixers, garnishes, a good bartending book (our personal favorite is *The Bartender's Bible* by Gary Regan), and ice—plenty of ice. Ask friends to bring over their spirit of choice and voilà! The party is on.

Whatever your choice, remember to drink plenty of water and take some aspirin before bed to help ease that morning pain.

A Day on the "Green"

With the Euro pounding the U.S. Dollar, a trip to weed-friendly Amsterdam may be beyond your unemployed budget. No, it's not legal everywhere in the U.S., but there are pocket sanctuaries for the use, cultivation and distribution of medical marijuana. You can find out each state's particular laws from the **Drug Policy Alliance** (www.drugpolicy.org, "State By State"). The **National Organization for the Reform of Marijuana Laws**, or **NORML** (www.norml.org) can get you up to snuff as well. Leaf through their informative website to find the latest on mary jane.

Why might this interest you, the edgy leisure seeker? As our friend "Ross" explains, "Weed will get you through times of no money better than money will get you through times of no weed." Perhaps true for some. If you're experimenting for the first time, we're sure you can find friends for advice, support, and, er, collaboration.

Livin' After Midnight

"Last all night or longer." No, it's not the latest Viagra slogan; it's the description of a Free Party, also known as a rave, doof, teuf or sometimes a teknival.

At a Free Party, you can dance, socialize and have uninhibited fun all weekend, whether you're in an empty warehouse or at the beach, in the middle of a forest or in the midst of a crowded club. The most authentic are organized by a group of enthusiasts sharing the tasks of supplying the power, the bar, the decor and the tunes—the bigger the sub-woofers, the better. The scene is above ground these days and the focus is on letting fans of the all-night electronic music scene do their thang.

The ultimate rave might be at Burning Man in the middle of a Nevada desert, where the only lights you'll see will be from lasers and strobes. Most raves attract a crowd closer in age to 20 than 30, and yes, there are often lots of drugs, of the supposedly social and recreational variety. Raves are usually free, in terms of both expression and cost. Even if there is a charge, ask nicely and you might get a non-employed discount. Pay if you can, though—events are expensive. If you can't give greenbacks, offer to give your time. Volunteers are generally welcomed. Get up to speed on rave culture at **Raves.com** (www.raves.com), where you can check out their calendar listing parties from Montreal to Melbourne.

GETTING EXTREME

Maybe you prefer the natural high of adrenaline. Why skate through the park when you could inline downhill? Why go for a Sunday drive when you could do time trials around the track? If the thought of jumping from a bridge, out of a hot air balloon, or off a giant crane attached to nothing but a giant rubber band gets your heart pumping, extreme sports could be for you.

Bungee Jumping

Kiwi wildman AJ Hackett could hardly have known that by jumping off the Greenhithe Bridge outside of Auckland, New Zealand in 1986 tied to nothing but a giant latex cord, he would ignite a worldwide phenomenon. But it wasn't until 1987—when the charismatic Hackett leapt from the Eiffel Tower in Paris with the worldwide media looking on, and was greeted on the ground with champagne and kisses by the Parisian women (in addition to handcuffs by the French police)—that the sport of bungee jumping captured international attention. Still, he can't take credit for inventing the sport. That can be traced back as early as the 1500s on the small island nation of Vanuatu, where for hundreds of years brave young men have launched themselves into a male rite of passage by "vine jumping" off the edge of a small cliff, anchored at the ankles by nothing but a long vine.

The modern bungee cord is, we're happy to report, a little more forgiving on the body. And at a cost of $50 per leap or even lower, bungee jumping makes for a relatively cheap thrill. It also appears Mr. Hackett's little publicity stunt paid off: AJ Hackett Bungy (www.aj-hackett.com, and yes, there's a dispute over the correct spelling of "bungee/bungy") is now an international corporation with operations in eight countries around the world, including the U.S., in Las Vegas. For a homegrown bungee starting point, try **Bungee.com** (www.bungee.com).

Hang Gliding

Ever wanted to fling yourself off a cliff and fly like a bird? The **United States Hang Gliding Association** (www.ushga.org) reports flights of more than 300 miles long and 18,000 feet high. Shave $3,000 off your starter costs by purchasing used equipment. *Used?* Just make sure that an experienced pilot inspects it first. See also **Adventure Handbook** (www.adventurehandbook.com) and select "Hang Gliding" from the pull-down menu.

Sky Diving

There's no rush like falling out of an airplane, whether it's a one-time tandem jump or the first of many solos. Just remember, when push comes to shove, you have to jump out of a plane strapped to a sack of silk. Bon voyage! To dive into more information, seek out the **United States Parachute Association** (www.uspa.org).

Auto Racing

Trust us, you won't be thinking of work when you're screaming around a racetrack at top speed. "The most enjoyable aspect of car racing is its intensity," says long-time racer George Portugal. "Unlike so many other pursuits in life, racing demands immediate—and often less than optimal—action. Drivers don't have the luxury of waiting to make perfect decisions." Or of being distracted by thoughts of the office!

If you've been itching to explore an off-camber turn, rev up your engine with a popular high performance driving school. You'll need your own street-legal car (we recommend a Porsche 911, but that's just us), a 3-point belt-harness for both front seats (i.e., the standard shoulder and lap strap), a Snell-rated helmet, and a cool leather jacket. Okay, the jacket's optional. For a more affordable ride, rent a performance car and join an auto club for a member-paid track day (try **UnlimitedLaps,** www.unlimitedlaps.com). You get to brag about the day's events over beers afterward with your new driving comrades.

Unauthorized: So you just finished watching *The Fast and the Furious* and *2 Fast 2 Furious* back to back, and your gas pedal foot is spasming uncontrollably against the floor while nitrous-fueled dreams are dancing in your head. Before taking it to the open road, know this: street racing is downright dangerous, and the cost of getting caught racing illegally is steep. That being said, all you speed and car nuts can tap into an underground scene. A number of websites offer a bevy of information, mainly provided by racers themselves, including **Street Racing Online Magazine** (www.sromagazine.com) and **Street Racers Online** (www.streetracersonline.com).

Vroom vroom.

Harley Riding

Some consider it edgy; others consider it a high form of patriotism. One thing's for sure, a well-maintained Harley is a rare example of American automotive ingenuity that didn't go down the tubes with the rest of Detroit. For a wild event to get in touch with your inner Harley, rev on down to Daytona Beach, Florida, in March for the perennial **Bike Week** (www.daytonachamber.com, then "Official Bike Week").

Shark Diving

Presumably, shark cages have come a long ways since the days of Hooper, Quint, and Brody (remember *Jaws*?). That doesn't mean, however, that your heart won't slam out of your chest at the site of a great white shark up close and personal. Save more than your pennies for this one, as the trips are not cheap, running $700–$2,500 per person.

"I didn't feel unsafe at all," reports Marlo Sarmiento, who traveled to Palau (oh, add another $2,000 for plane tickets) for a week on a diver's live-aboard. "We did a shark feed off the back end of the boat and stuck our cameras underwater, with no protection. If there's food in the water, the sharks aren't interested in you."

Research the latest in shark adventures with **Shark Diver** (www.sharkdiver.com), or preview the thrill with **Incredible Adventures** (800-644-7382, www.incredible-adventures.com, click on "Shark Adventures").

NUDITY

No neckties, no nylons, no dress code at all. Actually, the dress code is *no* dress. That's right, we're talking about nudist colonies.

In many ways, nudity isn't edgy enough to belong in this chapter. "Nude is not lewd!" declares the **Naturist Society** (www.naturist society.com), a 25-year-old organization that believes that to relax and be nude is to let yourself be totally free. Think of the innocence you feel when skinny dipping, for example, and you'll understand why it's perfectly appropriate for children to participate in most naturist activities. Class distinctions disappear along with your clothing as you learn to accept yourself and others more easily. What better antidote to office politics?

Most things that can be done clothed can be done unclothed, and usually it's a lot more fun. There are nude backpackers, canoeists, kayakers, scuba divers, skydivers—even enlightened Texans roam "free from the cares of the textile world" at Bluebonnet, a 66.5 acre naturist park in North Central Texas, an hour and a half from Dallas. Join in their "Bare as you Dare" 5K cross-country race and weekend campout and discover for yourself—nude running brings an exhilaration that can't be matched.

Some travel clubs fill an entire resort or live-aboard boat so that the whole group can be nude. No one is required to "skin" dive, but if you'd like to give it a go, contact **Buff Divers** (888-686-0006, www.buffdivers.com) and the club's coordinators, Dale and Fluffy Felton. Membership is $15 per year.

Short of committing to a new lifestyle, you can try a day at the beach (or hot spring, or swimming hole) or a weekend excursion to a nude resort or campground. Publicly owned sites like Miami-Dade County's Haulover Beach, Long Island's Fire Island, Toronto's Hanlan's Point, and San Diego's Black's Beach now welcome naturists, as do hundreds of clubs, resorts, and campgrounds across North America. The nude resort atmosphere ranges from rustic to luxurious to friendly, wholesome and family-oriented.

The **American Association for Nude Recreation** (800-TRY-NUDE, www.aanr.com) keeps tabs on close to three hundred private clubs, resorts and RV campgrounds in the United States, as well as 50,000 individual members. Note that "clothing-optional" is different from nudist. At a nude resort, you will have no option—those clothes *are* coming off! And with that, we will clothes this section.

MORE FUN WITH YOUR BODY

Many forms of cosmetic self-expression simply won't fly in an office environment, even if that office does have a ping-pong table. But if you're no longer reporting to The Man, it might be time for you to dye your hair a crazy color, stick a big ring in your nose, or get that cool snake tattoo you've been eyeing at the local ink parlor. A midweek field trip can help you research these various body alterations.

Tattoos

Tatt' calling your name? Just remember—tattoo removal is painful and expensive; anything inked into your skin at 25 should look just as good on you at 50. Try a henna tattoo for a temporary walk on the wild side.

Body Piercing

Lips or brow, navel or nipple, almost no body part goes pierce-free these days. And don't forget about those oldies but goodies, the ears! Does it hurt? Well…yes, but it can't be as painful as the overbearing boss you left behind at your last job. Poke around at **Body Modification Ezine** (www.bmezine.com) for every possible body mod you might imagine—and some you haven't.

Hair

Nothing signifies a break from conventionality like fluorescent spiky hair. "When I left the company I worked for, I colored my hair fuchsia and gave all my designer clothes to a woman's shelter," says Joan E. Phelps, a sixty-year-old publisher, business coach and communication consultant (www.joanphelps.com). "Now I change back and forth from fuchsia to blonde, depending on what shades of Nice 'n' Easy are on sale." Keep in mind when you're done with all that crazy hair, it was your idea, not ours!

SEX IN THE TIME OF UNEMPLOYMENT

Sexuality and unemployment go together like—well, let's just say they go together. "I try to have as much sex as possible," said Gina Clark, writer and speed meditation expert, when asked how she spends her time off. "An inexpensive bottle of wine, a decent home-cooked meal, a good DVD, fresh linen on the bed and a silky nightgown can be really exciting."

Randy D. agrees. "One of the nice side benefits to being unemployed and having carnal relations is that you can have a relatively sleepless night, see your lover off to work in the morning, then go back to bed and catch 40 more winks," he told us. Randy is also a big fan of the dual leisure model: "If you find a partner who is also unemployed, then every night is like a Friday night!"

Sexual pursuits take time, energy, and often a certain degree of, uh, flexibility...making now the perfect time for putting some zest back into your sex life.

Hooking Up

Is it an intense, immediate connection without emotional commitment, or a simple hit-and-run? No matter the vocab, the one-night stand is a time-honored tradition that fits right into a noncommittal phase of life. If the briefest of flings are your style, be safe and responsible—and then have a go at it!

It's a cliché to pick up at singles bars, plus they might not be your scene. Never fear. You can work it just as well at the local café, laundromat or grocery store. Singles websites such as **American Singles** (www.americansingles.com) have not only lost the cheesy image, they now rank right up there with an introduction from a trusted friend in terms of likelihood of hitting paydirt. **Craigslist** (www.craigslist.com) is free and even hosts a "missed connections" forum where you can get a second chance at saying hi to that hottie who was in front of you in line at the coffee shop.

places

Everybody has a favorite unusual romping ground (um, right?). If you don't, maybe it's time to get one. "I made a couple visits to the fifty-yard line in college," Karen X told us. "What can I say? My boyfriend was a football player."

For some, the pleasure is heightened by the fear of getting caught. Others return to their favorite sites year after year—or, in some cases, night after night. At the beach, in an elevator, on the desk in the office of your worst manager, perhaps?

How about on a cross-country flight? Rise to new heights with *The Mile High Club* (www.milehighclub.com).

deviant leisure

No, it's not the name of a cutting-edge punk band. "Deviant Leisure" is a term used in the field of Leisure Studies to describe diversions outside of societal norms. The practice of witchcraft, for example, or the recreational use of prescription drugs, are activities you're not likely to find on the local PTA agenda.

But where does recreation end and deviance begin? Group sex may be as normal for some as a belief in the occult is for others, while each sect sees the other as a fringe element.

So is it deviance, defiance, or just plain delight? All we know is that if it hurts you or others, don't do it. Beyond that, you'll have to decide for yourself what you're comfortable with, and what risks you're willing to take. If your idea of fun runs consistently afoul of the law, keep in mind that you could soon be *getting* booked instead of reading this book!

And speaking of your odds, we'll just note that the art of connecting can never get too much practice. Are you listening, gentlemen? Learn your lessons from **Seduction Science** (www.seductionscience .com) and you're sure to get high scores.

Bookstores & Clubs

There are more adult bookstores and theaters in the United States than there are McDonald's. Gives a whole new meaning to the term "quarter-pounder." You don't have to be alone in the dark to indulge your carnal nature, though. Strip clubs can be fun for boys and girls alike. Bargain hunters note—their daily happy hours often include free admission and drink specials. Find your personal utopia on the **Strip Club List** (www.stripclublist.com). If you're really looking to stretch your sexual boundaries, consider going to a sex club. Don't get into a compromising position without protection, though.

Erotica & Fantasy

Not only does Gina *have* as much sex as possible, she *thinks* about sex as much as possible too. "You know, thinking about it is sometimes better than doing it," she says. "Fantasizing is like a party in your own head." And great heads think alike. Joani Blank, who brought the buzz of vibrators into the mainstream by opening **Good Vibrations** (www.goodvibes.com), advises people to get as much sex as they can—with or without a partner. "If you do enough of it, it'll keep you slim and healthy," Joani says.

On masturbation versus going out to find sex, Joani asks a good question: "What takes more effort, for me to go out to a bar or dance club on the hopes that *maybe* I'll meet somebody who *maybe* will have sex with me after a few weeks of getting to know me better, or giving myself an orgasm?" Actually, we don't see any reason not to do both. Masturbate and *then* go to the bar!

Or skip the bar altogether and buy some toys online. Investigate a large selection at **bettersex** (www.bettersex.com).

WHEN LEISURE BECOMES SLEAZE-URE

What if you find yourself not on the edge but over it? Time off can be a great time to ditch bad habits, but as Gina reminds us, "The ones that are the most fun are the hardest to let go!"

The line between hedonism and deviance, self-indulgence and self-destruction, can be thin. Deviance is in the eye of the beholder, of course—one person's graffiti is another's street mural—but we draw the line at activities that are destructive to yourself or others. If you think you might be overindulging in drink, drugs, sex, gambling or any other vice, you probably are. Get some help. Turn the page!

Leisure Liz	Sleazure Larry
You like going out with your friends.	You no longer have any friends.
You wake up next to a stranger and say, "This could be the start of a beautiful friendship."	**You wake up next to a stranger and say, "Who the !\$#@ are you, and what are you doing in my bed? Oh—we're not *in* my bed?"**
You usually have enough money to pay for your entertainment of choice.	You constantly scrounge for jack to support your activities and owe several people money.
You enjoy telling your friends stories about what you did last night or last week.	**You're ashamed to tell your friends what you did last night or last week—if you can even remember.**

Time To Go On The Wagon?

It's amazing how fast an open tab can drain the budget—especially a sabbatical budget—and alcohol poisoning isn't exactly a walk in the park. So don't be stupid about how you party. In fact, consider a sojourn to sobriety. Amy gave up drinking after her high-tech employer laid her off, so she "could keep a clear head, and not get too depressed." It worked.

The same goes for other drugs. Dr. Anthony Liguori, assistant professor working in Human Behavioral Pharmacology at Wake Forest Medical Center, has given his monkeys large daily doses of THC (no, you can't get the monkey job). Guess what—it turns out that the constantly stoned really *are* less motivated. If "wake and bake" has become your free time motto, it's probably time to give your lungs (and mind) a breather.

Addictions

A pleasure becomes an addiction when you can't stop, even though you know you should and you aren't even enjoying it anymore. Almost any behavior can become addictive if you're vulnerable, especially if you're depressed. If you need it, help is available from these and other support organizations:

- **Alcoholics Anonymous** *(www.alcoholics-anonymous.org)*
- **Narcotics Anonymous** *(www.na.org)*
- **Gamblers Anonymous** *(www.gamblersanonymous.org)*
- **Nicotine Anonymous** *(www.nicotine-anonymous.org)*
- **Overeaters Anonymous** *(www.oa.org)*

EXERCISE THE POWER OF CHOICE

Whoa, some sobering thoughts to end on. But time off is all about choice, edgy or otherwise. Non-employment can and should give you a level of control over your life you've never had before. Use it to take charge, whether it's through experimentation or by setting new goals. If your new personal power includes the physical or metaphysical, turn inward for a stint of getting re-acquainted with yourself.

CHAPTER 7
REDISCOVERING YOURSELF

In our leisure we reveal what kind of people we are.

~ Ovid

LET'S revisit the subject of you. Or more specifically, you apart from your work. Establishing and maintaining a strong identity separate from your job is a challenge in today's work-centric culture. Likewise, self-reflection and self-improvement are undernourished practices in our dog-eat-dog work world. Yet all are crucial to our personal fulfillment and happiness. A rewarding career can bring monetary riches and a sense of accomplishment, but without discovering and focusing on your true passions in all aspects of your life, those successes can be as hollow and vapid as a mansion with no furniture inside.

Take this time to learn more about yourself, what's important to you in life, and how you can better position yourself to achieve that. "It's a time to recreate your life," says Rochelle Teising, psychotherapist and career coach, "a time to reclaim old dreams." Find out what really gets you fired up, as well as what makes you unique and interesting, outside of your profession. This can encompass mind, body *and* spirit.

Keep in mind, this type of exploration need not be an excruciating exercise that has you weeping in the corner, thumb in mouth in a fetal position rocking gently back and forth (Mommy?). It doesn't mean you need to shave your head and start singing "Hare Krishna" either. There are as many paths to so-called self-improvement as there are hammocks strung on a sandy, palm tree-lined beach in Mexico—which, of course, could be one such path. Ultimately though, self-exploration is a very personal endeavor, and the road you choose is up to you and you alone.

THE MENTAL YOU

We each soul-search in a different way, depending on our needs. Some of us decompress in a relaxing place, others reassess personal goals or seek out one-on-one professional guidance. What makes *you* tick?

Engage the Mind

Hobbies may seem like mindless diversions, perhaps useful as a temporary distraction and not much more. But consider what hobbies do for a person, and you'll see that they are nothing less than mind*ful*, offering a means to focus the brain and calm the soul at the same time.

take two hobbies and call me in the morning

Ernie Zelinski touts hobbies as a way to rejuvenate.

"If you have hobbies, you can get your mind totally removed from work," he says. "I think that's one of the best things you can do to be more creative at work, just remove yourself from it sometimes. And hobbies and other pursuits are what can get you there."

So there you have it, straight from Dr. Leisure, no less. Take the prescription, and dose up on pursuits that will engage your mind.

The first realization you might come to is that you don't have any hobbies. Doh! That's not anything to be proud of, but it doesn't mean you can't change in a hurry. Fire up one or more pursuits to wrap the ol' noggin around. Read some books, paint a picture, plant a garden, heck—learn how to pay the tuba! All these types of activities are good for the intellect, they teach patience and self-reliance, and perhaps most important of all they make you interesting—and sexy!

"I think I married my husband because he has such interesting hobbies," says Jessica, a book editor in California. "Even though they get on my nerves sometimes, he always has something to add to the conversation, always has something on the back burner that he is making for somebody or researching. It keeps him bringing something to the table, which is fun."

According to Cecile Andrews, founder of The Simplicity Circles Project, "Hobbies are something that we can really get absorbed in. Our breathing slows down. Everything else we do, we do to get ahead, to make money, to provide for ourselves, but hobbies—it's just fun." Sounds Zen-okay to us.

A True Test

Want to know more about yourself? Are you sure? Remember now, it's not always so pretty. Okay then, have some fun with personality and aptitude tests. Sure, they can be dripping with psycho-babble, but they can still tell you a lot about your true inclinations, as opposed to aptitudes that you may have inherited from past jobs, parents, teachers, or any number of outside influences.

QueenDom.com (www.queendom.com) reigns supreme in the testy world of the wacky and wonderful Web, and is, to quote their site, "seriously entertaining." They tout themselves as the world's largest testing center, and we're not going to dispute it. At any one time they host hundreds of personal little experiments to conduct on your brain. Take tests ranging from an emotional-IQ exam, to an honesty test, to the all-important accident-proneness assessment. Have fun with the analysis and brain fodder but please remember to screw the cranium back on when you're done.

A timeless classic in the field of personality tests is the venerable Myers-Briggs Type Indicator. The MBTI measures preferences based on four basic scales, the combinations of which result in sixteen different personality types. Myers-Briggs disciples can psych themselves up at a variety of websites, including **Personality Pathways** (www.personalitypathways.com), which will put subjects through their paces to get to their MTBI personality type.

If you're feeling more career-minded (so to speak), test your mettle with the **Self-Directed Search** (www.self-directed-search.com), developed by Dr. John Holland, a professor emeritus at Johns Hopkins University. SDS breaks down vocational personality types into six buckets, visually represented by a hexagonal model. Holland discovered that what people are good at often reflects the environment they grew up in and how much time they've put into certain skills—which does not always reflect what they're *able* to be good at. For that, they should explore all corners of the hexagon.

Dick Bolles, author of *What Color is Your Parachute* and a proponent of the SDS model, encourages career counselees to use this concept. "You ought to use free time to get a mental rest," Bolles says, "and the mental rest is found by engaging in tasks where you're using skills you didn't use in the strongest [SDS] corners. For years and years this is what I've advised people do when they have time off: be sure you're taking time to use skills that you don't use normally at work."

★ GREAT MOMENTS ★ ★ iN UNEMPLOYMENT ★

Paula Deen was suffering from agoraphobia, and her marriage was DOA. With no source of income in sight, she sought refuge in her heritage as a Southern cook. With the help of her sons and $200, Paula launched The Bag Lady, a lunch home-delivery service. Two Savannah-based restaurants (The Lady, and The Lady & Sons) soon followed. Paula now stars in The Food Network's *Paula's Home Cooking*, attracting millions of faithful viewers.

FROM BAG LADY TO FOOD STAR

Reassessing Success

Success can be a loaded term in our society, tangled with the trappings of material possessions, or assessed on a financial scorecard. We frequently measure our own eminence based on parameters set by others. And guess what? Those measures usually revolve around work. It's no wonder if we have difficulty enjoying a "success" that someone else has defined for us. That's why Ernie Zelinski believes it's up to each of us to set our own standard. "You really have to define what success is to you. That way you become successful on your own terms," he says. "Success then is not as elusive." Ernie recommends people ask three key questions to determine their own parameters for success: What are your biggest accomplishments? What do people compliment you about? What are your biggest talents?

After getting laid off early in his engineering career, Ernie put himself to the test. "For me, the answers were that I'm a risk-taker, I'm creative, and I'm good at living the flexible way that I do," he told us. "When I answered those questions I had this revelation that I absolutely could not go back to work at a regular job. I could not consider myself successful if I had to go work at a job nine to five." His realization enabled him to eliminate previously-held expectations, and go on to become a well-known author and professional speaker.

Rather than diving headlong back into whatever you were doing before you took time off, examine your goals, both personal and professional and, as simple as it sounds, determine whether you're doing what's important to you. Mike Norman, an insurance specialist from Fridley, Minnesota, was laid off in April of 2004 for the first time in his 26-year working career. Instead of racing out and finding a new job immediately, Mike was able to spend time with his two young children, aged six and four. His experience at home with his children changed his perspective and, ultimately, his aspirations about work. Because his wife had a growing interior decorating business, Mike was able to make the transition to stay-at-home dad, a change he doesn't regret: "Being a full-time dad at home with the kids has been an enlightening experience for me… I brag to a lot of people—men in particular—that I'm a stay-at-home dad and the looks of envy on their faces is something to behold, let me tell you!"

Treat Yourself

Without an employer to reward you with a paycheck or a professional pat on the back, you need to reward *yourself* sometimes. While treating yourself might not be as much about rediscovery as it is about self-affirmation, it is nonetheless important to celebrate your accomplishments during times of transition. What better reason for blowing a little didge than to enhance your personal well-being?

A self-granted bonus can come in many forms. Rachel Karagounis had a rocky start to her new life in Las Vegas, yet she was determined to make the transformation and was proud that she had found the courage to make the change. So after a particularly difficult stretch, she went into emergency indulgence mode. "I went to a $130-per-night suite for one night," she told us. "There was complimentary champagne—a little bottle, but it was still champagne, dammit! I took a bubble bath in one of those Roman tubs with jets, and when I jumped in the bed there were six pillows on there and the sheets were so thick—I felt like a princess."

The treat worked. "The next morning I woke up fresh again, and I was like 'Okay, nobody's going to run me out of this town...this is *my* town. I belong here!'"

Making a Plan

Once you've had a chance to assess and perhaps adjust your goals, create a plan for what you want to work on and how you're going to accomplish it. Cheryl Beck worked in the insurance industry for ten years but finally quit her job in order to figure out what she really wanted to do with her life. "If you are—by choice or not—laid off, use the time to really see where you want to be.... You've got time. It's easier to do than when you are working. If you're in that stage, definitely take the time when you're off to do it," she says.

PLAN TO CONQUER YOUR FEARS

Laying out a detailed plan helps alleviate fear, a common cause of inaction. "Far too many dreams have suffocated and died because of fear," says Gary Ryan Blair, **The Goals Guy** (www.goalsguy.com), a life coach and consultant. "Fear resides where knowledge does not exist; the more you know about anything the less intimidated you feel."

Professional Help

The stigma of going to see a "shrink" is long gone. These days, it almost seems abnormal if someone *hasn't* been to some form of therapy! Despite what you might have heard, therapy can be a very useful tool for self-analysis. If nothing else, it will force you to focus on you—the good, the bad and the ugly.

If you left your job because you're seriously discontent with your work or career path, therapy can help you analyze your angst. "Being unemployed is a really good time to look at what happened, what was it about the environment that made you unhappy or why did you not fit there," says Mari Bull (www.maribull.com), a psychologist out of Southern California. "If you can come up with a reason, you can come up with a place that you'll fit into. If you can't come up with an answer, talk to somebody about it."

Robert Rafferty, a chef from Pennsylvania, used his parents for counseling. "I graduated from Franklin & Marshall, one of the top twenty-five liberal arts schools in the nation, with a degree in political science, wanting to be a lawyer, but realized I was doing it for all the wrong reasons," he told us. "My father gave me the impetus to say, wait—my personality wasn't cut out to be a lawyer, even on the bleeding heart end of it. I had a heart-to-heart with myself, and with my parents' guidance, I decided to follow my heart and my passion and go to the culinary academy in Hyde Park, New York." Robert has been content in the kitchen ever since.

"What Should We Do, Coach?"

We employ coaches and tutors for all sorts of endeavors—sports, fitness, academics, career, even childbirth. Why not for life? The emerging field of life coaching is quickly gaining popularity. Generally speaking, it's a holistic approach to help you prioritize and manage your life, often transforming it in the process. Life coaches act as mentors, someone objective who is not just analyzing your decisions after the fact, but helping you plan out those decisions in advance, and then egging you on. A personal trainer plans a workout and then gets you to sweat; a life coach plans out a strategy for your life goals and then (hopefully) gets you to act.

"I see life coaching as making the assumption that for people in the current time, work and life and family has all sort of merged into one big bubble," says Hope Dlugozima, co-author of *Six Months Off* and a former life coach expert for **iVillage** (www.ivillage.com). "Where in the past there were career counselors and family counselors, now life coaching

upsides, downsides

A big downside of professional therapy is, of course, the cost. $100 an hour will eat up a sabbatical budget in a hurry.

Many modern health insurance plans provide at least partial coverage. This is where paying the higher cost of COBRA to continue a former employer's health plan (see **Chapter 3**) might benefit you in the long run.

If insurance won't cover you, ask if your therapist is willing to work on a sliding scale. Many will be flexible in response to your current financial position.

A nearby university or training center could have a graduate psychology program. Most allow therapists-in-training to see patients at low cost. You can also ask the **American Psychological Association** (800-374-2721, www.apa.org) what they recommend.

The "friends and family" plan is usually free—let the people closest to you provide you with feedback. It worked for chef Robert!

Finally, if you're brave enough to self-diagnose, have at a few online personality tests first.

the why and how of it

So why engage a life coach during your time off? For starters, they're particularly helpful during times of transition, when you may have difficulty identifying, prioritizing and managing what is—we hope—a world of new possibilities. And the voice of experience can be just as valuable as the voice of a therapist, without all the tears!

As for hiring a coach, it works a little differently than it does in the National Football League (and thankfully it's a bit cheaper). Finding a coach is a lot like finding a good therapist, and we all know how to do that, right? Seriously though, look at relevant experience and training, and ask around for personal referrals, which are always a good way to qualify potential counselors.

The Web can help you find some help as well. Try **The Coach Connection** (800-887-7214, www.findyourcoach.com), an all-inclusive coaching site that draws kudos from Dr. Phil (hard to beat that), or **The Coaching Hub** (888-597-4879, www.coachinghub.com), which maintains a straightforward coach directory.

is blending all those things together, and managing them on any given day."

Kiki Weingarten, a life coach and co-founder of the New York-based **Daily Life Consulting** (www.dailylife consulting.com), puts it more simply: "Life coaches help people bring out their best selves, the greatness within them, their unique talents; and help them identify those talents."

She believes that as people get caught up in life, they change dramatically—you probably aren't the carbon copy of who you were ten years ago. "Most people know they're not the same person, that their priorities are different," Kiki says. "You might realize what's important, but your perspective is different." Yet rarely do people pause to evaluate exactly how they've changed and what their new goals might be.

Kiki is quick to add that life coaching is different from therapy, even though many life coaches are trained therapists. "The best way to get the most out of coaching is to have your head together. If you need therapy, get therapy."

John McGrail, a performance coach based in Los Angeles, takes a more behavioral approach to coaching. He believes that transitions involve thorough self-examination. "The process of rediscovery and reinvention begins with instilling an understanding of how we as humans get to where we are in the first place," he says. "Most clients are surprised to learn that the bulk of this behavioral programming is completed by about the age of seven."

Yikes! Well, if you're making a dramatic transition, then you might have some reprogramming work ahead of you (don't we all). Don't rush it, as transformation takes time. "This is a process and we must give ourselves permission to go through it and embrace it, step by step; there is no silver bullet here," says John.

THE SPIRITUAL YOU

"Spirituality" can be a nebulous concept. In the context of rediscovering yourself, spirituality doesn't necessarily equate to religion—although religious practice is certainly one approach to finding yourself. In fact, one's "spirit" may or may not incorporate any type of metaphysical belief or experience at all.

We think of spirituality as a highly personal energy and state of consciousness that helps you connect to the world around you, however you choose to make that connection. It might be through loved ones, a passion for the environment, personal meditations, or yes, even a nod to a higher power.

If you choose to explore independently, there are plenty of resources at your disposal to help you discover, learn, and formulate your views. Should you choose to seek spirituality through more structured means, many organizations have religion ready-made for you—you'll just have to choose which one suits you best. With luck, you'll find a group that suits your needs (and is not just a cult with the proverbial Kool-Aid). Remember, there are always the Leisure Commandments from **Chapter 1** to guide you!

Seriously though, use your flexible schedule to explore introspective alternatives. John McGrail agrees. "Balancing mind, body and spirit is the key to the castle," he says. "We tend to get caught up in the vagaries of our extremely materi-al society, where we're constantly under pres-sure to do, produce, achieve, succeed—and the measure of that success is usually material possessions, social stature, etcetera. This is the world of the ego and it can be a very shallow world."

So repeat after us: "Let go of my ego!"

McGrail goes on to point out the importance of being true to oneself. "The point of acknowledging the spiritual side is to establish enough peace of mind so the individual can begin to think about doing and being what and who they really want to be rather than what they either learned or were expected to be," he says. "Only then can one choose a new direction that will allow them to be themselves and attract abundance in all areas of their life."

Organize Your Religion

Maybe you're one of the many people who are just trying to find out what makes you tick, not looking for a higher power, per se. That's cool. But if you're already down with a particular religious affiliation, now might be a good time to get more involved to give yourself a social, communal *and* spiritual boost. Why not see if one of the Christian, Buddhist, Islamic, Jewish or other religious organizations near you is a good fit?

If you already have a church, then you're one step ahead of the altar. Find out what you can do to get engaged, so to speak, in volunteer opportunities or social events. Most church groups provide ample social prospects as well as an existing community to plug into. This isn't exactly breaking news, but the point is, now you have the time to participate more actively. An added bonus: your religious community can serve as a much-needed support network during what can be a difficult time. "I can't imagine going through this transition without having friends and the network of my church," Cheryl Beck told us.

We're hardly able (or qualified!) to exhaust the topic of religion in the confines of this book, so if you want to dumb it down a bit, call upon *The Complete Idiot's Guide to World Religions* by Brandon Toropov and Luke Buckles. Think of it like a crib sheet for theology. Remember: spirituality resides not within a group, but within an individual.

Meditation

There are various forms of meditation, quiet time, alone time. Whatever kind of time you care to call it, these personal moments come when you allow yourself to stop running around and sit still, and can provide much-needed balance to our fast-paced lives...particularly if you're coming off a stressful bout of overwork. Slow it down! As the traffic cop says, "What's your hurry, mister?"

Meditation has helped bring sanity to more than a few sabbatical souls. "It took some time," said Gina Clark of New York, "but I eventually realized I could be leisurely just laying in bed looking at the ceiling, sitting on a park bench looking at the sky, or camping out on my sofa, staring at nothing in particular." Gina had to fight the forces of a fast-paced city. "We spend most of our waking hours moving in some way; we should also take some time to be still so that there's balance. That's what I call leisure."

For Rachel Karagounis, meditation was more of a way to keep her from freaking out about her transition to a new town, and a new life. "Meditation kept me sane, kept me believing that things were going to work out," she said. "It felt like it was going to work out in my heart, but my head was saying '*what* are you *doing*?'" Meditation helped Rachel thrive, not just survive, in her new environment.

i MUST BE iN THE FRONT ROW!

Spending time alone is an important part of the rediscovery process but it's not without its worldly perks. "I showed up by myself at a Lyle Lovett concert once—no ticket in hand—and asked for whatever was the best seat they had left," says country music fan, Jane. "The seat was front row center! I swear, Lyle was singing right to me. It was like my own private serenade. Well, me and the other five thousand fans in the amphitheater." Jane is sure she would have missed this opportunity had she been unwilling to show up solo. "No one I know would have risked not getting a ticket, plus there was only one seat left up front." Talk about putting yourself center stage!

CyberZen

Are you a little more laid-back, a little more Zen? Then don't search the Web, let the Web come to you. Cyberspace is full of resources on Zen philosophy and living, where you can choose to remain in a meditative virtual world or link back to the corporal, and then perhaps even forward yourself into the metaphysical. The **Buddhist Network** (www.buddhistnetwork.org) will plug you into Buddhism and Zen study, catering to both beginners and advanced practitioners. The site provides, among other services, a first-rate search engine to help you find teachers and centers in your area.

DailyZen (www.dailyzen.com), where you're asked to "enter in peace," is another such domicile. You can practice daily meditations at the site, and read up on Zen quotes and teachings.

Red Alert
If while pursuing your spiritual longings you find yourself suddenly in the wrong organization, there are groups that can help. Research the **International Cultic Studies Association** (www.csj.org), whose mission is to study, educate and assist people in relation to cults. Also see **CultsOnCampus.com** (www.cultsoncampus.com) for general information and resources on cults.

THE PHYSICAL YOU
Physical fitness helps keep you out of the doctor's office, a boon if you're under-insured. It makes you look good. More important, it makes you feel good, and it's the perfect way to maintain a sense of achievement when you don't have an employer to reward your accomplishments.

> *Leave all the afternoon for exercise and recreation, which are as necessary as reading. I will rather say more necessary because health is worth more than learning.*
> ~ Thomas Jefferson

Free Your Body
Just about everyone understands on some level that fitness is an important component to a healthy lifestyle. But just how important?

Psychologists and other experts overwhelmingly agree that for depression, exercise is one of the most important things a person can do. "Keeping your body in its best condition goes a long way to keeping your mind and spirit in good shape, too," says Dr. Jan Cannon, a career advisor and author who works in Boston, Massachusetts.

In fact, staying fit will be more important than ever if you suddenly have fewer commitments. "I got up at 5am every single day and went to the gym," Marsha Converse told us. "It was one of the best things I did for myself after I got laid off." Friends might come to the rescue if you blow your sabbatical budget, but no one else can work out for you.

Fitness and exercise have the same mental effect as other hobbies—they focus your mind, they give you a sense of accomplishment, and they improve your physical conditioning at the same time. This all conspires to further build self-esteem and a stronger non-work identity. Exercise keeps you moving, keeps you happy, keeps you focused and keeps you healthy. Consider it a crucial obligation—to yourself. And oh yeah, it's fun!

Goal Setting

Let's face it, getting in shape doesn't happen overnight. Fitness takes time and dedication. Experts prescribe a minimum of three sessions a week, so get on it! (Sorry, schlepping to the corner store to buy new batteries for the remote doesn't count.) Set a modest goal if you're just starting—to lose ten pounds, to run a 12K race—or simply to look good naked. If you're already reasonably fit, choose something more aggressive like competing in a marathon or triathlon. Either way, shoot for a pattern that you can stick with whether your schedule is rigid or flexible.

The next choice will probably be where to work out. Gyms are a reliable option. Look for special introduction deals offered by fitness clubs. National chains like **24 Hour Fitness** (www.24hourfitness.com) are constantly offering promotions to entice exercise newbies. In fact, if you're clever you might be able to work out for free.

burn, baby, burn

You might think you'll get in the best shape of your life with all this time to pump iron. Funny thing is, you'd burn calories just reading, or sunbathing in the park—even rolling a joint! Your basal metabolic rate (BMR) measures how many calories you use to maintain normal body functions like breathing, heartbeat, and staying warm. It accounts for 60-70% of the calories you burn off each day.

So if you're firmly planted on the couch watching Oprah, why bother?

Because even at rest, a pound of muscle burns 25 times more calories than a pound of fat. Increase your BMR by building muscle, and you'll be shaping up even while you're sitting behind a desk!

Use the BMR Calculator at **Global Health & Fitness** (www.global-fitness.com, "Free Fitness Tools") to find out how many calories you can consume without gaining weight. It factors in the burn from key leisure activities such as Strolling (210 calories hour), Golfing with a Pull Cart (300 calories hour), and Square Dancing (350 calories hour—yee haw!).

gym slutting

Can't decide where to work up a sweat? Try "gym slutting"—going from one free trial membership to another. Most chains offer two weeks gratis to first-time local guests. Hit up five franchises and that's 2+ months of gym membership, for free!

Dana Magenau did just that when he was new in town. "I felt it was in my best interest to thoroughly investigate the pros and cons of each and every gym out there," he told us with a wink.

The gym isn't the only option. Weather and location permitting, hit the great outdoors with your bike, your bathing suit, or your hiking boots. Playing outside is fun, it's healthy, there's all that fresh air you hear so much about, and, for the most part, it comes at the low, low price of free. Woo hoo!

Choosing a Fitness Hobby

A hobby doesn't have to be collecting ceramic figurines or building popsicle-stick castles. One way to stay motivated with exercise is to find an appealing fitness hobby. Fitness hobbies are serious leisure, so get serious! This will transform your workouts from arduous labor to labor of love. Okay, so maybe more like love-hate. We can't tell you what physical pastime to pursue, but we can suggest some leisure-friendly options—activities where the price is right (cheap or free), and the exercise is of a more, like, organic nature, dude.

Yoga

Strike a pose with yoga. It has the relaxing benefit of incorporating mind and body, and can be just what the doctor ordered to replenish the non-working soul. In fact, you might find yourself stretching (and bonding) right alongside your non-employed brethren. Why? Perhaps because it's a relatively inexpensive way to achieve a dynamic mental and physical workout. Or, perhaps because people just need a place to go and hang out and a nice warm yoga studio seems as good as any.

There is a dizzying array of yoga types. Hatha and Ashtanga make good starting points, and you can take your practice from there. Don't let them call it Hot Yoga, though, unless they're paying dues to Bikram Choudhury. He founded *and copyrighted* the routine of 26 Hatha yoga poses performed in a very warm room and known as Bikram Yoga. Bikram is not a battle—many instructors tailor their sessions to newbies and pregnant women—but advanced practitioners revel in the more competitive environment.

To read up on all your yoga options, start your research at **Yoga.com** (www.yoga.com).

Jogging (Or Is It Running?)

Perhaps the easiest place to start exercising is straight out your front door. For the price of some decent running shoes (try **Road Runner Sports** at www.roadrunnersports.com), you can jog, run, skip, trot—whatever you want to call it—literally anywhere and at any time. Just remember how to find your way back home when you're done!

Lara Nicol Usinowicz, a sales rep and traveler extraordinaire from Evergreen, Colorado, uses running to stay in shape both at home and abroad. "Running is such a great form of exercise because it's so versatile," she says. "It can be social or solitary, on a trail or the road, a twenty-minute outlet to clear your head or hours and hours of training. And you can go right out your door or anywhere else in the world you might find yourself. It's very pure."

To add a little fun to your run (or run to your fun), look up your local chapter of the fabulous and wacky **Hash House Harriers** (www.gthhh.com) running club, quite possibly the most eccentric athletic club in the world. Keep in mind the emphasis is as much on the social as it is on the athletic. The fact that they are sometimes referred to as "a drinking club with a running problem" should tell you all you need to know.

A DRINKING CLUB WITH A RUNNING PROBLEM

The Hash House Harriers was formed in 1938 by a British expat living in Malaysia, and has grown into a global organization with more than 1,500 chapters in nearly every major city in the world. Based on the original concept of hare-and-hounds style chases, hash trails are set up by "hares" who set clues for the following pack of "hounds," who run from clue to clue, with everyone finishing at what's called the "On-In" or finishing point. A variety of social tomfoolery ensues there, including ample drink and song.

Neophytes are sure to receive plenty of attention from the gang, including a rite of passage called the "Down-Down," which we'll leave up (or down) to your imagination....

go tell it on the mountain

Otis Guy, Gary Fisher, Tom Ritchey, Joe Breeze and friends could hardly have predicted that their enthusiasm for chugging up the steep slopes (on one-speed bikes!) of Mount Tam north of San Francisco and barreling back down again would earn them a place in local lore. After all, they weren't the first ones to do it.

A group of cyclists known as the Canyon Gang held their earliest races on Mount Tam in 1971, aided by the "balloon tire:" a tire phat and knobby enough to handle the punishment of rapid off-road descents.

Five years passed before the first official race on October 21, 1976, down the east face of Pine Mountain just north of Mount Tam. The blistering speeds so hammered the riders' coaster brakes that they had to re-pack their hubs with new grease in order to make the ride again. The trail itself became known as Repack, still a popular and intense 2-mile, 1300-foot downhill bomb for the fearless.

keep pedaling...

Hiking (Or Is It Walking?)

Healthy feet can hear the very heart of Mother Earth—or so said that Sioux sage, Sitting Bull. We couldn't agree more.

Jogging's first cousin (or is it the other way around?), hiking is another low-maintenance outdoor activity that helps you get your feet back on the ground. You'll want some decent shoes or boots (see **REI** at www.rei.com), but after that initial investment, you'll be rambling across the countryside as far as your healthy feet care to carry you.

"Hiking allows you to slow down a little and get away from the hustle and bustle of life," says Lara. "It's slow enough that you have time to take it all in—the scenery, the sounds, the smells—but can be strenuous enough to give you a great workout. And the views...that's always what makes it worthwhile, the view from the top!"

Add a social dynamic to your trekking if you're tired of walking that path alone, and link up with one of the thousands of hiking clubs. The **Appalachian Mountain Club** (www.outdoors.org) is among the oldest and largest, focusing on the northeastern United States. **The Sierra Club** also (www.sierraclub.org) dishes a fabulous, if crunchy, bite of hiking adventure. When it's time to take those dusty boots off, tiptoe on over to **Barefoot Hikers** (www.barefooters.org/hikers), which has loosely affiliated chapters across the U.S., Canada and the U.K.

Can't bring yourself to put your stompers back on? Then curl up with

...and now the descent!

the shoeless manifesto, *The Barefoot Hiker,* or look into the prestigious **Society for Barefoot Living** (www.barefooters.org), another leisure-minded group—albeit one with soiled tootsies. Walk on!

Biking (Or Is It Cycling?)

"Vive Le Lance!" has been the worldwide cycling rally cry for the past six years, as American cyclist Lance Armstrong has ridden the sport's popularity to astonishing new heights with his run of six straight Tour de France victories. But Lycra jersey or no, recreational cycling has always been a great way to get around and get your blood pumping at the same time. With the advent of the mountain bike to complement the road bike, there's nary a terrain around that can't be navigated on two wheels. The best news is, with a minimal equipment investment, you can be off and riding like the wind or—even better—*with* the wind.

jumping the stumps

A San Jose, California, manufacturer released the first mass-produced mountain bike in 1981—the Specialized Stumpjumper. Mountain bike sales tripled every year for several years after that, and annual unit sales since 1984 have averaged close to ten million. Even the Olympic Committee has cashed in on the action by offering a medal in cross-country mountain bike racing.

Road Biking

Your cycling choices will be more varied on a road bike than with a knobby-tired downhill bomber. Your two-wheeler could be anything from a laid-back beach cruiser to a LeMond Tête de Course titanium/carbon racing bike (the yellow jersey costs extra). Sport a helmet to protect the noggin, and perhaps some ultra-tight shorts (but we ain't necessarily promoting those here!). Gear up at REI or **Performance Bicycle** (www.performancebike.com).

Meg Lynch, an avid cyclist and tour guide for **Backroads** (800-462-2848, www.backroads.com), an adventure travel company that leads cycling trips all over the world, likes to feel free on her bike. "Cycling offers me freedom—freedom to discover nature and cultures on two wheels. Early in the morning, late at night or perhaps even in the daytime, it's great to get some exercise while giving yourself some time to reflect." There's a nudge for your mind, body and spirit all in one shebang!

CRITICAL MASS

Despite a bit of road rage from gridlocked drivers and over-zealous cyclists, the "unorganized coincidence" known as *Critical Mass* (www.critical-mass.org or www.talkfastrideslow.org) still rolls through many American towns each month, reclaiming public streets for bicycles with the rallying cry, "We're not blocking traffic, we *are* traffic!"

In most locations, the holiday from cars starts after work (anywhere from 5pm-7pm) on the last working Friday of each month. Most participants cheer and holler wherever they roll while most onlookers smile and wave them on.

From its humble beginnings in San Francisco with 48 riders in Year One, Mass has spread to 300+ cities around the world. In its heyday, you could trace the route by watching where the TV choppers flew. More than 10,000 cyclists turned out to celebrate the San Francisco tenth anniversary on September 27, 2002.

Find out more in *Critical Mass: Bicycling's Defiant Celebration*, an anthology edited by Chris Carlsson, one of the original riders.

Mountain Biking

The dirt and rocks of Mount Tamalpais in Marin County, California, prompted custom bike-manufacturer Gary Fisher and his friends to deck out their rides, which led to the first formal, timed downhill race and seeded the growth of a whole new industry: mountain biking. To this day, Mount Tam remains one of the country's most visited mountain biking spots.

What does this mean to you, the leisurely fitness hound? It means get yourself a bike and hit the trail! Newbies to the sport can get themselves up to speed with the **International Mountain Bicycling Association** (www.imba.com), where would-be cyclists can read about "Epic Rides" or use the handy "Trail Finder."

Swimming

At the risk of making a sweeping generalization, we'd say swimmers are pretty happy peeps. Could it be the chlorine or saltwater exposure to the brain? The freedom of wearing tiny Speedos? We're guessing it's the dedication involved, and the Zen-like nature of the sport. Swimming for an hour gives you a lot of time to think without much distraction.

Depending on the climate, swimming will go down in a pool, lake or ocean. A good lap pool is a score at a gym; otherwise, look for one at a public rec center or the neighborhood **YMCA** (www.ymca.com).

Open water swimming in a lake or ocean is an entirely different kettle of fish. The bad news is that depending on where you live, it can be cold. Really cold. Particularly in the wintertime. The good news is that wetsuit technology has come a long way, and neoprene suits are warmer and more comfortable than ever.

Some aqua souls, such as members of the **Dolphin Club** (www.dolphinclub.org), actually thrive in cold water. "Besides being an instant cure for the worst hangovers," says long-time polar bear Deirdre Hussey, "swimming in the sub-60 degree waters of the Bay offers the best views of the Golden Gate Bridge, Alcatraz and other spectacular sights." If icy water is truly your calling, you can get a lot colder than that with polar bear clubs in places like Coney Island, Boulder, or Vancouver. Brrrr....

Temperature aside, the competitive-minded can deepen their knowledge of open water swimming by dipping into **oceanswims.com** (www.oceanswims.com).

Rock Climbing

Purveyors of leisure—at least those who don't mind dangling hundreds of feet in the air from a sheer wall—can practice the same art of focus and determination it takes to claw their way to the top of a career, by climbing their way up a rock (and you won't have to step on any heads!). It'll get you outdoors to some magnificent areas, bring you closer to Mother Earth (you'll be clinging to her, in fact), and talk about a challenge—many say the quest lasts for a lifetime.

Let's all say it together: we love the Web! If you're just starting out or want to connect with the climbing community, scramble over to **Rockclimbing.com** (www.rockclimbing.com), where you can read articles, find routes, look at cool photos, and connect with other climbers. You can also blog to your heart's content, as many climbers do. Onward and upward!

TRANSFORMATION

Whether you use your free time to transform yourself completely or to reinforce what's already important to you, enjoy the process of self-discovery. It can be fun and rewarding to explore new areas or passions. It's even more fun to share them. New passions can create new friends *and* new relatives. Time to rev up your social life!

CHAPTER 8
FRIENDS & FAMILY

*There was a definite process by which one made
people into friends, and it involved talking to them
and listening to them for hours at a time.*

~ Rebecca West

FULL-TIME work and a healthy social life can be frustratingly at odds for many of us. Long hours, the daily pressures of demanding jobs, and business trips conspire to sap our relationships.

Time off, on the other hand, presents a chance to revitalize your social life, whether you're married or single, young or old. Now is the time to turn favorite acquaintances into friends, and favorite friends into even better friends. It's time to go out on that date, cook for your spouse, or host that long-awaited dinner party. And if you're a busy parent, you already know how precious extra hours with your kids can be.

Reconnect with loved ones and make new friends during your hiatus. After all, our social connections truly are the zest of life!

CONNECTING

Many people curtail their social life during periods of non-employment. Some suffer from the "work-as-identity" syndrome, losing confidence and self-esteem during sabbatical stints. Others focus on cutting back their expenses, and automatically assume that socializing will cost them considerable coin and therefore shorten their sabbatical.

But a social life need not break the bank, nor should unemployment break your spirit. That's for people who don't read this book! There's truly no need to hide out in the bedroom, guarding the cash you've stashed under the mattress. It's time for recess, kids!

Friends

Ethan Watters profiles the changing dynamics and increasing importance of friendship in younger generations in his insightful book *Urban Tribes: Are Friends the New Family?* According to Watters, these friendships now form the foundation for loosely affiliated "tribes," which act as a closely-knit community as well as extended family.

So treat your tribe with care. Organize rallying events—a weekly "friends dinner," for example, or a movie night or games party. Consider a retreat with friends who also have flexible schedules, allowing you and your cohorts to get to know each other in a different environment. Road trips allow ample bonding time (see **Chapter 4**). Backpacking, spas, sporting events, camping—all are great ways to rally a small group into spending dedicated time together.

Rob organized a weekly guys' movie night with his friends, many of whom weren't working at the time. They chose a different theme each week. "It was a great way to get everyone together," he told us, "although you could definitely tell who was working and who wasn't. We'd host it on a weeknight, and the employed guys wouldn't drink much and would slip out relatively early. But those of us who weren't working, we'd sometimes tear it up into the wee hours, and we definitely bonded around that."

Communities

The need for unemployed bonding during our nation's last economic recession created a whole new category of social event. Dot-com era pink slip parties come to mind—they were, in their heyday, great forums for commiserating with fellow fired folk. Today, however, the non-employed network in a way that has evolved beyond just griping and pressing resumes.

The sophisticated forum of **Craigslist** (www.craigslist.org), for one, serves as a de facto community for the unemployed, self-employed, or fluidly employed. Their regional sites cover just about every urban area in the U.S., as well as big cities around the world. The sections on "jobs" and "community" key into non-working needs, as does the "personals" section (if you're so inclined).

The Kingdom of **Bojon** (www.bojon.com), created and maintained by Tom Haan, has also created community buzz. "What's better than your dream job?" asks the King of Bojon. "No job!"

Tom is quick to set his site apart from those that express bitterness about being laid off, explaining that Bojon is not an ephemeral concept. "Somebody who is uptight about not having a job and who is running around pressing resumes is not truly bojon," Tom explains. "Conversely, somebody who loves his profession and is passionate about his work *can* be bojon."

Tom quotes the Chinese philosopher Chang Ch'ao:

Only those who take leisurely what the people of the world are busy about can be busy about what the people of the world take leisurely.

The Buddha couldn't have said it better himself.

the tao of...no job?

Brian Cox, a friend of Bojon founder Tom Haan, coined the term "bojon" in the early 1990s. The college sophomore found himself surrounded by upperclassmen boasting about the great gigs they had lined up for after graduation. Wanting to sound equally sophisticated, he told them he was going to work for Bojon. "It's a French company," he claimed.

And it's also "no job"—spelled backwards!

CREATIVELY ODD

Wondering what to do when you find yourself sitting in front of the tube all day, with no real work or social life to speak of? You read this book and snap out of it! Then take your creative energy, combine it with some minimal Flash development skills and a wicked sense of humor, and create the most popular Internet cartoon series ever. Set up a tip jar on the site, and sit back and watch the money roll in—along with book and other development deals.

Todd Rosenberg did just that, and may be the one having the last laugh. His site, **Odd Todd** (*www.oddtodd.com*), has received millions of hits from more than forty different countries, and Todd himself became a media darling, appearing on CNN and the *Today* show, among others. His subsequent book, *The Odd Todd Handbook: Hard Times, Soft Couch,* has further solidified his position as a true Leisure Legend.

Odd Todd has become an underground icon in the land of layoffs, and has grown to symbolize the culture surrounding the post-dot-com bust. When your laughter subsides after viewing his online cartoons, connect with like-minded folks through "Laid Off Land" or "Odd Todd Tribe," linked from the Odd Todd homepage.

FOOTLOOSE AND FANCY FREE

Be Open at All Times

A horse with blinders sees only the racetrack; an overemployed American sees only the job. Downtime rips those blinders off, leaving us open to new encounters—and once you're open, you might be overwhelmed with opportunities.

Seth, a California-based attorney, finally had the energy to meet new people during a recent period between firms. He chose to focus on dating, so much so that he found himself dating two women at the same time—something he doesn't exactly recommend!

You might be surprised at how many new people you can meet on any given day, and how little you know about the people you've already come across. Try this exercise: during your daily routine, whatever it may be, introduce yourself to each and every person you interact with and spend a moment to learn something about them. Start at the coffee shop in the morning; include the bus driver if you take public transportation, the gas station attendant, the florist, the bartender, and so on. Josh McHugh, a writer for *Wired* magazine, took the opportunity to do just that during a recent break between assignments and found it refreshing—and a good muse!

Flirt Before 5pm

People are surprisingly approachable during the day. Instead of "picking up" at the typical night spots (i.e., bars and clubs), try an afternoon jaunt to a museum, retail shop or gallery—any place where your reason for being there isn't solely to pick up.

"Finding somebody new who's also free during the day is always a treat," says Joani Blank, author and founder of **Good Vibrations** (www.goodvibes.com). "It's important for people to find lovers who likewise don't have to get up early in the morning!"

Consider going shopping during a weekday (or *reverse* shopping—see **Chapter 4**). You don't need to do a lot of buying; browsing works just fine. Those who think you'll run into nothing but housewives might be surprised. In fact, shop at Good Vibrations, where you can find books, toys, erotica *and* maybe a new friend, all in a clean, well-lit space that won't leave you feeling embarrassed or sleazy.

josh finds his muse

Josh McHugh, a technology and business journalist, recently spent the better part of a Friday tooling around his neighborhood, using his local coffee shop as home base. Among those he met were a construction foreman, a professional musician, a forced-retiree-turned-coffeehouse-manager, and a baby-toting mom doubling as a caterer and tripling as a home IT network administrator.

"Talking with humans, face to face, is by far the best way to get brand-new ideas bouncing around," Josh reports. "Plus, shooting the shit with people in a coffee shop is a lot more fun than squinting at a screen."

He adds, "As a writer, you always need fresh ideas to play with. The ideas that come to you via media, whether TV, print, or even the Web, are, by definition, processed and, as a result, a bit stale. The good stuff comes from live conversations."

How a-*muse*-ing!

CREAM OR SUGAR?

Want some nourishment that's social as well as edible? Try the local café. In addition to being the de facto home away from home for the fluidly employed, cafés serve as a modern-day community center. Don't whiz in, grab your coffee, and buzz off to work; linger a while. Get a table. Peruse the morning paper. Soak in the atmosphere. If you drop by at various times of the day, rather than just during the morning work commute, you're likely to encounter a whole new ambience with an entirely different cast of characters. Plus anyone you *do* meet will probably be geographically desirable!

Local art galleries and museums make great midweek outings for finding kindred culture-seekers in your community. The literary-minded might also try bookstores to browse for more than the latest bestsellers. Note that we're not just talking *When Harry Met Sally*, here—according to a recent American Express survey of about a thousand New Yorkers between the ages of 25 to 35, the best singles scene in the city turned out to be Barnes & Noble. Your hometown independent bookseller likely offers the same attraction, if you don't like to be shackled by the chains. "I always meet people in bookstores," says Sharon, an avid reader from Boston. "I'm not necessarily hitting on guys mind you, just making friends. It's easy—you're there for a common purpose, and most people who are *browsing* have time on their hands by definition."

Josh Briggs, a Chicago-based landscape designer who took a year off from work to finish his degree, was at first nervous going to a bookstore to meet people. "When you walk in with the intent of getting a phone number or something, it's so obvious," he told us. He found it helpful to forget he was there to meet women. "It feels strange, kind of disingenuous, but once you get there, you start actually getting into the books. You see somebody looking at a book that you have already read, and all of a sudden it is the easiest thing in the world to say, 'That's a great read!'" Josh suggests browsing where a café is close by, to give you the chance to chat over a cup of coffee.

Enroll in Activities

You'll save nine stitches with one if you pick up the thread in time, and you'll meet people who share your interests when you do things you like to do. Those old adages (you probably heard them from your grandmother) are trite but true. Think of your interests as your thread—pick it up now and enroll in a class, join a group, or take up a new sport.

Male leisure seekers take note: yoga classes have gender ratios tilted wildly in your favor. Not only will you be in a class packed with women, but the atmosphere is soothing and relaxed. Just be friendly and don't intrude on others' space during their practice.

"You have to be careful," says Justin, a marketing director from Texas who took up yoga while between jobs. "You don't want to be seen as that cheesy guy who's hitting on all the girls in the class. That being said, there

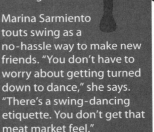

shake it

Develop a fun skill that can serve you in dating and beyond: dancing.

Marina Sarmiento touts swing as a no-hassle way to make new friends. "You don't have to worry about getting turned down to dance," she says. "There's a swing-dancing etiquette. You don't get that meat market feel."

Salsa is also kicking up big-time in cities across the country. "Salsa dancing is a fabulous way to meet and mingle in a diverse crowd, says Lesley from Seattle. "Many dance clubs offer lessons before the live band starts and I get to learn a few new moves while meeting other *salseros*."

Lesley enjoyed the freedom of midweek Salsa during a recent transition from teacher to tutor. "I like going dancing during the week because the clubs are less crowded. And not having to wake up the next morning makes dancing the night away a no-brainer."

To find some shaking maracas near you, shake your booty on over to *SalsaWeb* (www.salsaweb.com).

were a lot of cool, attractive women in my class." Justin managed to perfect a manly Sun salutation and cross that fine line between leering and alluring. "I finally got the nerve up to ask this one girl out. We ended up dating for about three months." Unfortunately for Justin, it didn't work out. Perhaps she wasn't flexible enough?

For more on stretching your boundaries, see **Chapter 7** under "Yoga."

Single women, don't despair; team sports tilt the odds back in your favor, whether you're watching or playing. Sports bars during football season are packed on weekend afternoons; tackle them all. Then bring your own game to a local sports league. **Sport and Social Club** (www.sportandsocialclubs.com) is the premier organization for adult sports leagues across the country, offering everything from softball to street hockey in most major cities. Coed football teams frequently match five men with three women—see, your chances are already improving!

Volunteer

That's right, volunteer; the hidden perk is social interaction. Work at an event that instantly throws you into a common cause with a new group of people, such as the **Cystic Fibrosis Foundation's** GREAT STRIDES (www.cff.org) event, or one of the **American Cancer Society's** (www.cancer.org) evening galas. You'll meet a ton of new people, usually in a relaxed setting, and you get the bonus of knowing you're helping a cause.

Camille Turrey and Peter Kellogg met at a "thank you" party hosted by the international youth hostel where they volunteered as baseball tour guides. "The four years that I led groups on this outing," Camille told us, "no two were ever alike. I remember the mobs of Japanese fans coming to cheer as well as British tourists drawing comparisons to cricket." But she remembers meeting Peter most clearly of all.

"Peter and I talked about volunteering and what it meant to us to lead the baseball tours, and I do believe I fell in love right then!" she said. So not only did Camille's volunteering stint get her into major league ball games where she got to share her love of the sport with people from all over the world, but she also hit romantic paydirt! She and Peter have gone into extra innings, and are now pitching their wedding.

For more on social volunteering and ways to meet and greet, see "Working the Room" in **Chapter 9**.

Host Parties

Now's the perfect time to throw that singles dinner or cocktail party. Become the hostess with the mostest. Entertain to entertain! Small gatherings are a great way to meet and greet new faces, as well as to reconnect with friends and family. Mix up the group by asking your friends to invite some new people, then you do the same—how 'bout that interesting guy or gal you met at the bookstore? How 'bout your new teammates from the soccer club you joined?

Hosting parties begets numerous other fringe bennies. For one, it's cost effective. Why spend copious capital on fancy restaurant dinners or high-priced cocktails at bars? Learn a few appetizer recipes, snag some cheese and crackers, stock plenty of ice, and rally your friends to enjoy a more intimate setting—your home! Playing the host also sets you up for some serious karmic payback. After you've wined and dined others, invitations will magically begin floating your way. Trust us, people will appreciate and remember your generosity, and will reciprocate one way or another.

Marina Sarmiento became legendary among friends for her enticing singles parties. "I got the idea from *Sex and the City*. They had a 'recycling' party, but I didn't want to call mine that. So I named it 'The Single, Mingle, Tingle, Wine Soirée.' Everyone was required to bring a single friend and a bottle of wine, or they weren't allowed through the door." The parties are on hiatus now: Marina's first four were so successful, she's no longer single!

Not looking for a date but sniffing about for a new job or career? You'd be hard-pressed to find a more relaxed setting for talking shop (or turkey) than a dinner party hosted by you or one of your good friends. No need to dine with your resume pinned to your shirt, but do seize the occasion to let others know what you're looking for.

tastes like chicken!

"We had a group of small publishers whose goal was to go to as many parties at the ABA *[American Booksellers Association]* as we could, whether we were officially invited or not," said Bill about his party-chasing posse. "We dubbed our group the 'ABA Gleaners and Grazers Association.' Our motto was 'You provide the raw materials and we'll provide the party!'"

They hit a few surprises en route: "In Vegas, we crashed what we thought was an ABA party. At the entrance, we gave our business cards that showed we were all publishers, we signed the guest list, and they let us in to this poolside party at Caesars Palace with great music and great desserts and booze. We were conversing with people for ten minutes before we looked at their badges and realized it was the American *Poultry* Association. The APA logo looked like the ABA in our drunken haze. It was then that we concluded that somebody could just crash parties at various conventions around the country and live a great life."

So glean and graze away, be courteous to your hosts, and enjoy your escapades!

Janice, a public relations manager from Atlanta, was part of a rotating dinner party group during tough economic times. "My friends and I organized a monthly gig," she told us, "that doubled as a way for us to meet new people and keep our spirits up at the same time. This was when quite a few of us were out of work, so we needed something to keep us going." She and her friends rotated hosting duties, and invited someone new to dinner each month. And yes, several diners parted with job leads as well as doggie bags.

Crash Parties

It's not always apropos, but party crashing is a time-honored social technique dating back to the days of Plato and Socrates. With a little invention and daring, you too can be mixing with a new crowd, often on someone else's dime. And talk about being around new people—you won't know *any* of them!

There are various forms of crashing, and of course varying degrees. Novices would do best to start with large, anonymous events, where the chances of being outed are minimal. Corporate functions make an easy target, and industry events are an even bigger bull's eye. Business-sponsored social mixers and hosted cocktail hours already spell "boondoggle" for company employees, so no one's going to get too bent if you tip back a few, or nosh on appetizers at the company's expense. Carry some business cards and feign at least a remote interest in the company's products or services, and you're golden.

Dating Services and Social Clubs

We know, we know—modern dating services and social clubs aren't for everyone. But many of you have claimed success, or at least positive experiences, so we're going to pass along a few recommendations.

Online dating services have emerged as the overwhelmingly preferred vehicle for structured meeting and dating. The preeminent service is **Match.com** (www.match.com), where users can peruse thousands of potential "matches." This includes any combination of genders: boy meets girl, girl meets boy, girl meets girl, boy meets boy—and perhaps combinations in between? It takes a while to read all the postings but hey, time is what (we hope) you've got!

There are dozens of friendly networking and dating services, many of them completely free, and some free until you want to contact another member. **Yahoo! Personals** (http://personals.yahoo.com) has thousands of members, and it's free; you can also check out the "catch of the day" under the personals at **Salon** (www.salon.com); or look for something spicier at **Nerve** (www.nerve.com). The exponentially expanding **Friendster** (www.friendster.com) promises "a fun and safe way to organize your social life." We'll buy that, but add that reliable sources tell us that "social life" usually means meeting and dating.

Be warned if you're looking for a geographically desirable mate: your anonymity won't be assured. Just ask Ken, a technology strategist whose

the need for speed

Speed dating is a new idea that might be zooming to a bar near you. An LA rabbi invented the concept in 1999 to help connect Jewish singles, and it's now blossomed into a full-fledged industry.

Single men and women of pre-determined age ranges go to a bar and meet each other through a series of rapid "dates," usually ten minutes or less. After the meetings, potential matches indicate whether they'd like to contact the other person again; if both parties agree, they trade digits.

Bachelor J.J. Dillon recently experienced this social phenomenon. "Any woman who asked me what I did outside of work stayed on my list," he told us, "and any woman who asked what kind of car I drove did not."

Believe it or not, dozens of companies would like to whisk you around the dating block. One of the biggest and best-run, *8minuteDating* (www.8minutedating.com), hosts speedy events in cities across the U.S.

You'd better be quick—they sell out fast.

degree of separation from a woman he met on Match.com was just one: "I couldn't believe it—I had just started using the service. I went out on one date, and it turns out the girl was my friend's roommate!"

LOVE IN THE TIME OF UNEMPLOYMENT

Think about the last time you fell in love. Somehow you found the time to dream, plan, hope and strategize about your blossoming relationship. Okay, you probably anguished about it as well! But while you might not have realized it at the time, you undoubtedly dropped less pressing pursuits to focus on the new person in your life.

Scott Phillips negotiated a partially paid sabbatical with his employer and was able to spend valuable time with his Czech-born wife in her home country, much of it at her family's home in the woods of Bohemia. Such an appropriate place for leisure! According to Scott, "We got to know each pretty well during that year, without any job-related stress to get in the way. I think it's made us a stronger couple. In terms of shared experiences, it was like having five years of American time together."

Erik Wohlgemuth, an environmental consultant, was working a flexible twenty hours a week when he first met Arah, who had recently left her job at Booz Allen. He says they probably wouldn't have ended up together if they hadn't had that free time. "We laugh at how much we progressed in two months," Erik told us. "We even introduced our families in that short time. Most couples don't get there; they're working the typical fifty-hour-per-week jobs, and they just don't have the time or energy to invest in dating. They're lucky if they see each other two or three days a week."

Arah's and Erik's flexible schedules allowed for more caprice, as well. "We were able to take off on spontaneous dates and trips, such as a last-minute visit to New York over the holidays to meet my family, and a one-month trip to Chile," Erik told us. Arah and Erik were engaged within a year and recently married. And for their honeymoon? They took a break from their jobs to go on a two-month trip through the South Pacific.

In researching an article on unemployment and relationships, Ann Marsh, a freelance writer from Los Angeles, met several young career-driven individuals who had either deferred serious relationships or neglected them altogether. It was only after they'd become disillusioned with their jobs or been laid off (or both) that they had finally gotten romantically involved. Considering her own status, Ann took these words to heart.

After getting laid off from her job as a staff writer for *Red Herring* magazine, Ann decided that the time had come to have a serious relationship of her own. Employing an ambitious, systematic dating strategy, she went about the process of finding the right man with all the zeal of an industrious entrepreneur. Six months later, she claimed to have gone on dates with no fewer than one hundred men—and had herself a great story for *Oprah*. And the "research" paid off: Ann met Johanne, and they married last year. No one ever said that dating couldn't be a full-time job!

UNEMPLOYMENT AND POPPING THE QUESTION

Ted Witt credits a recent stint of unemployment with taking his relationship to the next level. He fell in love with Shauna while they were working for the same company. After both were laid off, Shauna found another job relatively quickly but Ted decided to enjoy a full year off. Rather than put a strain on their relationship, Ted's unemployment energized it.

He didn't wait for *Re-Employment* before asking Shauna to marry him. Though concerned about how his jobless status would look to his in-laws-to-be, Ted did secure the blessing of Shauna's father first (okay, so he fibbed a little about some "consulting" projects) and then had plenty of time to plan the engagement, before and after he popped the question.

Shauna and Ted are now married and living happily ever after.

PUT A SPARK IN YOUR LOVE LIFE

How many times have you heard your partner say "I never see you anymore," or "We never spend time together!" Whether you're married, just dating, or somewhere in between, take this opportunity to recharge your relationship. Here are some ideas to get you cooking.

Think Romance

Love is eternal, but romance takes time. With some extra hours you can plan all sorts of little surprises. Delight your loved one by decorating the house with candles, preparing a fragrant bubble bath, and offering your services as a masseur or masseuse. Or sneak off to some natural wonderland together—perhaps to the beach to watch the sunset, or on a picnic in the woods. As clichéd as it may sound, the simplest efforts are often the most romantic.

"I didn't mind hanging at home at all," said Cathy, a publicist from New York, about her recent "mandatory" time off. "In fact, I kind of reveled in being a stay-at-home wife for a while. I would prepare little surprises for my husband when he'd get home from work, or plan our evenings out in the city."

Out to Lunch

You can be all about spontaneity when you don't have a clock to punch. So why not stop by your lover's workplace (if there is one!) for an impromptu lunch date? Lunching together is unusual for most couples, so it makes for a nice treat. You'll score major brownie points, maybe even impress the co-workers. Add in the possibility of networking opportunities, and you might make this a regular occurrence!

Terrance was working for a technology startup in Boston and getting a lot of grief from his wife of two years for not having enough

time for her. Then the tables turned. Faster than he could say "venture capital," his employer was out of business and he was out of a job.

"At first, I didn't know what to do with myself," he told us. "So I would go downtown at lunchtime to see what my wife was up to." She was thrilled.

"To be honest," Terrance admitted, "it started off as just a way for me to get out of the house and around people, but I saw my wife loved it so I just kept doing it."

Cook For Your Lover

Cooking for someone is a wonderful way to show you care. Use your extra time in the early evening to prepare a scrumptious meal so you can enjoy dinner together. You'll save money, spend quality time in the privacy of your own home, even be able to choose your own music!

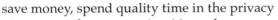

Derek in Atlanta used the power of the pan to sizzling effect with his would-be girlfriend on Valentine's Day. "It was at that point in the relationship where I was ready to put both feet in," he recounted. "I'm not that big of a cook, but I have to say I pulled out all the stops on that dinner. I took the day off, did all the shopping and advance food prep, then went to her apartment and cooked her a five-course dinner, including several appetizers."

And how was the dinner received? "Let's just say I had a fancy dessert all ready to go, but we never got to it." Spicy!

For some altogether luscious ideas about cooking and romance, check out **Sex and the Kitchen** (www.sexandthekitchen.com), a website dedicated to culinary and romantic delights.

Plan a Weekend Getaway

Choose a place you've both wanted to go: the mountains, the coast, or maybe wine country. Make it a surprise and you'll be a star in your partner's eyes for sure. You have literally thousands of choices, particularly if you're willing to throw down some cash. If you're not, you'll certainly find some less expensive—albeit alternative—escapes within striking distance.

Camping is easily one of our faves, an inexpensive option that is as adventurous as it is romantic. A tent, sleeping bags, and a few other basic supplies are all you'll need—oh, and a target destination, which you can find with **GORP** (the website, not the trail mix: www.gorp.com, click on "Camping" under "Activities"). Munch on their extensive recommendations such as "Where to Camp," "Know How" and their "Summer Camping Guide." Predictably, they detail plenty of ways to gear up as well.

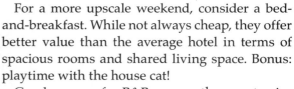

For a more upscale weekend, consider a bed-and-breakfast. While not always cheap, they offer better value than the average hotel in terms of spacious rooms and shared living space. Bonus: playtime with the house cat!

Good sources for B&Bs across the country include the definitive *Bed & Breakfasts and Country Inns*, 15th Edition, by Deborah Edwards Sakach, and the excellent web resource **Bed & Breakfasts Online** (www.bbonline.com).

Another option: stay at a hostel for an adventurous refresher. Meet people from all over the world while winding your way through romantic, thrifty days. Will you have to share a room with ten others in bunk beds? Probably not. Most hostels now sport private rooms as well as dorm-style accommodations.

The U.S. is home to one of the largest hostel networks in the world, and you don't need to be foreign-born to reap the benefits. Plan your getaway at **Hostelling International USA** (www.hiusa.org), where you can also book a bed. Actually, make that a bed for two....

FAMILY

You know what romantic weekends lead to, right? Family! Maybe you have one already. You all had parents, of course, and some of them were even human. Perhaps you're from a family of six with lots of aunts and uncles and several sets of grandparents (think of all the leisure loan potential!), so it could be time for you, like Chevy Chase, to load up the family truckster and hit the road—but please, leave the crazy aunt at home. Or, if you're still unattached, perhaps you'd prefer to drift in your parents' pool, contemplating your future à la Dustin Hoffman.

Whatever avenue you choose to get some quality time with your family—kids, spouse, parents, siblings or others—understand that it might take an extra effort to adjust. Your family can be a tremendous source of support during weeks, months, or even years of unconventional living, but keeping up the role you filled when you had a job can be trying. Your spouse, parents, or even kids may have certain expectations of you, and taking time off doesn't always fit neatly within those parameters. Maybe you *never* want to go back to work. What would your family think about that?

Below are some suggestions on how to relate, where to take your children, how to organize family activities, or how to take a family vacation—Griswold-style!

Adjusting

Being out of work can allow you to spend more time with your family, but it can also cause domestic turmoil. The myth that equates unemployment with laziness or underachievement can strain the marital relationship, creating a lack of respect and understanding, and ultimately animosity. Ironically, according to career counselor Rochelle Teising, dual-income couples are likely to feel this tension the most: the partner that's still working full-time perceives the other as loafing at home. "It's hard for anyone living with a partner who is enjoying time off not to be jealous," Teising says.

Former software sales executive Matt Green experienced this first-hand, admitting it was tricky to be around his family all the time after he quit his job. "Now that I'm not working, my wife's and my kids' lives haven't changed," Matt says, "but I'm out riding my motorcycle, meeting my friend for a beer, and that's something I have to be sensitive to. Jealousy's too strong a word, but my wife is thinking, 'I still have to do what I do and you get to go play.'"

Matt's wife eventually asked him to take on more of the household responsibilities. The transition was difficult, as Matt didn't feel he was skilled at anything around the house. Take doing laundry, for example. "During this motorcycle trip I was just on, I thought about going to a laundromat, and I said, nah, I'm going to wear what I have on for three days and then go back to Vegas and just buy new clothes. And that's what I did."

But once Matt was able to relax and regain his patience, the family slipped into a comfortable routine, and Matt was able to spend more quality time with them—the reason he'd quit his job in the first place. Looks like all that clutch work on the motorcycle served as good training for operating the vacuum cleaner after all.

Moms and Dads

Is life different for parents when one or both aren't working? Remember *Ozzie and Harriet*? *Leave It to Beaver*? Dad earned the dough and Mom spent it—on the family and the home, of course. While that may now seem archaic, it did give the heads of the household the luxury of more free time, or at least the appearance of it. Without debating gender roles and family values, we'll just observe that the parent who is not working (regardless of why) will have more time and energy to focus on family.

"Mothers are so exhausted when they come home," says Ann Crittenden, author of *The Price of Motherhood*. "Parents do everything they can to spend time with their kids—so what suffers is time with their own friends, time for their own leisure, and time with their spouses. Their marriages are put on the back burner." We hope you can avoid this fate!

Mike Norman of Minnesota is thankful his wife was able to pick up the slack when he got laid off. "My ego is not so inflated that my pride is crushed because my wife is making the money to support us. Admittedly, it was something to get used to, but as time went on I came to the conclusion that since our marriage is a partnership of love and family, which we agreed on early in our relationship, what difference does it make which one of us brings home the dough?"

GREAT MOMENTS IN UNEMPLOYMENT

My Pretty Po-Knee

Stay-at-home dad Robert Klick was bouncing daughter Maddi on his knee when he had a vision: an adorable stuffed pony he could attach to his leg, letting her ride in style. The Po-Knee was born, was featured on *Oprah* and sold 2,500 units during its first three minutes on QVC. The Po-Knee has given Klick more time to indulge in his favorite activity of all: playing with daughter Maddi and son Cameron.

Kids

Now that you have more time for your children, what are you going to do with them? Slouching in front of the boob tube hardly equals quality time. Of course, some of you may be looking for the reprieve! Kidding aside, it's been a delight and inspiration to hear of so many people who've taken sabbaticals to become closer to their kids.

Steve Wozniak of Apple Computer fame has long preached the virtues of society's paying more attention to children. After taking a rather extended period "off" from Apple (way back in 1985!), Woz helped found several organizations supporting children and education, including the Children's Discovery Museum of San Jose and The Tech Museum of Innovation.

Stacie Parker, an entrepreneur who owned two retail clothing shops, sold both to focus on raising her children. "Retail is no life for a parent," she said. "I had a 24-hour-on-call schedule. And I poured myself wholly into the daily grind, traveling to tradeshows and working late nights and weekends in the stores. But at 35, I had waited a long time to be a mom. So, at that point, I felt no guilt in giving up my business."

Tykes and Travelin'

If you enjoy taking life's journey with your family, why not hit the road for real? Make some new memories at a dude ranch in Wyoming. Camp out in Yosemite National Park. Rent a sleeper van and roll the whole fam-damly down the coast of Baja!

Travel for Kids (www.travelforkids.com) is a site for kid-friendly travel prep that also suggests numerous international and local destinations. Check their regional recommendations for specifics. *Educational Travel on a Shoestring: Frugal Family Fun and Learning Away from Home* by Judith Waite Allee and Melissa L. Morgan is another highly educational manual to add a bit of knowledge to your family adventure. Just remember, while traveling on a shoestring, be sure keep the tykes' shoestrings securely tied. In fact, go ahead and double knot those baby sneaks!

Teachers Karin and Joe Dixon didn't let parenthood slow them down. Karin pursued a Fulbright scholarship in Stockholm and Joe came along for the ride to take care of their infant son, Amos, who was eleven months old at the time. They traveled through parts of Norway and Germany in addition to living in Stockholm, all the while toting Amos along in the BabyBjörn. For preparation, Karin and Joe recommend *Lonely Planet's Travel With Children* by Cathy Lanigan. Karin also recommends taking a high-quality stroller, a good plastic pouch bib, backpacks instead of suitcases, and plenty of emergency snacks. She adds that breastfeeding (if your child is still nursing) can make traveling more leisurely for both parents and child.

The *Unofficial Guide* series (John Wiley & Sons, www.wiley.com) includes numerous regional titles for traveling with the rugrats, and the books will benefit locals too.

For destinations closer to home, check out **Activities for Kids** (www.activitiesforkids.com). Organized by state, the site suggests a myriad of options, some of them low-to-no cost. Explore "Places to Go" and "Just for Fun" for tooling around with the tykes. Or, if you're exhausted chasing the little ones around, you might strategically (mercifully?) consider letting someone else take care of the kids for a while through "Camps" or "Educations & Classes."

CONGRATULATIONS ON THE BABY!
(NOW WE HAVE TO LET YOU GO)

Micki Karrer's maternity leave had a rude beginning. Then-head of marketing for telecom startup Sigma Networks, Micki got laid off two weeks before she was to go on leave—right before her due date! Because the company shut down soon thereafter, she lost her health insurance as well.

Lucky for the whole family, Micki's husband's insurance kicked in to cover most of the maternity expenses and, much to her credit, she was able to adapt quickly. In retrospect, she sees the sudden time off as a blessing. "The timing worked out great," she told us, "as I was able to take about nine months off, which was perfect. Also, with a baby on the way, I had more perspective than many of my colleagues did, and could just focus on being a mother."

Not all new mothers will be so lucky, of course. Don't count on your employer to create quality time for you and your family. It's still up to you to strike the balance, which means being prepared to leave work behind when you have to.

From Here to Maternity

Being a new parent is no vacation, but parental leave is at least somewhat institutionalized, which makes it pretty much the only type of time off that's legitimate in the eyes of the mainstream. So do what you can to take advantage of time allowed.

The process of maternity and paternity leave has evolved over the years. The federal Family and Medical Leave Act (FMLA) of 1993 stipulates that certain employers (generally, public agencies and businesses with fifty or more employees) must grant eligible employees up to twelve weeks unpaid leave for the birth and care of an employee's newborn child. For more information on the FMLA, check with the **Department of Labor** (www.dol.gov).

Some larger employers do offer paid maternity-leave benefits, but sadly these perks aren't universal. If your employer is more family-neutral than family-friendly, think about staggering your leave: Mom takes four months off, then, as she transitions back to work, Dad takes six weeks.

Most mothers use some combination of short-term disability, vacation, sick leave, and unpaid leave at the birth of a child. Short-term disability covers all or a portion of your salary during times when you are unable to perform your job due to a disability (like giving birth), and is offered by some companies, unions, and certain states, such as California and New York.

Andrea Ghez, a professor and scientist at UCLA, took advantage of the university's flexible maternity-leave benefits, and used a combination of time off and flex-time during her baby's first six months. "There wasn't much precedent for me to follow. If you can believe it, I was only the second woman in my department to take maternity leave as an active, full-time professor."

Unfortunately for everyone, this type of benefit is usually available only to mothers. Some companies, however, do offer personal leave above and beyond the federal law. Maureen Feeney works at Agilent Technologies, one of the more

single parents

A single parent won't have much wiggle room when it comes to taking time off, but that doesn't mean it can't be done. Careful planning and a strong support network will help.

Adrianna, a high-tech professional, spent many months of involuntary time off. As a single mother of two, she didn't enjoy her time off so much as survive it, but she did feel it was important to present her situation positively to her children. "I didn't feel guilty, but I was worried about finances—and my kids noticed I was sad." She managed to maintain a positive outlook during a challenging time, in part by working out "a ton." Way to hang tough!

Marsha Converse, also a single mother, lost her job with NorthPoint Communications during company-wide layoffs. Despite serious financial and personal turmoil, her son noticed the before-and-after: "She came out of the whole experience less stressed and more level-headed," he said. And *she* says she now knows what's important: family. "I feel like getting laid off made me a human being again."

progressive employers in the country; she recommends negotiating for your leave. She did just that, received ten weeks of paid maternity leave, and was able to tack on another six months of unpaid leave, for a total of nearly nine months. Her husband Jeff, however, who also works for Agilent, wasn't so lucky; he had to use his vacation time in order to get paid time off. Unfair!

Californians are thankful for the recently-passed law, **Paid Family Leave** (www.paidfamilyleave.org), which extends partially-paid paternity leave to fathers through the State Disability Insurance Program. We can only hope other states will follow.

Regardless, we encourage all mothers and fathers to ask for extended leave during their newborn's first year and beyond. Look at it this way: you're not just asking for yourself, you're setting a precedent for all your future-parent colleagues. Your employer may surprise you; many are, if not sympathetic, at least open to negotiation.

Some terrific sources on the subject delve into much greater detail. *Everything a Working Mother Needs to Know About Pregnancy Rights, Maternity Leave and Making Her Career Work for Her* by Anne C. Weisberg and Carol A. Buckler has been the babymaker's bible for years. Also cherished is *Life After Baby: From Professional Woman to Beginner Parent* by Wynn McClenahan Burkett, which focuses on professional women entering parenthood. Web-savvy moms can study up at **BabyCenter** (www.babycenter.com, search "maternity leave") for a good rundown on the basics.

LASTING CONNECTIONS

Time off is not always a smooth road, but a willingness to stay flexible combined with an optimistic attitude usually keeps the sun shining. If you care to share that positive impact, get out there and volunteer. It's only right for you to start sharing the leisure!

CHAPTER 9
SHARING THE LEISURE

*Never doubt that a small group of thoughtful,
committed citizens can change the world;
indeed it is the only thing that ever has.*

~ Margaret Mead

IF YOU'VE hopped off the job train and spent time at the leisure station, chances are you've been focusing on you, and "getting" a whole lot of good stuff in the process. There comes a time, however, when most of us yearn to spread that good fortune around, like peanut butter on a slice of Wonder Bread. As Winston Churchill famously said, "We make a living by what we get, we make a life by what we give."

Giving to a worthy cause creates an upward spiral of swirling dividends that enrich the community at large. If you feel frustrated, anxious, angry, or just fed up with the world's problems, there's no better antidote than to get off your keister and do something to help. Volunteer for a cause you believe in and you'll know that you've moved from the ranks of the rankled to the echelon of the engaged. It's a sure-fire way to get those warm fuzzies that your old cubicle could never provide.

Volunteering then triggers one of the great paradoxes of the universe: the more you give, the more you get. We're not talking just the personal satisfaction of knowing you've made a difference, here. We're talking perks. Bennies. Righteous reimbursement. Donate your time and you could learn new skills, make influential contacts, score free food and drink, augment your T-shirt collection with the customary freebies (and let's face it, who actually goes out and buys T-shirts anymore?) and get a desk, a phone, even a new title of your choosing.

Give, to get, to give more, to get more…good gravy! It's a wonder we're not volunteering all the time.

EVERY VOLUNTEER OPP UNDER THE SUN

VolunteerMatch *(www.volunteermatch.org)* is a highly-touted online resource founded in 1998 by Jay Backstrand, a one-time marketing manager at computer giant Sun Microsystems. He witnessed firsthand the power of the Internet in coordinating Sun's corporate volunteer efforts. "Before VolunteerMatch," Jay told us, "it was often very challenging to translate volunteer inspiration into volunteer action. With the service, it has become much, much easier to simply get involved."

VolunteerMatch has generated nearly two million referrals to tens of thousands of non-profits nationwide since its founding. "It's incredible to see that the organization is having a positive impact and making such a tremendous difference," Jay says. "Because of our service, more and more people are choosing to volunteer, and to me, that's extremely rewarding."

Fill out your profile and VolunteerMatch will send you periodic emails about organizations in your area. You can customize the type of gigs you're looking for: working outside, working with kids, teens, seniors, animals—even "virtual" opportunities for those who don't or can't leave the computer. You can also enter your zip code for results based on the distance you're willing to travel. A quick zip code search of Boise, Idaho, for example, yielded 63 results, from hospital couriers and tour guides to IT specialists. Even the zip code for Jellico, Tennessee, a tiny town of 3,300 people in the Appalachian Mountains, produced several results.

GETTING STARTED

Given all the worthy causes, it's a challenge just deciding where to start. Russ Finkelstein, associate director of **Idealist.org** (www.idealist.org), a global clearinghouse for the non-profit sector, recommends that people do some introspection before they commit.

"The most important thing is to think about what matters to you," Russ says. "What's the thing that's going to get you out of bed every day, whether it's for a couple of hours a week or for a couple days a month? What will you be excited to do? How much time are you willing to give in terms of days or hours per week, and for how long?"

In other words, be honest with yourself. Do you want to be the person on the front lines—the one walking the dog, ladling the soup, answering the phone, passing the tray of champagne, clearing the bike trail? Or do you want to be the person in the background—updating the database, stuffing the envelopes, organizing the fundraising gala? And how much time are you comfortable giving? Think about time not because you need to test your level of altruism, but because some volunteer work can be emotionally draining or physically demanding. The last thing you need is to suffer volunteering burnout!

Once you've narrowed your volunteering goals, use a centralized resource to help you find specific opportunities. **The United Way of America** (www.unitedway.org) oversees about

volunteer etiquette

True, volunteer jobs don't pay and you can't really get fired. That doesn't mean the normal rules of courtesy don't apply. We're talking *karma* here!

Here are some etiquette reminders from Russ Finkelstein, associate director of *Idealist.org* *(www.idealist.org):*

Before you commit, talk to the volunteer manager or whomever is in charge and ask questions:

* Do you offer any training?
* Why do people drop out?
* What kind of skills are you looking for specifically?

Visit the actual work site before volunteering, to see if the job is something you can or want to do.

Once you've signed on:

* Take it seriously; it does affect a lot of people.
* Make sure you are prepared when you arrive.
* Be on time, and call if you are running late.

Remember that if you don't show up, you are making it harder on the people who do. If it's not working out, let them know that it's not the right fit—and let them know why.

1,400 community-based organizations nationwide, and that means ample opportunity to get your "volunteer" on. Their search engine, (www.volunteersolutions.org) can deliver opportunities sorted by your skills, interests and availability. Don't overlook the ubiquitous stand-bys (such as the **American Red Cross**, www.redcross.org) that have served our communities for years but are always in need of volunteers. If you find yourself long on altruism but short on time, don't forget about donating blood. It's easy, it's quick, and the need never ends.

Dr. Jan Cannon (www.cannoncareercenter.com), career advisor and author of *Find a Job: 7 Steps to Success*, suggests that you don't have to go far to find an opportunity—many are not even advertised. "You can find volunteer work in everything from a sports team to local government or regional government," Jan says. "It doesn't have to be United Way or some other large organization. You can volunteer to help your local police or fire department—do their filing, for example—or shelve books at the library. Look up your local parks and rec department; they always have something." For job-seekers, it's not a bad way to gain entrée into an organization you'd like to know more about.

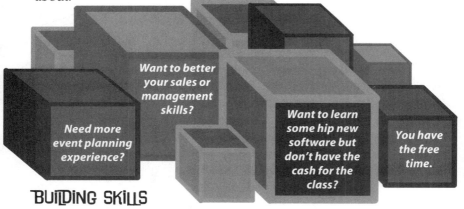

Want to better your sales or management skills?

Need more event planning experience?

Want to learn some hip new software but don't have the cash for the class?

You have the free time.

BUILDING SKILLS

On that note, if you've been looking to change the direction of your career—or explore other types of work, buff up your skills, or break into the non-profit world—volunteering is your ticket. Team up with a non-profit and learn how to raise funds, or volunteer to organize a special event for a philanthropic organization and build your public relations moxie. Countless non-profits will provide you with training in return for your effort.

Trying to break into management? "If you can manage volunteers, you can manage anybody," says Dr. Cannon. "You have to plan, negotiate, direct. All of those skills are extremely valuable."

Yet, according to Dr. Dory Hollander (www.wiseworkplaces.com), a career coach in Arlington, Virginia, some career-minded individuals don't understand how donating their time can improve their professional prospects. Some even fear that volunteering could be perceived as a sign of failure. "Even though the benefits of volunteering are real, so are the perceived liabilities. When people don't have any sense of what volunteerism involves, they may fear that they will be confused with dilettantes and those who have failed at finding paid work," she says.

Eliza Barrios is a West Coast-based artist who gets it. She volunteered to teach photography to high-school kids in the California school system not only because she believes strongly in supporting creative education, but also because she wanted to improve her teaching skills. "I've come to a point in my career where I want to do something worthwhile with the artistic skills and experience I've acquired," Eliza told us. "I feel teaching is the best way to infect the masses with information and skills that will allow them to expand in ways that are unlimited." She now has the experience and credibility to add "teacher" to her resume.

THE GREAT OUTDOORS

Everybody needs beauty as well as bread,
places to play in and pray in, where nature may
heal and give strength to body and soul alike.

~John Muir, *The Yosemite (1912)*

You'd be hard-pressed to enjoy a more rewarding experience than pulling on your boots, rolling up your sleeves and burrowing your hands in the soil to help protect Mother Earth. John Muir's legacy, the **Sierra Club** (www.sierraclub.org), wouldn't be a bad place to start. They need people for all manner of earth work—from saving wild tigers and leading hikes to helping preserve forests, wetlands, and watersheds. If you like the outdoors, get out there and spruce it up!

The **National Parks Service** (www.nps.gov) could also use your help, considering they manage over 84 million acres of parkland hosting approximately 270 million visitors annually. Do you want to feel important? Then join the ranks of their **VIP Program** (www.nps.gov/volunteer). It may not be the most exclusive club in the world—140,000 volunteers donated their time in 2004—but you will find just about any outdoor opportunity imaginable, from maintaining park trails in the Sierra Nevada to assisting in historical preservation and community outreach on Ellis Island in New York.

To take it a step wilder, check out the hip outdoor trips at **Wilderness Volunteers** (www.wildernessvolunteers.org). Their one-week excursions will cost you a few hundred duckets to cover food, equipment and other incidentals, but they'll take you to some of the most amazing spots in the continental U.S., Hawaii, or Alaska. We challenge you to find a more economical and rewarding vacation option through your local travel agent.

COMMUNAL GIVING

Volunteering was temporary diversion got so fired up at the **Burning Man** office (see "Participate" at *www.burningman.com*) that he continued to contribute on weekends even after he found a full-time job. "It was a great way to connect to an amazing community," he told us. His burning passion to volunteer even inspired him to found an educational non-profit of his own: *Senior Surf* (*www.senior-surf.org*). like Dave did? You Burn beforehand, too, by making the ticket gate, or of other activities. Just to your hometown

more than a for Dave Casuto. He *Computer Education* Want to feel the fire can contribute to the or at the event itself playa signs, working performing any number remember to come back playa when it's all over!

VOLUNTEERING ABROAD

A volunteer stint abroad can find you tutoring kids in a rural village, working for a non-government organization (NGO), helping to preserve the rain forest, or rebuilding houses after a disaster. Those are but a few possible endeavors; the options are as varied as volunteering in your own community, with the added benefit of immersion in another culture.

Work Camps and Placements

Generally speaking, overseas volunteer options fall into one of two categories: "work camps," which are bare-bones volunteer groups that usually have projects ranging from one week to one month and are relatively inexpensive; and volunteer placement organizations, which are more costly but also provide extensive support and amenities. Some organizations charge fees that can stretch your leisure budget a bit too far, so this is one crusade you definitely want to do your homework on.

Don't forget to ask for answers that seem obvious, but aren't. (Are room and board covered? Who pays for the flight?) Below are a couple of homework assignments, after you finish the required reading: *How to Live Your Dream of Volunteering Overseas* by Joseph Collins, Stefano DeZerega, and Zahara Heckscher.

Work Camps:
Volunteers For Peace (www.vpf.org)
Service Civil International (www.sci-ivs.org)

Placement Organizations:
Global Volunteers (www.globalvolunteers.org)
Amizade (www.amizade.org)

Elective Elections

Want to promote freedom and democracy around the world without donning battle fatigues or toting a weapon? Volunteer to help monitor an overseas election. The need is out there (just like the truth), and you'll play a critical role in helping to ensure that elections are both free and fair.

Jason Julian, an attorney in California, has made monitoring elections a habit over the last decade, venturing overseas six times to regions of emerging democracy such as Bosnia, Liberia and Ukraine. It has been a reality check.

"As United Nations Volunteers, we had to do a lot of organizational and logistical support work relevant to the election, as opposed to just watching for fraud or other irregularities," Jason told us. "My most memorable experience was in Liberia in 1997 just after the end of the civil war there. The whole country had a post-apocalyptic 'Mad Max' feel and landscape to it. One day I saw two young girls fist-fighting in the street and one picked up a large gray object to hit the other. When I got a bit closer I could see (to my shock and surprise) that she was wielding a human skull. I asked a Liberian mechanic in our post where she got the skull and he nonchalantly replied, 'Oh, they are all around.'"

If this has you scratching your head, take it as a sobering reminder that people still sacrifice their lives in other regions of the world to fight for basic freedoms that many of us take for granted.

For more information:

United Nations Volunteers (www.unv.org)
The Carter Center (www.cartercenter.org)
PAE React (www.pae-react.com)
Organization for Security and Co-operation in Europe (www.osce.org)

Dr. Jones, I Presume?

Jessica Burnette-Lemon, a magazine editor from Tennessee, took her interest in conservation all the way to Ecuador as a volunteer for *Jatun Sacha* (www.jatunsacha.org), an environmental NGO. "After finally extracting myself from a soul-sucking admin job," she told us, "I was unemployed, restless, and ready to learn something new. I was interested in environmental issues and improving my Spanish, so I researched environmental volunteer opportunities in Latin America. I found a biological research station where I could live in Ecuador's remote coastal forest while planting trees, helping visiting biologists with research, practicing my Spanish, and meeting people from all over the world."

more...

More?

For more information on volunteering abroad, including organizations that specialize in placements with more of a vacation bent, see "Volunteer Vacations" in **Chapter 4**.

Still thinking globally? Whet your international appetite by helping **Global Exchange** (www.globalexchange.org) with international human rights issues and policies. Their programs include study tours, retail stores promoting alternative trade, educational development, media outreach, and human rights campaigns.

ACTING LOCALLY

...cont'd

Helping your neighbors might not have the glam appeal of a stint overseas, but it comes with the added benefit of plugging into and making an impact in your own community. Look up your local Parks and Recreation department on the Web or in the phone book. They need volunteers year-round for help with everything from coaching kids and teaching art classes to raking the leaves and cleaning up the beach. Local opportunities in education and health abound—use a tool like **Volunteer-Match** (see "Getting Started" earlier in the chapter) to find out who needs help within your zip code. They might be right around the corner!

For $200 a month, the station provided Jessica with housing, meals, and educational sessions in local ecology, history and economics. In exchange, she got a once-in-a-lifetime experience and a perfect home base for exploring the rest of the country on weekends.

"I woke up every morning to the sound of howler monkeys on distant ridges," Jessica told us. "I rappelled down waterfalls and spelunked in caves big enough to house whole colonies of bats—very Indiana Jones.... I now know the Spanish words for 'mud,' 'spider,' and 'be careful, that bites.'"

Jessica might not have found the Lost Ark of the Covenant, but she did find an extremely gratifying overseas experience for relatively little money.

Reading Is Aloud

If you've gotten this far, we know you can read. Help others learn to read too. After all, a lack of literacy affects people's ability to succeed in society, and that affects us all. Volunteers are a vital part of what has been dubbed the "literacy movement," so read this: being a literacy tutor helps people get their

GEDs, improves kids' self-image and grades, and gets parents more involved in their children's education.

Launch your research by launching your browser to **Literacy Connections** (www.literacyconnections.com) and going to their "Volunteer Links." Their site alone is a worthy teacher, and includes extensive resources to prep you as a tutor.

Can you hear me now? Good, because Verizon Communications is getting the word out with the **Verizon Literacy Campus** (www.literacy campus.org), which is all about volunteering for literacy. Connect to opportunities by going to their "Volunteer Now" section, where you can review the types of contributions you can make as well as plug into their handy volunteer engine. They also host a virtual "Campus Center" complete with an online library, bulletin board and bookstore.

Word: your regional search may very well lead you directly to your local public library, which wouldn't be a bad place to start.

Nurture Your Neighbors

Consider yourself fortunate if you're not suffering from abuse or AIDS, and doubly fortunate if you can help those who are. Keep in mind that volunteering your time for causes such as preventing domestic abuse or helping those with severe medical conditions is a serious commitment, and is not for everyone. The rewards for these types of volunteer positions are often more character-building than social.

Domestic Violence

Want to help stop domestic violence or assist victims? The **National Domestic Violence Hotline** (800-799-7233, www.ndvh.org) is just a phone call away. Although they are located in Austin, Texas, they have the ability to patch volunteers into their hotline remotely, so that you can take calls from wherever you are. Most other domestic violence volunteer opportunities are regional, but you might find what you need from the **National Coalition Against Domestic Violence** (www.ncadv.org, see "Resources," then "State Coalition List"), or turn back to the handy Web engine at VolunteerMatch.

AIDS

Healing hands can get involved with the local treatment and pre-vention of AIDS. Start with the **American International AIDS Foundation** (www.aids.com) and hone in on their extensive "Official Directory of AIDS/HIV Sites." You'll find an abundance of resources arranged by category, including community organizations, where your efforts can range from delivering meals to teaching sex educa-tion courses to organizing public awareness events.

Little Brothers and Sisters

If you never had a little brother or sister to pick on, this is your chance. Bond with a little one through **Big Brothers Big Sisters** (www.bbbsa.org). The oldest and largest youth mentoring group in the U.S., Big Brothers Big Sisters is a serious program for seriously committed individuals. Volunteers generally pledge a minimum of one year—training requirements and minimum commitments vary regionally—to befriend and mentor a young boy or girl. No noogies allowed! Community-based Big Brothers Big Sisters is their standard program; Big Brothers Big Sisters in Schools, their other core program, applies the same concept to the specific task of helping a youth with schoolwork.

Tess Roering, who grew up in the Midwest, reveled in being able to devote more energy to BBBS of San Francisco and The Peninsula dur-ing a recent six-month hiatus from her marketing career. "I've worked with Big Brothers Big Sisters for years," Tess told us. "Now I've been able to invest a little more time, spend more time in the office, do more specific projects. I've been on the board for a couple of years and it's always been something I've cared about; now to be able to spend time in the office, have meetings with the staff—I feel like I'm getting a better handle on the day-to-day workings. I think it makes me more effective going forward."

CASA

Tackle another rewarding challenge by contacting your local office of **CASA** (www.nationalcasa.org), an organization that pairs volunteers one-on-one with children living in foster care. "CASA" stands for Court Appointed Special Advocate. Each volunteer advocate becomes a sworn court officer who works to understand the interests and legal needs of the child they represent, and to make sure that lawyers, the courts and social services agencies are protecting that child. Becoming a CASA advocate is an intense but potentially life-changing commitment.

Ashley Arledge Hamlett, SFCASA Case Supervisor, tells us that "you don't have to be a lawyer or social worker to become a CASA volunteer. As a CASA volunteer, you will receive training from professionals in the legal and child welfare fields, and you'll have the complete support of your CASA organization to help you get through each case." You won't ever be left wondering whether your efforts matter, according to Ashley; you'll know you're not wasting your time with these kids. "You can make a lifelong difference for these special children," she says, "the difference between homelessness and a safe home, between dropping out and completing school, between jail and becoming a productive member of society. And you'll be rewarded with some of the most powerful and fulfilling experiences you can find."

Habitat for Humanity

To help others get a roof over their heads, don't your carpentry wear, and build a house with **Habitat for Humanity International** (800-422-4828, www.habitat.org). Together with countless volunteers, Habitat has built hundreds of thousands of houses in communities around the world. Find your own volunteering home with one of their thousands of local affiliates.

WORKING WITH KIDS

Perhaps no one deserves your charitable attention more than children. If teaching or mentoring is your bag, help tutor students, read to children or chaperone field trips.

Ahoy matey! A fantastic opportunity awaits you if you have an interest in teaching kids to write. **826 Valencia** (www.826Valencia.org), founded by renowned author Dave Eggers, has been providing free tutoring for kids ages 8-18 from one of the hippest locations in San Francisco, the back of a pirate store! The organization provides instruction in expository and creative writing, songwriting, poetry, drama—almost any genre imaginable. If you want to rub elbows with some real professionals in the field, 826 has been attracting star volunteers since its inception. It's expanding nationally, and currently has centers in LA (www.826LA.org) and New York (www.826NYC.org), with plans for more. 826 has an ongoing need for volunteer teachers, writers, cartoonists, and filmmakers to help teach kids how to express themselves.

Trips For Kids (www.tripsforkids.org) is a fun way to introduce the great outdoors to inner-city children (as opposed to goats) through cycling. Their "Rides" program exposes kids to the outdoors via two wheels while their "Re-Cyclery" program teaches them employable skills such as bicycle repair. Contact one of their local chapters if you're interested in leading a trip or, if no local chapter exists, wheel through their website to learn how to start your own.

WORKING WITH SENIORS

Do a little role reversal and become a little brother for a change (but please, no bratty behavior). Benefit from the wisdom of experience by befriending a senior through **Little Brothers—Friends of the Elderly** (www.littlebrothers.org). With programs ranging from regular volunteer visits, which require a one-year commitment, to special events and parties that can be done on a one-time basis, you're sure to find a good friend fit. You can even volunteer as an entertainer, in case you were looking for an audience for that new song, comedy routine, or magic act you've been working on. What better opportunity for budding performers to gain a dedicated audience and to strut their stuff? A word to the wise: go easy on the grinding speed metal or punk rock lyrics.

To help deliver the basic necessities of life to the elderly, hop on board with **Meals On Wheels** (www.mowaa.org), one of the most successful charities around. Food for thought: donate a lot or a little, and see clear and immediate results demonstrated by the smiles on seniors' faces. Search "Finding a Local Program" off their home page to connect with your local chapter of MOW.

WORKING WITH ANIMALS

Today's urban dogs and other animals have it tough. Their numbers continue to grow without a corresponding increase in homes or services. Plenty of wayward pets and animals need your assistance. First stop should be your local **SPCA**, a group focused on saving and caring for our homeless canine and feline friends. Unfortunately, regional SPCA offices don't seem to work together, at least not on the Web. SPCA.com is the site of SPCA Canada, while SPCA.org is maintained by SPCA Texas. Texas? Sounds like a digital land grab to us. In any event, use a search engine to find the SPCA in your community—or go retro and check in the phone book.

WORKING THE ROOM

That's right: work it. Work it *real* good. Want to meet and greet while you're volunteering? No problem. The concept of singles or social volunteering is becoming more popular and highly refined.

Just about all volunteering creates a congenial environment—strangers are brought together to give to a worthy cause, and the affair is usually a great bonding experience (see also **Chapter 8** under

"Volunteer")—but certain groups *specialize* in social volunteering, giving together as a way of getting together, so to speak. The epicenter of singles volunteering is a group called, you guessed it, **Single Volunteers** (www.singlevolunteers.org), where "a single person can make a difference," and they have a nationwide network of chapters to mingle through. Can't find one in your area? Their website guides ambitious self-starters through forming a new chapter.

GiViNG AND LIViNG LEISURE

That's a lot of giving going on! And getting, and giving…. The more good vibes you share through volunteering, the safer the world becomes for leisure. Keep that generous spirit in mind as you transition into your next big life endeavor, whether that's heading for the halls of academia or (gulp) going back to work.

swanky parties

"Night-of" assistance with special events is fun, on site, and very social. It helps in raising boatloads of money. Sound like your scene? Then don your tux or evening gown, and help the rich and notable loosen their grip on their wallets.

Start with the swanky events of the *American Cancer Society* (www.cancer.org), which can double as great networking opportunities. Continue with the *Cystic Fibrosis Foundation* (www.cff.org), which uses special events as one of its primary fundraising vehicles and is always looking for volunteers. You can hobnob the evenings away in between!

leisure vineyards
star of leisure

1996
Vintage Champagne

PART THREE

RE-ENTRY

CHAPTER 10
BACK TO SCHOOL

Woo-hoo! I'm a college man!
I won't need my high school diploma any more!
I am so smart! I am so smart...S-M-R-T!
I mean, S-M-A-R-T....

~ Homer Simpson, "Homer Goes Back to College"

YOU might be wondering what to do *after* your Unemployed Odyssey. Hopefully you'll score some stress-free fun before facing this decision, but what if you're still not ready to go back to work? What if you loathe your career and aren't sure what you want to do next? Don't panic. There *is* a solution. It's time to go to school.

Going back to school is a major undertaking, especially if it means foregoing a high-paying job. The possibility of debt and career derailment can loom large. You might wonder if it's worth the investment. But think about it this way: you have the rest of your working life to earn dollars, but you may never have a better chance to further your education. Most fellow earthlings are lucky to get a high school degree, much less finish college or go to grad school. From that perspective, consider any type of schooling a privilege.

Higher education can serve as a panacea for that which ails the leisure seeker. You get to ditch the pressures and responsibilities of a job (temporarily) while working toward a worthy goal: greater knowledge. But being job-free is not the only benefit—if you've longed to study the classics like history, art or literature, the books are waiting for you. Looking to change careers? A new degree can open doors as well as your mind. Maybe it's a trade that appeals to you. Become a certified bartender. Go to beer school!

You can never learn too much. If you can fund more school, get thee to thy registrar and get those neurons firing.

GRADUATE SCHOOL

Lisa Turner decided to apply to a graduate journalism program after getting laid off from her dot-com job. "The prospect of giving up a big salary to go back to school was daunting," she told us. "But coming from a position of unemployment or self-employment, it was more realistic."

Robert L. Peters' book *Getting What You Came for: The Smart Student's Guide to Earning a M.A or a Ph.D.* can help you weigh the pros and cons of becoming a student again. But don't limit your calculus to the practical; some of life's most enriching experiences result from factoring in the whimsical, too.

Gena Bilden, assistant dean of student services for the graduate programs at **Saint Mary's University of Minnesota** (www.smumn.edu), realizes that most students go to grad school to advance their careers and increase their salaries, but advises applicants to seek personal growth too. She cautions against going to grad school for the wrong reasons. "I've sat in class with individuals who proclaim that all they want is a piece of paper," she told us. "If they don't come away with the knowledge, they have only wasted their time and money."

Research

You'll find comprehensive information on programs in the U.S. and abroad at sites like **GradSchools.com** (www.gradschools.com). The site is funded by sponsoring universities, which means the information is free but might be skewed in favor of those sponsors. **Peterson's** (www.petersons.com) produces another free education portal with a good search engine; just be prepared for them to hard-sell you one of their many books. A more neutral source of U.S. graduate program rankings is *U.S. News & World Report* (www.usnews.com, "Rankings & Guides," then "America's Best Graduate Schools").

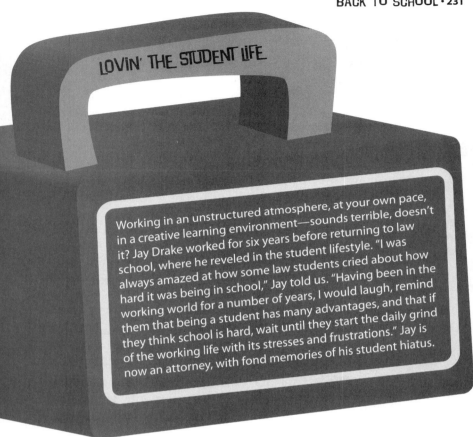

LOVIN' THE STUDENT LIFE

Working in an unstructured atmosphere, at your own pace, in a creative learning environment—sounds terrible, doesn't it? Jay Drake worked for six years before returning to law school, where he reveled in the student lifestyle. "I was always amazed at how some law students cried about how hard it was being in school," Jay told us. "Having been in the working world for a number of years, I would laugh, remind them that being a student has many advantages, and that if they think school is hard, wait until they start the daily grind of the working life with its stresses and frustrations." Jay is now an attorney, with fond memories of his student hiatus.

The Admissions Process

Applying to grad school and getting accepted are two entirely different steps. The admissions requirements and application process will be much more stringent than the hoops you jumped through for your undergraduate study. Don't be intimidated—you won't be the first or the last to go through the rigors. In fact, guiding applicants through the admissions maze has become its own thriving industry.

If you have your eye on the business world and making tons of money, for example, you can buy the book by Matt Symonds and Alan Mendonca, *ABC of Getting the MBA Admissions Edge*. If you aspire to heal others, check out Andrew Goliszek's straightforward *The Complete Medical School Preparation and Admissions Guide*. And if you advocate justice for all, pony up for *Law School Admissions Adviser* by Ruth Lammert-Reeves.

Entrance Exams

No institutional process would be complete without good old-fashioned standardized tests. Welcome to the wonderful world of acronyms: GRE, GMAT, LSAT, MCAT, TOEFL...YIKES! Those who dwell in the neo-acronym world of high-tech will feel right at home.

As with research, there are companies that can help—for a not-so-nominal fee. **Kaplan** (800-527-8378, www.kaplan.com) and **The Princeton Review** (800-273-8439, www.princetonreview.com), two preeminent test preparation companies, offer live and online courses for all common standardized tests. Live course fees start at a whopping $800. Even the more economical online courses with self-study materials will soak up anywhere from $100 to $500 of your freedom funds. If you're the self-disciplined type, practice some frugality and go with materials from the bookstore.

Are the pricey courses worth the money? Ted Witt bumped up his GMAT score a modest 30 points after taking a live course. He admits, though, that he might have been a little preoccupied—his second try was only six days before his wedding!

"I decided to take the test again four weeks later with no studying," he told us. "One hundred and ten points higher that time." Guess it took a while for the course info to sink in, or maybe the test is just that random. Ted's final answer? "Prepare with books or a class, and if you aren't happy with your score, take the test again."

WHO'S GONNA PAY?

Most university programs require serious cash. Never fear. An intrepid trailblazer like you should be able to mine at least one of the following sources.

---

the perpetual student

Can't get your socks to match? Harbor a secret propensity for wearing corduroy sport coats? Whether it's a convenient hiding place or a passionate extension of your life's mission, academia allows you to dress as you like, set your own schedule and philosophize until the wee hours of the morning. Sabbaticals are not only allowed, but encouraged!

Academia can make a superb cocoon for the leisure connoisseur. "Gradual" programs can go on for years and years. Not bad, considering how numerous the funding possibilities are. You could even focus your studies exclusively on the subject of leisure, like *Professor Benjamin Hunnicutt* (www.shorterworkhours.com) at the University of Iowa—perhaps the most scholarly leisure seeker in the nation.

Scholarships

First step: think "scholarship." Scholarships are fantastic, untapped resources, and many garner little competition. But these treasures won't stay hidden much longer, as the Web makes it infinitely easier to ferret them out.

Folks we know rave about the **Catalog of Federal Domestic Assistance** (www.cfda.gov) as a starting point. One of the least commercial online sources is **Scholarships.com** (www.scholarships.com), whose sophisticated search engine helps you manage their extensive database. **BrokeScholar** (www.brokescholar.com) boasts a database of more than 650,000 scholarships worth over $2.5 billion. And **FastWeb** (www.fastweb.com), owned by the career website Monster, lets you search for colleges as well as scholarships, for free.

Dr. Stephen Jones, scholarship expert and author of *Seven Secrets of How to Study*, advises students to go beyond the Internet to try some lesser-known funding sources, like a credit union, the neighborhood hardware or grocery store, or your local legislator. Many private and public scholarships never make it to the Web. If you can sell yourself convincingly, Dr. Jones suggests an even bolder approach: make a scholarship appeal on a local radio program, and receive funding from their listeners. To tune into his other ideas, send him an email at stephenjoness@rcn.com and he will send you a free ten-page scholarship guide.

Student Loans

If you've squeezed out whatever scholarship or family money is available and you are still short on tuition, consider a student loan. Most are offered at exceptionally low interest rates, many are subsidized by the federal government, and repayment schedules are usually flexible.

ph.d. pleasures, ph.d. pressures

Brian Collier enjoyed teaching high school at a Native American boarding school, but left behind the long hours, low salary and inadequate respect to pursue a Ph.D. at Arizona State University. His schedule is now flexible enough to allow him to take care of his son at home part of the day, while teaching at the college, writing and researching. "I just love it!" he says.

If you too are intent on completing a full-bore Ph.D. program, more power to you. Be advised, however, that while academia can appear to be "the life" looking from the outside in, it does have its share of organizational politics, bureaucracy and inflexibility—just like other work.

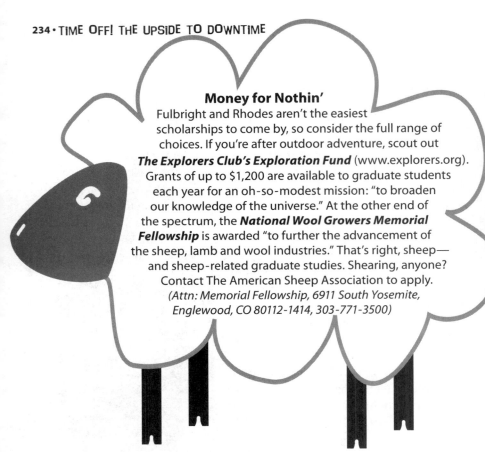

Money for Nothin'

Fulbright and Rhodes aren't the easiest scholarships to come by, so consider the full range of choices. If you're after outdoor adventure, scout out *The Explorers Club's Exploration Fund* (www.explorers.org). Grants of up to $1,200 are available to graduate students each year for an oh-so-modest mission: "to broaden our knowledge of the universe." At the other end of the spectrum, the *National Wool Growers Memorial Fellowship* is awarded "to further the advancement of the sheep, lamb and wool industries." That's right, sheep— and sheep-related graduate studies. Shearing, anyone? Contact The American Sheep Association to apply. *(Attn: Memorial Fellowship, 6911 South Yosemite, Englewood, CO 80112-1414, 303-771-3500)*

A loan is still a loan, though, no matter how attractive the terms. Do the math and make sure you're comfortable with how much you'll owe once you've earned your degree. Consult the **U.S. Department of Education** (www.ed.gov, under "Financial Aid") for information on grants and direct loans from the federal government.

Other Federal Government Aid

Get back some of your hard-earned tax dollars by taking advantage of other forms of government aid. The National Science Foundation has developed a program called the **Integrative Graduate Education and Research Traineeship** (www.igert.org), designed to improve the graduate school experience by providing interdisciplinary training in the sciences, mathematics, engineering and technology. Students accepted into the program receive (gulp hard) $30,000 per year, plus tuition and fees. And of course, veterans should remember the **GI Bill** (www.gibill.va.gov).

Employer's Tuition Reimbursement

Think of it as the GI Bill for the private sector: some companies will pay for or reimburse your tuition to attend grad school (with a promise of you returning to your job for a certain time period), so make sure not to pass up this employment perk. Not all companies have formal tuition reimbursement programs, but that doesn't mean you shouldn't ask.

The Source of Last Resort

That's right, the parents. Paying tuition is a legitimate use of their money, right? Wrangling financial aid from your folks might take some fancy persuasion, however.

Mary Mangold's father was skeptical when she asked for a loan to go to film school, so she got creative. "I brought Dad to an open house at the college for extended learning downtown," Mary said. "My future film teacher was so inspiring that my dad agreed to support me."

When you're making your pitch, highlight the ways that the university experience will make you a better person and increase your earning power in the long run. Don't forget to mention how it could boost your ability to care for your elders in their retirement: a little leisure for you now means greater leisure for them later. Isn't it nice how that works?

LOANS THAT CAN BRING YOU TO TEARS

About six months after joining her first-choice law firm, Erica found herself crying in her office one night. "Practicing law was nothing like studying it," she told us, "and I realized I was handcuffed to working at this place I didn't like, in order to pay off the huge private loans I took, in order to get the education I got, in order to get this job—that I didn't like!"

All's well that ends well, though: Erica funneled a huge portion of her big firm salary into paying down those loans as fast as she could, knocking off almost a *hundred thousand dollars* in less than three years. Two years later, she changed careers and has now happily returned to academia, working for a university while earning her Masters in Education.

GOING TO SCHOOL OVERSEAS

Miss out on that undergraduate semester abroad? Go now! You'll reap the benefits of travel and education in one neat package. Brian Pollack went on exchange to Madrid for six months during his MBA program at the University of Washington. "It was one of the best times of my life," he says. "Madrid is an amazing city, and the Spanish culture suited me perfectly." Most universities offer foreign exchange options to their graduate students in addition to their undergrads, but don't despair if you're not already matriculated in a degree program. Any number of programs offer standalone international study. Check out **StudyAbroad.com** (www.studyabroad.com) and **Road2abroad.com** (www.road2abroad.com) for comprehensive directories of programs.

PROFESSIONAL PROGRAMS

Not everyone aspires to become a doctor, lawyer, or business executive, but few can deny the broad-reaching benefits of a professional degree. Win entrance to any of these prestigious programs and make Mom and Dad proud.

Business School

Future titans of industry can earn an MBA just about anywhere, but they won't be alone. The good news is that applications for full-time programs have trended down the last two years, according to the Graduate Management Admission Council. The bad news is that the decrease is mostly just a fallback from a record spike of applicants in 2002. The bottom line: you'll have some company applying to business school.

Peter Johnson, co-director of admissions at **Haas School of Business at UC Berkeley** (www.haas.berkeley.edu), says they've seen a greater number of recently-laid-off applicants than in past years. "Job opportunities in technology are fewer and the venture capital market for entrepreneurs is not good at present," he says. "As a result, many people feel that it is an ideal time to step out of the workforce and enhance their management skills while they wait for the economy to improve." We're liking the sound of that.

Medical School

Despite insurance companies' continued squeeze on the entire medical profession, becoming a doctor remains a noble calling. Acquire the power to heal at a world-class school of medicine. You can apply online via the new, computerized **American Medical College Application Service** (www.aamc.org, click on "AMCAS"), but remember to write your essays in a word-processing program first, and *then* paste them in and send them through.

GREAT MOMENTS IN UNEMPLOYMENT

12

Fake It Till You Make it

It seems "Colonel" Harland Sanders was a jack of all trades. He worked as a lawyer without having a law degree, and delivered babies without a medical degree (and does anyone know if he really *was* a Colonel?) before operating a gas station in Corbin, Kentucky. He also loved to make fried chicken. The home-cooked meals he served at a table in back of the gas station would eventually evolve into the Kentucky Fried Chicken franchise we feed off of today. A testament to career trial and error, the Colonel wasn't afraid to take chances, something we could all stand to emulate. However, if you're dying to go out and pull teeth, please, do us all a favor—go to dental school first!

6

Law School

Maybe you've always dreamt of arguing your case in front of a jury or suing the pants off of your neighbor. Consider getting a law degree first. Students who have lived a little before taking on this arduous endeavor are particularly well-suited for the daunting task.

Jason Julian filled up an entire decade before embarking on law school. "I did all the fun stuff first," Jason says. "I figured I should do it while I still could, before I had a family." He certainly took advantage of his footloose status, spending two years in the Peace Corps, several months-long sessions monitoring elections in emerging democracies, and four years living and working in our nation's capital—where he met his wife. Jason is now rising through the ranks at a prestigious law firm, proving the model of responsibility for his two children. *Ergo, res ipsa loquitur.* Get your apps in! Tech-savvy sorts should check whether your law school of choice accepts applications online.

NIGHT SCHOOL AND NON-DEGREE OPTIONS

Rachel Karagounis recently moved to Las Vegas to start a new life and career, and is taking advantage of her transition time to learn some new tricks. "I've decided to learn Spanish and horseback riding," she told us. "My friend and I are also going to sign up for a computer class because we only know the basics." We're biased toward full-time programs, ourselves—no work!—but if you absolutely must, consider night school or continuing education. You can customize most programs to accommodate your (pending?) work schedule.

LEISURE STUDIES

The scholastic study of leisure is multi-disciplinary, drawing from fields such as history, sociology, economics and politics to describe how people spend their free time. Many reputable universities have Leisure Studies departments, including **San Francisco State University** *(www.sfsu.edu)*, and the **University of Iowa** *(www.uiowa.edu)*. You can even specialize in "therapeutic recreation" to become nationally certified as a recreation therapist. Now that's a program we can get behind!

If you think leisure might be the field for you, try your hand at an actual course. Heidi "Queen of Leisure" Wells took one as an undergrad. "I got a 'C' on my first paper," she told us. "A 'C' in leisure?! I couldn't let that happen. It was odd taking leisure so seriously, but I ended up with an 'A' in the class." Heidi continues to reign supreme, currently volunteering in Peru.

"Leisure studies have flourished rather more strongly in Canada than the U.S.," says Robert Stebbins, a semi-professional double bassist when he's not professoring social sciences at the University of Calgary. "Life centers on work in the U.S. more than the rest of the world, and as Canada is still much more tied with Europe, we have a more European style of work." Perhaps a study abroad stint is in order....

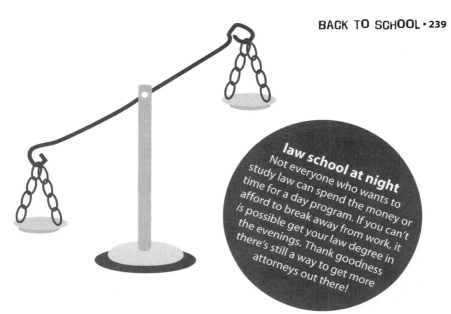

law school at night
Not everyone who wants to study law can spend the money or time for a day program. If you can't afford to break away from work, it is possible get your law degree in the evenings. Thank goodness there's still a way to get more attorneys out there!

Executive and Part-Time MBA Programs

Executive MBA programs, which allow students to earn MBAs without quitting their day jobs, are increasing in popularity. Just think, you get to work full-time and go to school—double the fun! A word of caution: most executive programs charge as if an employer were footing the bill. And on that note, don't forget to find out if your company provides tuition reimbursement.

Continuing Education

Continuing ed can spark your intellect and open up new cerebral worlds—or it can teach you how to taste wine, repair your car, or do your taxes. Either way, it expands your horizons, and that's a big part of the practice of leisure.

Most universities offer some form of continuing adult education. Their courses include certificate and special programs as well as a broad variety of general ed classes. Some of the spicier courses found in recent course catalogs include "Love, American Style: A Cultural History of Sexuality in the United States," and "The Greatest Wines in the World."

Classes at community colleges might be the best bargain around. For-credit courses are available on just about any subject imaginable, and non-credit division courses at some colleges are tuition-free. That's right, tuition-*free*. Students need only show up on the first day of class and buy their own books and supplies.

Drop-In Schooling

The loosely defined concept of "course auditing" gained popularity in the 1960s. Gone are the days when any inquisitive soul could sit in on a class of choice, but auditing remains a very cost-effective method of study. You can study what you want and the admission requirements are quite lax—as in, nonexistent.

Policies vary among universities and professors, so you might have to check around a bit before choosing your "major." Generally speaking, the larger the university and the bigger the class, the easier it will be to audit.

If you ask the professor up front if you can audit the class, you risk being asked for proof that you're enrolled in the university. This is where holding onto that old student ID card would come in handy! Stealth mode might be an option for larger classes, but that means skipping exams and other graded assignments. Whether or not you have the professor's permission, one major drawback of auditing is that there's no chance for credit or to bring home an "A" on your report card. No extra allowance for you!

Jeremy Cantor audits at least one class a semester. Of course, it helps that he works for a university. Although he has an insider advantage, he trusts that most professors will be happy to accommodate an auditor if the class has space, and you approach them early, with a genuine interest in the subject. Jeremy recently audited a graduate-level course in Public Health Policy with the professor's permission. "It's a great way to break up my week," he told us. "A good class is a stimulating, challenging environment—and when you audit, there's no required work. I've been able to check out a number of career and grad school possibilities."

take two

Susan Logas, a 52-year-old mother who retired early from a career in telecommunications, returned to school to study computer science. Several years later, she had completed one certificate program in Unix System Administration and another in Web Administration. "I love being an adult student," Susan told us. "It's a whole different perspective. I know how to study. I know how to listen. And I know how to support the teachers."

Thanks to her fine new education, Susan is now contemplating re-entering the workforce as a system or web administrator.

TRADE SCHOOLS

Vocational schools can get you where you want to go if you want to acquire a set of skills quickly. The nationwide **University of Phoenix** (800-697-8223, www.phoenix.edu), among others, presents a variety of practical programs for working adults, including business, technology, healthcare and education programs. Other schools specialize in a focused trade, such as design or culinary studies. All promise to prep you for success.

Construction

Put your back into your wages with construction work. It's not only well-paid, but trade unions usually provide free training. Apprenticeship programs can get you started in carpentry, tile setting, drywall, painting, plumbing, you name it. You'll be tired at the end of the day, but you will definitely have the satisfaction of working with your hands. Work your way over to **Construction WebLinks** (www.constructionweblinks.com) to nail down a school of your choosing.

What's Cookin'?

Earning your Associate's in Occupational Studies from culinary school takes about twenty-one months. Robert Rafferty chose the culinary academy in Hyde Park, New York. "The New England Culinary Institute is a great school, and the California Culinary Institute is also a great school, but I looked at only Hyde Park," he said.

Robert describes the teaching kitchen as "a weird dynamic but a great mix," with students fresh out of high school, and doctors and lawyers going back for another career. "In the middle of your studies, you have to do an internship," Robert explains. "You can do it in a lot of different places—I chose Key West, who wouldn't?—then you come back and you finish your studies."

After graduating, Robert worked all over the country as a professional chef and culinary school instructor, from Manhattan to Alaska to the Poconos. Now he is teaching culinary arts at a county vocational-technical school. "Teaching is the best, it's even better than being a professional food service person. My dad owns a bar, still does after 26 years, and service is what I've always known. That's why I chose to pursue food service as a professional."

Sounds tasty to us! For more information to stew on, check **CookingSchools.com** (www.cookingschools.com).

Another Round!

Bartending can make for a lively career or a quick cash stop-gap, with evening hours to assure plenty of lounge time during the day. Higher education in the field is available at the **American Bartenders School** (800-532-9222, www.barschool.com), which offers degrees in the time-tested field of "mixology." But wait, there's competition in the world of cocktail education. The **National Bartenders School** (800-556-6499, www.national bartending.com) is also eager to train you. Formal training costs from $500 to $1,000 and will have you drink-ready in about two weeks.

KEEP THE MIND BREWING

Remember surveying the drunken crowd at an all-school kegger and thinking, "Man, if only I knew how to make my *own* beer…I could make a fortune!" Time to bring that fantasy to life—if not for the fortune, then at least for the beer. Beer making has graduated from backyard to big time. Want to go old-school? Hop in the footsteps of beer giant Dan Gordon (of Gordon Biersch) and head to the prestigious *Weihenstephan (www.wihenstephaner.de)* in the heart of Bavaria, the birthplace of brew. Take a more modern approach at *UC Davis (www.ucdavis.edu)*, where you can earn an undergraduate or master's degree in brewing science, or just enroll in an extension program. Total new-schoolers can follow virtual courses at *American Brewers Guild* (www.abgbrew.com), which includes apprenticeships in brewpubs throughout the U.S.

ALTERNATIVE EDUCATION

"Alternative education" is a peculiar expression, really—sort of like "alternative rock." What exactly constitutes "alternative?" Who decides what is "alternative" versus "mainstream?" Damned if we know, but if this chapter has said nothing but "yawn" to you until now, jump to one of these more vivacious options.

Holistic Services

Have you always dreamt of laying your hands on others? Poking needles through someone else's skin? (Minds out of the gutter, please.) You might be a born holistic healer with the untapped potential to treat your fellow human. There is no time like the present to explore the healing side of yourself.

Massage Therapy

Who doesn't like a massage therapist? (Especially one you're dating!) They spread more joy than perhaps any other class of professionals, and feed off that joy in return. So get paid to be popular. Massage therapist Liz King finds her career very fulfilling. "I know that I'm positively influencing people's lives, and helping them relax," she told us.

Teaching Yoga

Barbara MacMillan, a self-proclaimed yoga fanatic, enrolled in an intensive four-week program for yoga instructors. She now teaches at several studios and gives private lessons at her home. "The best part of teaching yoga is that it provides the most fulfilling work atmosphere I've ever had," she says. "The energy is positive and everyone leaves the lesson feeling better than when they arrived."

Michele Hecht kept her day job as a systems analyst while learning to become a yoga instructor, training every weekend for ten months in order to fulfill her dream. Then she quit to teach yoga full-time. She still manages to enjoy long walks in between teaching at a community college, a corporate lunch program, and gyms, and is developing a program to help special-needs kids. Michele revealed that she has "many other irons in the fire to see what works out." Leisure is all about figuring out what's best for you, right?

Many instructor programs sponsor scholarships or charge tuition on a sliding scale. That way, you can learn to teach others to stretch their boundaries without stretching your budget!

Chinese Medicine & Acupuncture

Are you a stickler for acupuncture? This and other alternative health practices have flourished in the U.S. during the last 20 years, as more and more people explore the healing power of ancient Chinese therapies. *The Journal of the American Medical Association* reports that the number of visits to alternative practitioners has increased recently by more than 40%. In fact, more and more U.S. medical schools offer elective courses in alternative or complementary medicine, and some require them. "Alternative" medicine may not be so alternative after all! Check out **Natural Healers** (www.naturalhealers.com) for a comprehensive listing of schools that offer training in Eastern therapies. They list massage and yoga schools, too.

Belly Dancing

Last but not least, we come to the study of belly dancing. What back-to-school discussion would be complete without touching on this incomparable art? And you thought all those dancers were *born* with rolling stomachs and gyrating hips. *Au contraire, mon frère*—they trained for years to master their craft.

Belly dancing has its roots in Middle Eastern culture. The traditional dance was re-putedly taught to young girls as a way to strengthen their abdominal muscles in prepara-tion for childbirth, and is quite conservative: practiced by women, for other women only, as part of a fertility cer-emony.

Leave it to Western cul-ture to add the erotic touch. Apparently the hip and abdominal movements were too risqué for conservative Western views at the end of the 19th century, so the dance was branded as immoral—which only piqued the public's interest. Hollywood contributed the seduc-tive costumes and naval jewelry that prevail among belly dancers today.

Why the heck do we care about the history of belly dancing? We're not really sure. All we know is that we like it, and we're all for the modern sensual versions, too. Further, we encourage the leisurely study and practice of the art. Learn to mesmerize with your navel at **Yasmina's Joy of Belly Dancing** (www.joyofbellydancing.com). "It's not just a workout," says Liz King, who takes regular lessons and hopes to begin performing soon. "It's a reconnection to my femininity."

FINAL EXAM

Powerful stuff indeed. Whether reconnecting with your femininity or your ability to mix drinks, studying queuing theory or organic chem-istry, you'll never go wrong furthering your education. However, if you must (and we do mean must) go out and get yourself a job, read on to learn how you can find fulfilling work without giving up your hard-earned sense of leisure.

CHAPTER 11
THE LEISURELY JOB HUNT

*You've achieved success in your field when you don't
know whether what you're doing is work or play.*

~ Warren Beatty

LOOKING for a job can be a major drag. What's leisurely about job hunting? But exploring career possibilities can also be exciting and cathartic, particularly if you're able to re-evaluate your skills and passions, and remove what we call *Work Inhibitions*. No, we're not talking about the corporate decorum that keeps you from photocopying your bare bottom after too much champagne at the office holiday party. We mean self-imposed restrictions based on those pesky little "S" words: salary and status.

Take this time to think, inhibition-free, about your ideal job. Do you want to work for yourself or someone else? A big organization or small? A business, a non-profit, or something altogether different? If you just want to fund more leisure, this meditation won't take long. But if you're ready for deeper career soul-searching, it deserves significant time—in fact, it's a lifelong pursuit.

We'll admit that talking about jobs in a book on leisure is ironic. But we wholeheartedly believe that not only do most people need to work, they want to work (that's right, we said it)—as long as the work is something they feel good about. Look for work that will feed your spirit as well as pay the bills. Remember, nothing anchors a life of leisure more than a job you can't wait to get to each day!

CAREER = LIFESTYLE

Plenty of great resources expound on career transitions, career self-analysis and the like—including the venerable *What Color is Your Parachute* by Richard N. Bolles (www.jobhuntersbible.com) and *I Could Do Anything If I Only Knew What It Was: How to Discover What You Really Want and How to Get It* by Barbara Sher—but few address the importance of lifestyle in choosing your path. Separating work and play, vocation and vacation, can be a paramount mistake if your goal is to create a healthy work-life balance.

"All planning should begin with personal planning," says Gary Ryan Blair (www.goalsguy.com), a specialist in goal setting. "Any choice one makes regarding career will affect their quality of life. Therefore it is imperative to determine quality of life first and then create the opportunity that best supports your personal life agenda."

It's never too late to point your career in a new direction and do something that supports a more rewarding lifestyle.

ZEN AND THE ART OF JOB HUNTING

Like dating, job searches obey a natural rule: the harder you pursue, the more elusive your quarry. We've all experienced the phenomenon of being more attractive to others when we're already in a relationship. The same holds true in the work world: potential employers find us more attractive if we're already involved with another organization. Great, but what if you *don't* have a job? Remember that you don't have to *be* taken to *seem* taken—or at least desirable. By conveying that you're not desperate for a job, you'll come across as confident, secure and in demand, whether you really are or not. Easier said than done, but definitely worth a try.

Work is love made visible.
~Kahlil Gibran

Let the beauty of what you love be what you do.
~Rumi

Your work is to discover your work, and then with all your heart to give yourself to it.
~Buddha

leisurely work & the wisdom of the ages

Whatever your circumstance, keep reminding yourself that you are a valuable, unique asset—because you are! Your job search is simply a matter of figuring where your talents best fit within the work world, not about whether you will be hired by a particular industry or organization.

So don't look for a job, at least in the traditional sense. Let the job come to you, Zen master. Radiate the aura of a survivor. Even though you're searching for work, your world won't end if you don't land a given job.

Staying calm about your job search is not to say that you can sit and wait for the phone to ring; it just means that job searching is not a competition that you win or lose. You won't earn points for talking to the most HR people, scheduling the most interviews or garnering the most offers. You will score by landing a job that you love.

seek the zone

What do you do when you can do anything you want to? Can you translate that into a paying job? Maybe not, but then again— maybe you can. When time disappears and not a thought enters your mind but what you're doing at that moment, what is it that you're doing? Look for a job that includes those activities and skills.

"If you have to settle for less than your dream job in the short term, stay committed to what you ultimately want to create in this world," says Joel Garfinkle, founder of *Dream Job Coaching* (www.dreamjobcoaching.com). In other words, seek the zone.

"What Do You Do (For Fun)?"

Untraditional job hunting tactics range from going to parties to taking ski weekends to playing golf. Sound like fun? Sound leisurely? It can be. No one ever said searching for a job meant sending out hundreds of resumes, or spending long hours at home in front of the computer. Leave the career fairs to those who feel the need to don a business suit and stand in long lines with resume in hand.

Do you like parties? Find some! In fact, go out and have fun at whatever it is that you like to do. Depriving yourself of your favorite activities or interests in favor of an extra hour in front of the computer is hardly going to benefit your search. Indeed, driving yourself crazy with the job hunt is not only detrimental to your frame of mind, it can actually hinder your search.

"I firmly believe that looking for a job is *not* a full-time job. I don't think anyone can sustain that kind of pace," says Terry Karp, career counselor and co-founder of the **Bay Area Career Center** (www.bay areacareercenter.com). "If you sit at home in front of the computer all day you're going to burn out really quickly, and you're not going to have the stamina that you need to stay in it for the long haul—which you might need to do."

Career advisor Dr. Jan Cannon agrees. "Don't make yourself a slave to the job search. You need to change your scenery by going to a museum, taking a walk in the woods, spending time with friends in a social setting, even going to the movies. Balance is key." So if you like to snowboard, go snowboarding. If you like to golf, get a foursome together. Better yet, invite a friend to bring along an associate who might be a good contact. It's remarkable how many people find a job, or at least a connection leading up to a job, by pursuing their natural ambitions.

FIND THE FUN

Socially speaking, the good gigs are found where the fun is. If the job hunt is getting you down, crib these hip tips.

Cafés. Where does the working set get their daily dose of caffeine? Find out, and schedule that half-caff, double-shot, soy latte accordingly.

Dog Parks. Whether in dating or in job hunting, trust man's best friend to break the ice. Dog parks, particularly ones strategically located near business offices, can get you talking "doggie snacks" with the vice president of marketing in no time.

House Parties. A pillar of the social job hunt strategy—get yourself on those invite lists, and go easy on the pesto dip.

Team Sports & Clubs. Time to join the local softball soccer volleyball team. Find one affiliated with a company you want to work for, and you're golden. Not athletically inclined? Then the local computer club, perhaps.

Golf. They say a significant portion of business deals get closed on the links, why not close on a job?

Homecoming. Employ your family and friends. They know you better than you think, and they have your best interests in mind. And you'll get a home-cooked meal out of it!

Skiing/Snowboarding. Plenty of quality time on the ski lifts interspersed with periodic adrenaline rushes make for ideal bonding conditions.

Reunions. Visit your alma mater to reconnect with your fellow alums. College, high school, fraternity, sorority—heck, even your Tuesday night poker buddies—bring people back together man. After all, most of them have jobs. You don't! And if a few beers happen to be involved….

Employment by Osmosis

Much like a groupie backstage at a rock concert, you too must be a "hanger-on" to the employed set. As much as we laud the cafés and other weekday hangout spots in the leisurely sense, you might want to curtail those three-hour coffee sessions now (we know, it seems like sacrilege!). When your goal is to find an employer, you need to share a table with someone who's working. Call it employment by osmosis.

Short of hanging out in your best friend's office all day, try timing your meals to catch the working set during morning coffee, lunchtime or happy hour. Find out if any of your friends need a date to a company cocktail party or holiday gathering and volunteer your services. If you can afford it, join a health or social club. Anything to get yourself out of the house and around those with jobs!

Mine Your Friends & Family

Surprisingly, a lot of people shy away from reaching out to friends and family while they're job hunting. Check this impulse in yourself, for this is a time when you could really use their help.

Don't be shy. Ask those closest to you to assist. You'll surely return the favor when the time comes. Get your friends and family working for you and follow up with them diligently. They are your emissaries as well as your support team and can make your search a lot easier. Who better to market your value than the people who know you best? You

put on your party hat

Sitting at home watching *Desperate Housewives* is not going to broaden your network or expose you to new career possibilities (although it might expose you to something else). Get out and socialize, be it at a bar in the evening, a book club every Thursday night, or a fundraiser at your local museum. Iron your slacks and get yourself out!

House parties are a job-search gold mine, particularly those thrown by your friends. The guest list itself reflects a subtle screening process: you'll enjoy a built-in trust based on the fact that you're all friends of the host. Talk with people about their jobs and let it be known that you're looking for work yourself.

Don't walk around with your resume, but do ask questions, and be receptive when others offer information. They will probably help if they feel they're able. Remember, people want to work with other people they like. If they like you in a social context, they're more likely to support your working for their company.

could be surprised to discover how many people they know in high places.

Adrianna, an attorney who was *Limbo-Employed* for six months, asked her friends and family for honest feedback on her strengths and weaknesses. "It got them involved without blatantly asking for their Rolodex," she said, "and it helped them to understand better to whom and to where they could recommend me."

Right Place, Right Time

Several job hunters we spoke with let slip that they strategically plan their morning coffee sessions—geographically, to be near companies they want to work for; and time-wise, when they know employees will be stopping in for their morning jolt. Perhaps you won't have to curtail those coffee sessions after all, although you may have to get up a bit earlier!

Going to business conferences is another great way to get you in and around employers. You'll learn about the industry to boot. While their time may be limited, decision makers often float around the company booth, where you can chat them up. Your attending the conference in itself shows them your interest in the industry.

"I had a client who walked into the booth of a company she wanted to work for and just sat there until someone

WINE, DON'T WHINE

Will Eagle's wage fell from $135 an hour for high-tech consulting to $8 an hour selling wine, but his passion for the grape kept him going. He rapidly earned buying power at **The Wine Club** (www.thewineclub.com), met more people in the industry, and expanded his already impressive knowledge of fine wines. Drank his fair share of them, too! Will eventually landed a job in wine public relations but The Wine Club lured him back with a management and in-house public relations position of their own.

"Sometimes you've just got to look around," Will says. "I was in The Wine Club making a purchase one day, and there was a 'help wanted, no experience necessary' sign on the back of the door. When the clerk asked if there was anything else he could get me, I responded, 'Not unless you want to get me an application.' I was working there within a week, and I considered it a tremendous education. The only bad thing is, now everyone hands me the wine list when we go out!"

would talk to her," says Deborah Brown-Volkman (www.surpassyour dreams.com), career coach and mentor. "She was very polite and friendly with everyone. And it worked."

BARK, BUT DON'T BITE

Terry Karp, co-founder of the **Bay Area Career Center** (*www.bayareacareercenter.com*), had one industrious client who used her cute and playful Jack Russell Terrier to full advantage. She wrote up a target list of companies in Silicon Valley, and "coincidentally" walked her dog past each company building at lunchtime. Her adorable Terrier worked like a magnet. She was inevitably approached by company employees wanting to play with her dog, and eventually she networked her way right into a plum job. So there you go—add "cute dog" to your list of jobhunt resources. You might even consider renting one for the day!

NETWORKING

Every person and every book you turn to when you're looking for a job will stress the value of "networking." You might get sick of hearing it. While we don't dispute its value—even "hyper-networking" has its place—not all networking was created equal.

"Some networking is as useless as can be," says Dick Bolles, author of perennial jobhunt bible *What Color is Your Parachute*. "Most people understand networking to mean going to as many cocktail parties as possible and collecting business cards from everyone they meet, which is, of course, stupid." Bolles advises people use a more focused approach instead, and build up their own "grapevine" to take advantage of the large proportion of open positions that never make it to the job boards. "In seventy-five percent of all job vacancies, the employer fills it by talking to his or her network," he says. "The resume just isn't going to find those jobs."

Several of the networking tools that have emerged in recent years are worth mentioning. **LinkedIn** (www.linkedin.com) is designed to connect people professionally. The way it works is fairly straightforward: every person who signs up on the LinkedIn website puts together a profile as well as a list of others they'd like to invite to join their network. The "network effect" essentially takes over and people connect up with colleagues of colleagues in a variety of professional interests, including job hunting and hiring. **Friendster** (www.friendster.com) is focused more on the social and less on the professional, but operates to similar effect.

♪ "FREE BIRD!"

Why would you want to work for free? Think of it as a dry run—an ideal way for you and a potential employer to decide whether there's a good match. Say you're attempting a lateral transition. Even though you're confident that your skills will cross over, your future employer might not be. Mitigate the risk by offering to work unpaid for a 30-day trial period. If both you and the employer are pleased, you'll be hired. Put this agreement in writing ahead of time if you can. Even if you're fully qualified for the job, an unpaid trial period might be the way to go in a tight market. Think of it as *Pre-Re-Employment*. Fred Jasper, working out of Santa Monica as Special Projects and Media Director at Sugar Hill Records, did this to harmonious effect. "There I was, 24 years old, managing an independent record store near a college and trying to figure out what to do with the rest of my life," he told us. "I cold-called the record label and told them I was a big fan and owned several CDs of theirs in my music collection…. The next day I went in to meet with the general manager of the label and I was volunteering in their office within a week." His persistence paid off. "After toiling away for no pay for a little over a year, with the chorus of friends and relatives gradually getting louder and louder in their criticism of me getting 'taken advantage of' and 'wasting my time,' the record label offered me a full-time job. I've now been with Sugar Hill going on eight years." That's definitely music to our ears.

ELIMINATE EXPECTATIONS

As we mentioned at the beginning of the chapter, dealing with expectations poses a real challenge in any employment re-immersion process. If you have a strong idea of what you want to do next, set yourself free to pursue your goals. Let go of your salary expectations. Be ready to sacrifice responsibility or stature in return for greater personal fulfillment. As career coach Joel Garfinkle reminds us, "Finding your dream job brings you fulfillment. It allows you to feel lighter about your life and what you want to give to the world."

Erik Olsen, a producer in New York, left a television job at ABC so he could further pursue his passion to write. The change cut his income significantly. "You only go around in life once, so you better choose carefully what you're going to do with your time here," says Erik. "Some people see money as the goal, but it's always seemed to me that unless you actually enjoy what you're doing, unless you actually create something cool, you've wasted your time."

Erik is now working purely as a freelance producer and writer, a tough profession he says, but something he loves to do. "Sadly, lots of jobs that are enjoyable don't pay well. That's just the nature of supply and demand. So often, to do what you want to do, you have to forgo big money and prestige. At times, that can suck—being poor is often a drag—but in the end, you'll be happier."

Victims of the technology crash in 2000 and 2001 had to take several steps backwards before moving forward. Ted was the co-founder of an Internet startup and worked as head of operations for nearly four years. Despite this experience, he had a difficult time transitioning to a different industry.

"People looked at being at a dot-com as a joke," he told us. "As far as potential employers were concerned, it was as if those years didn't even exist." But once Ted released the memory of his old salary and status, he landed a gig in organic produce, an industry that has always intrigued him.

GET CREATIVE

According to a survey by **The Creative Group** of Menlo Park, California (*www.creativegroup.com*), job seekers use some downright wacky tactics to stand out in the crowd during a tight job market.

Advertising and marketing executives were asked the most unusual tactic they had seen. Among the responses: singing telegrams, resumes written on softballs, and lottery tickets included in place of cover letters. One eager interviewee even followed up by sending a pair of socks to the hiring manager. Their lucky interview socks, perhaps? We just hope they were washed!

if *i* won the lottery...

What would you do if you won the lottery? Would you follow Steve Martin's lead in *The Jerk* and get a house with a bathtub shaped like a clam, a solid red billiard room with a giant stuffed camel, and a disco room complete with its own disco dancers? Would you donate money to Mexico to stop the spread of the ugly sport of cat juggling? Okay, so maybe you'd do something a little more productive (not that there's anything wrong with a clam shell bathtub, mind you).

As goofy as it sounds, contemplating an unexpected financial windfall can give you insight into where to steer your career. If money were suddenly not a concern, what *would* you want to do for work?

Of course, money *is* a reality that factors into the final equation. But removing it initially, and then working backward to solve the financial piece of the puzzle, can help free you to follow your passions.

STAYING MOTIVATED

Keeping your spirits and motivation up during the job hunt can be extremely challenging, particularly in an employment market where job searches can take six months or more. Maintaining a positive attitude, in addition to keeping you healthy and sane, is critical to presenting your very best self to prospective employers.

Dr. Jan Cannon agrees. "Staying 'up' during a job search of any length is important, but especially when the search is extended. If you find yourself slipping into despair, take a break and do something totally different for a day or so. Clear your head. Renew your spirit. And then get back to work."

She recommends several techniques to keep yourself motivated, including joining other job seekers for support, setting up a formal schedule to achieve a sense of accomplishment and control, and maintaining a healthy body. "As clichéd as it might sound, get enough sleep, eat properly and get daily exercise. Keeping your body in its best condition goes a long way to keeping your mind and spirit in good shape, too."

Your personal support team, whether friends, family or other job hunters, will be paramount. Peter Hannah, a former technology worker who went back to school to become a career counselor, speaks from both personal and professional experience. "I cannot emphasize strongly enough the importance of a support network. And be honest with these people. If you're feeling down, or stuck, or apathetic, you can be sure that they all have at one point too."

GREAT MOMENTS iN UNEMPLOYMENT

Richard Bolles, author of **What Color Is Your Parachute**, wrote his best-selling treatise on job hunting after a budget crunch cost him his own job as canon pastor at Grace Cathedral in San Francisco. No sooner did he find another position than did he recognize the same career anxiety among the campus ministers he was now supervising. To help them with job switching and procurement, Bolles self-published 100 copies of his 168-page job hunter's "bible" in 1970 and handed them out for free.

Over 30 years later, *Parachute* sells 15,000 to 20,000 copies each month and, in 1995, made the Library of Congress's Center for the Book's list of "25 Books That Have Shaped Readers' Lives." Bolles pioneered the concept that the best way to find a job is to focus on the skills and talents you want to use and then find an organization that needs them. An ordained Episcopalian priest, Bolles is considered the father of career soul-searching.

LOST TIME ON THE RESUME

Are you worried about gaps in your resume? Don't be overly concerned. **Monster** (www.monster.com) reminds us that one in every five workers is unemployed at some point each year. Odds are, that crowd includes some of your potential employers. If that doesn't make them sympathetic to your situation—we forbid you to work for them!

But back on this planet, the sad truth is that not everyone who receives your resume will see your time off as the major accomplishment that it is. *We* know that you weren't just on vacation, you were building leadership skills through travel and outdoor adventures, presentation skills through karaoke...but it might take some ingenuity to convey the extent of your dedication to your future employer.

Dick Bolles has long opposed the use of resumes to begin with, and argues that you should always handle the gap issue face-to-face.

i *think* i can, i *think* i can

Scot Montagnino had worked for years as a chef in catering companies and restaurant kitchens. He had fine wine training and French service finesse. His dream job? Private chef. But he couldn't muster the pluck to translate his skills into a resume. "Although he actually had all the experience and skills he needed for the job, they weren't 'traditional' in the sense that we could list them from A to Z," his friend Dylan de Thomas told us.

So Dylan helped his nervous friend with a re-write. "I had watched his career progress and I knew he had what it took," Dylan said. "It took hours but I finally convinced him that he was as good as I knew him to be."

After enhancing his resume, and writing a sincere and honest cover letter, Scot landed that dream job. He's now a private chef to a big city bigwig.

"I would always explain it in person, and not try to explain it on a resume," he says. "It's important to tell employers what the results were [of taking time off]. Just saying 'I took time off and thought about what I wanted to do with my life' is universally perceived as a pretty lame excuse. They know the person really wanted to see Yosemite and Hong Kong and other things like that. But if the job hunter says 'I took it off for this purpose and here are the results' and they've done the self-inventory before they put themselves out there in the job market, then that is a reason I think everyone understands and would applaud."

Deborah Brown-Volkman agrees that it isn't the time that matters, it's what you did during the gap. "You're making a case for yourself to the employer," she says. "It always matters, they will always ask, sometimes just out of curiosity—but again, it depends on what you did. People get scared by the question. It can feel like an interrogation, but just make your case."

"Making your case" can be a challenge. When you look back at how you've spent your time, get creative when filling in those resume gaps. *How* creative is up to you, but the following tongue-in-cheek suggestions should help get your hamster wheel spinning....

Leisure Leo
1392 La Playa
San Francisco, CA 94122
leo@leisureteam.com

Key Qualification: Master of Leisure
Objective: To marry my passions with my work.

PROFESSIONAL EXPERIENCE

Dec 2004   **Marine Biology Researcher**
[*Translation:* sat on the beach]

Nov 2004   **Public Speaker**
[*Translation:* karaoke bar junkie]

Oct 2004   **Restaurant Management Intern**
[*Translation:* sat at the bar]

Sep 2004   **Construction General Contractor**
[*Translation:* built a rolling bar for Mardi Gras parade]

Aug 2004   **Volunteer Worker**
[*Translation:* constructed papier mâché palm trees for Burning Man theme camp]

Jul 2004   **Change Management Consultant**
[*Translation:* helped best friend get over breakup]

Jun 2004   **Subject of Monitored Health Study**
[*Translation:* friends watched me drink too much and then fall down]

May 2004   **Employed by the State**
[*Translation:* collected Unemployment Insurance]

April 2004   **Employed by the State**
[*Translation:* incarcerated]

Mar 2004   **Freelancer**
[*Translation:* "freelancer"]

Feb 2004   **Healthcare Consultant, Financial Counselor, Expert Time Manager and Personal Assistant to Busy Executives**
[*Translation:* raised a family]

Jan 2004   **Teacher**
[*Translation:* taught little brother to snowboard]

EDUCATION

Training [surfed the Net]
Continuing Education [surfed the Net]
Executive Education [surfed the Net]
Adult Education [slept around]
Cultural Exchange Student [ordered margaritas in Cabo]

i'm paying you for what, exactly?

Back in high school, Mary Mangold sought advice on how to make use of her talents. "I always knew I was creative but I never knew how to get there," she said. "I talked to my high-school career counselor about all the things I wanted to do. When I stopped talking, he looked at me—stared at me—and said, 'You have just got the longest eyelashes I've ever seen.'"

Thank goodness, most of today's career counselors are more professional. If you're having a difficult time charting a new career path or finding the right job, consider hiring one. They're not recruiters or "headhunters" but trained professionals who focus on counseling and coaching. Services range from low- or no-cost job placement assistance to in-depth life coaching that requires a significant financial commitment.

Choose your guidance wisely, as there's a range of advice available, not all of it useful.

GETTING SOME COACHING

Dick Bolles puts it bluntly when it comes to career counselors. "Some of them are wonderful, others should be shot at sunrise," he says. "Everything depends on who the counselor is."

"A career counselor will never tell a person anything that they don't know about themselves already," says Terry Karp. "But all the information gets tangled up in the brain, and people don't have perspective on it.... A career counselor can help the client gain access to that information and relate it to the world of work."

The greater the transition you're attempting to make, the more likely some type of coaching is going to be helpful. "Retooling yourself can be a daunting task," says Dr. Jan Cannon. "You might have the feeling that you're starting over from scratch, but that's not true. You do have experience that will be valuable in your new job—things like knowing how businesses work, getting along with co-workers, work habits, etcetera. They'll give you an advantage over workers with no experience."

Bolles strongly advises people to shop around—especially considering what counseling costs. "If they charge you a huge fee up front, I run for the door and I advise everyone who appreciates my council to do the same," he says. Bolles does acknowledge that the right advisor is worth every cent.

Do yourself a favor before shelling out big bucks for a full-blown analysis from a Ph.D., and consult the **National Career**

Development Association (866-FOR-NCDA, www.ncda.org). Their "Need a Career Counselor?" section recommends ways to choose the right counselor, and their search engine catalogs individual professionals by state. The site also lists a wealth of Internet resources for career planning, most of them free.

FREE HELP

Chances are that you're in cash-conservation mode if you're looking for work, making free resources pretty attractive. Your quest for more free help should begin with **The Riley Guide** (www.rileyguide.com). This stellar, well-organized site is compiled by career consultant Margaret F. Dikel, and provides, to her credit, largely unbiased job search information. Its sections such as "Prepare to Search," "Execute a Campaign," and "Target & Research" can add structure to your task, if nothing else. Oh yeah, they also have links to hundreds of thousands of jobs.

Our friendly neighbors up north at the University of Waterloo in Ontario, Canada have developed a comprehensive self-assessment tool called the **Career Development eManual** (www.cdm.uwaterloo.ca). The entire manual, comprised of six multiple-part steps, can be viewed, downloaded, and printed—all for free. Score one career goal for those crazy Canucks!

If you're the testing type, a good self-analysis site for career and beyond is **QueenDom.com** (www.queendom.com),

a bit of free advice

Terry Karp recommends two steps that are vital to successful career development and job searching.

1 The first is a thorough self-assessment. You have to analyze your talents and skills, obviously, but just as important is pinpointing where you get real meaning from work. "Introspection allows you to confront any fears you have about a transition, and to identify what kind of resistance to change you might have," she says.

2 The second component is an external process, or "market assessment," which involves taking what you've learned from looking within and comparing it to what's actually available in the job market. "You have to bring that [introspection] to the marketplace and say, 'Okay, this is what's most important to me. What is the reality of this?'"

The reality might be that there aren't many jobs in the areas you've identified, in which case you need to adjust your strategy—and expectations—accordingly.

which offers "an interactive avenue for self-exploration with a healthy dose of fun." Works for us! Their career section includes book recommendations, counseling referrals, discussion boards, and more tests than you can shake a number-two pencil at. It's worth noting that the site includes both free and pay-for content, but the pay-for material is good and relatively inexpensive ($14 per month or $30 for three months).

Another option to consider is your old alma mater. Leverage their career resources and extensive alumni network for your personal analysis and search. Although they may gear their services toward graduating students, universities are normally more than happy to help cheery—and potentially money-donating—alumni.

THE SHOPKEEPER EFFECT

Empirical evidence supports the theory that periods of high unemployment directly correlate to periods of increased entrepreneurial activity. Economists call this the "shopkeeper effect"—workers are in transition, labor is cheap and abundant, and many people are forced into self-employment. What does this mean to you, the leisurely job hunter? That a lagging economy shouldn't keep you from incubating that business idea you've been sitting on for years. Deanndra Eggers, sole proprietor of a specialty pet supply store, received plenty of warnings from well-meaning friends not to start a business in a down economy, but she did it anyway. "People will always need to feed their pets," she told us, "and I always wanted to open a pet store, so I did. I figure it's a risk whether the economy is down or not." A well-calculated one, it seems. She received a "best of" nod from her city's weekly newspaper after only six months.

Let's Get It Started

If you want some help to get started on your way to cutting your own paycheck, turn to **Nolo** (800-728-3555, www.nolo.com), with their great selection of "how to" books for the blossoming entrepreneur, and the **Small Business Administration** (800-U-ASK-SBA, www.sba.gov), which can assist with loan guarantees and advice. To get yourself in a risk-taking, entrepreneurial frame of mind, nothing beats the inspiring guide, *Making a Living Without a Job: Winning Ways For Creating Work That You Love* by Barbara Winter.

Rest assured that you won't necessarily need a huge bankroll. "You can start a business on peanuts," says Joe Gilmartin, proprietor of the White Horse Trading Company, a small pub in Seattle. "I sold my motorcycle to pay for my initial beer license. It cost five-hundred dollars." Joe then secured an SBA-backed loan to grow his business. "The most beautiful thing about the SBA loan," he says, "is that you don't have to pay principal for the first two or three years. You pay interest only, so you have time to get ramped up."

Do be prepared to log in some serious hours if you start a company. You'll have to make other sacrifices, too—Joe slept on a friend's couch for a year. "You gotta have that mental game that you're willing to work around the clock for very little," Joe advises. "The longer you stick with it, the better your chances are going to be to make it. All big businesses have to start as a small business."

Can I Fire Myself?

So is the toil of starting your own business worth it? Joe thinks so. "The bottom line is, I have job security," he says. "I can control how long I'm going to have a job." Yes, being your own boss is *the* outstanding perk of self-employment, and it's often a one-way street for that very reason. "I don't think I'll ever work for someone else again," Lisa Turner, principal at **Word, Inc.** (www.word-inc.com), said after breaking free from corporate life to become an independent marketing and public relations consultant. "I finally came to terms with the fact that it never was my style and likely never will be."

Gordon, a former sales rep who is now a self-employed day-trader in Los Angeles, finds setting his own agenda to be the biggest benefit of working for himself, explaining, "If I want to go surfing that day, I can go surfing."

Reinventing the Cube

"I don't miss working in an office at all," Gordon told us. Deanndra seconds the sentiment. "As much as I liked the company I worked for, it was still Cubicle World. Just a maze of cubicles. Not looking at those walls, that drab tan and gray—that's one thing I like about working for myself."

"Finding work that aligns to you will make work feel more like leisure, because you'll be doing what you do naturally and effortlessly," says career coach Joel Garfinkle. "It brings you fulfillment, and allows you to feel lighter about your life and what you want to give to this world."

What the professionals predict, the entrepreneurs live: "I think I work the same amount in seven days that I did in five," says Deanndra, "and I don't have any days off, but it doesn't feel like work. I am very relaxed."

How very leisurely!

CHAPTER 12
BACK TO WORK

Oh, you hate your job? Why didn't you say so?
There's a support group for that.
It's called everybody,
and they meet at the bar.

~ Drew Carey

YOU'RE not sure what it is, but a distant rhythm is beating ever louder in the back of your head: thump-bump…thump-bump…thump-bump. Is it the latest over-hyped, over-marketed single from U2? The pounding of an aboriginal drum from the deserts of Australia? No. The far-off thumping you hear is the alien call of employment, creeping slowly back into your psyche.

Of course, if you've gotten close to the bottom of your freedom funds, the noise could be merely the resounding clank delivered from the hollow depths of a depleted bank account, in which case the thought of a regular paycheck would be a welcome relief.

But while work might relieve one type of anxiety, it could very well cause another—the fear that your days of leisure are gone for good. After all, even the most fulfilling work is still work.

Ultimately, though, we are no more slaves to our work than we allow ourselves to be. The key is to bring a relaxed mindset into the workplace, and to keep it there. Setting proper boundaries creates a more tranquil—and in turn enjoyable—work atmosphere, which keeps the pressures of the job manageable. You *can* foster a culture of leisure at work, and you can band with your employer and colleagues to do so—but it all begins with you.

BE EFFECTIVE, NOT AFFECTED

One of the toughest aspects of shifting from full-time leisure to full-time work is the feeling that you've lost control of your agenda. Being constantly in reaction mode is quite un-leisurely. Lend more order and sanity to your day with the following "work smart" tactics.

Start Work Before Work

There's no need to start your day with an emergency. Yet, in many jobs, if you arrive at the official beginning of office hours, the red light on your voicemail box will already be lit and people may even be lined up at your door. Try getting in fifteen or thirty minutes early, and don't answer the phone or take any appointments before 9am (or whenever your shift starts). Maybe you'll be able to return one of those voicemails with a message saying, "Thanks for calling about that project. It's done."

Even better, start tomorrow's work yesterday—take fifteen minutes at the end of each workday to set six goals for the next day, so that you won't get sidetracked fighting fires when you come in. Prioritize. Stick to your plan. You'll sleep better for it.

GREAT MOMENT IN RE-EMPLOYMENT

The World's Shortest Retirement?

In 1963, Mary Kay Ash was looking forward to retirement after a long career in the male-dominated world of direct sales. Bored one night, she sat down at her kitchen table. She made two lists. The first list contained the positive qualities of the companies she had worked for. The second list was of the qualities that could be improved. Looking at the lists made her realize (with apologies to Mark Twain) that reports of her retirement had been greatly exaggerated. She launched Mary Kay Cosmetics on Friday, September 13, 1963.

Time After Time

While it may not be possible all of the, er, time—leave at a reasonable hour each day. Leaving on time will do a couple of things. First, you'll get a reputation. Your co-workers and colleagues will learn not to task you with projects right before you leave; they'll come to you sooner in the day with their requests, which will make it less likely that you'll be stuck working late on a deadline.

Second, being more disciplined with your time can help you to become better focused. How many times have you frittered away large chunks of the clock because you assumed you would have to work late anyway? Leaving on time forces you to be more efficient. You'll also be more likely to ask others for help when you need it.

Your exact hour of departure will depend on your situation, but there's nothing wrong with leaving a 9-to-5 job at 5pm. There, we said it—and we'll be happy to write your employer a note.

TALK ABOUT RECOMPRESSION

A high-level executive client of career coach Dr. Dory Hollander's increased her productivity—and in turn, her performance—by reducing her work hours in order to spend more time volunteering outside of work.

"She had to discreetly time-compress whole chunks of her job, doing in a day what used to take three," says Dr. Hollander. "She had to position her successes so everyone would see that she was a contributor to corporate success. While she spent more and more time fighting for the community causes she believed in, she became more sought after and valued at work. Paradoxically, by compressing her job in order to free up time for her causes, she became *more* work-focused when she was there, not less."

See if you too can compress your work, and utilize the time saved not to do more work, but to stow away precious free time for yourself. Most people don't realize how much time they actually waste until they take close inventory of how they spend their work day. And if too much compression gets your spine and nerves (not to mention your undies) all in a bunch, remember to use relaxing activities, both physical and otherwise, as a way to decompress.

Stay Late

Leave work on time, but stay late. Come again? It might sound contradictory, but spending the occasional evening at work (assuming that you work standard daytime hours) can allow you to catch up without constant interruption—no colleagues to distract you and no phones ringing off the hook. You can concentrate on more proactive projects that would otherwise be difficult to focus on if your day-to-day job involves putting out a lot of fires.

Daniel, an architect working in Chicago, occasionally stays late on Friday nights to catch up on work, as well as to unwind from a long week. "It's not like I do it all the time," he says, "but sometimes when everyone is rushing out for the weekend, I just like to stay and chill for a while. It relaxes me, and it's one of the few times I can clear my head."

Finishing your work-week at your own pace can allow you to enjoy the weekend to its fullest. Unfinished tasks won't nag at your conscience all weekend. You won't be harried and rushing out to a Friday night dinner with friends who are probably just as tired as you are. Wouldn't it be more relaxing to get together on a Saturday night instead?

You can even take some time for yourself: pay bills, answer some personal email, read a magazine. We're not suggesting spending every night at the office, just consider it once in a while. It could be the most peaceful time you'll spend at work, even if it means missing happy hour every now and then.

Beware of False Deadlines

Jane once stayed in her office literally all night finishing a project for some dud who'd put her on a deadline, only to admit later that he'd just wanted her to work on his project first. He went on to boast that he ended up not needing her work at all. Jane then lost even more precious hours plotting her revenge!

Don't be a Jane. If your co-workers are well-intentioned but prone to panic, ask what will happen if the task is not done by tomorrow. Take a moment, light a candle and chant this mantra: "There is nothing, and I mean nothing, that cannot wait until tomorrow." Surely you can work together to set a more reasonable deadline. And if your colleagues really are that devious? Consider keeping a copy of Sun Tzu's *Art of War* on hand.

Delegate

If you want something done right, do you really have to do it yourself?

Mastering control over your working hours means regularly asking yourself, "How important is right versus done?" If you're facing a task that only you are genuinely qualified to do, so be it. If you're keeping work to yourself out of expedience, turn the project over to a colleague and act as their coach. Taking those few extra minutes now will save you time in the long run, especially for recurring tasks.

Not incidentally, delegating will help you move up the ranks more quickly by multiplying your productivity and freeing up your time to learn new skills. This concept is nothing new, but it's key to creating a leisurely workday.

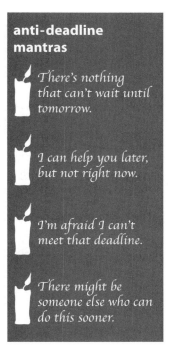

anti-deadline mantras

There's nothing that can't wait until tomorrow.

I can help you later, but not right now.

I'm afraid I can't meet that deadline.

There might be someone else who can do this sooner.

Schedule Downtime

Working smart and not long includes scheduling breaks. "Taking breaks allows you to get the perspective to make decisions that support and honor you," says career coach Joel Garfinkle, founder of **Dream Job Coaching** (www.dreamjobcoaching.com). Psychologist Dr. Joyce Brothers says the same thing: "No matter how much pressure you feel at work, if you could find ways to relax for at least five minutes every hour, you'd be more productive." A well-timed break will keep you from sitting there, stalled, trying to force inspiration on yourself.

Instead of frittering away work hours on procrastination, use that time to do something more satisfying. See a matinée, go home an hour early and garden, or take a class. Jeremy Cantor, an employee at UC Berkeley, has a friend who schedules at least two hours into her Palm Pilot each week for pure downtime. "Now I do it too," Jeremy says. "It's great. I take it as seriously as any other appointment."

You can schedule breaks inside the office as well as out. If you have a desk job, set aside thirty minutes a day to answer personal email or surf the Net. You're going to do it anyway. This way, you'll know it's coming up. You'll be less distracted thinking about personal tasks or entertainment when you could be getting work done. Whatever you do during a break, plan your day to include plenty of them.

Mix It Up

Can't decide if you're a morning or a night person? You don't have to. If you have enough flexibility to alter your hours during the day, trade off between being an early bird and a latecomer. Varying your schedule will keep things fresh. Vince, a financial services director, does this to relaxing effect; take a page from his day planner.

"You can come in early and leave early—maybe go for a swim, a hike in the foothills, or maybe a relaxing drive," Vince suggests. "Or pick a morning to hang out: read the paper, go for a run, make a breakfast burrito, whatever. Leave late if you need to, but mix up the routine. It gives you something to look forward to, especially if you don't do any travel for work."

Catch a Leisure Nap

What do you miss most about your work-free days? For Andrew Riley, a high-tech worker who recently started a new job after a layoff, that would be naps. "I miss my naps even more than my previously inflated salary," he says.

So why not nap at work? Fewer than one percent of American employers promote it, yet 36 percent of Americans say they do it, according to a recent human resources management study. We endorse each one of these sleepy rebellions. If the stars of ER can hide in the back office of the emergency room and catch some short-term winks, why not the rest of us?

Several government agencies use nap programs for employees who work in high-risk environments. Naps can increase alertness, reduce errors and absenteeism, improve effectiveness and generally keep a smile on your face. "Workplace napping is a natural, no-cost way to increase worker productivity," say Dr. William Anthony and Camille Anthony, the authors of *The Art of Napping at Work*.

A nap can be as simple as a 15-20 minute siesta in your office, or a few minutes of zoning out while appearing to study your email. Naps can be taken while you're "on the phone" too.

Find more tips on how to nap and how to lobby management in favor of napping from **The Napping Company, Inc.** (www.napping.com). And on the first Monday after we spring forward into daylight-savings time, don't forget to celebrate National Workplace Napping Day!

Care For Your Mental Health

Remember all those personal chores you took care of during the day when you weren't working? There is no reason to give them up when you're back at the job. Translate "doctor's appointment" into "mental health break" and take a few hours off. Savor a late breakfast, catch a baseball day game or relax at the beach if you live near the coast. Go ahead, play hooky now and then.

In fact, take a whole weekday off. Don't go anywhere. Just hang out. Or, if you want to take a day trip—say to a popular weekend spot—you can avoid the crowds. If your company allows for telecommuting, take two weekdays and work remotely yet close by, just as if you were working from home.

Not all of this has to be off the record. Wouldn't your boss allow you a short respite after an exceptionally hard stint of work? You never know until you ask.

Keep your breaks clean in this sense though: don't squander your leisure. If you already take lengthy lunches or fritter away hours at the water cooler,

bosses need naps too

Howard, a mid-level manager, wasn't a big fan of annual reviews, but who is?

He had accomplished a few things that year, so he wrote himself some notes, entered the boss's chambers and began to recite. It got quiet. He looked up and saw his boss's head nodding— further, further—until he was out!

Howard waited quietly for a full fifteen minutes, just about the perfect length for a refreshing snooze. Then his boss woke up. "Anything more?" his boss asked. "Nope," Howard said.

Howard left his "review" and got a raise two weeks later.

If you're a manager who wants to protect your budget, stay sharp. Take naps!

realize that you're just extending the overall amount of time you spend at the workplace. The more you focus on work while you're at work, the more you can get away from it entirely and enjoy the rest of your life.

LEAVE WORK AT WORK
Let Your Brain Work Without You

You can go one better than finishing the day's work on Friday—try planning ahead for the next week, too. It takes only minutes to make a list of things to do first thing Monday. The act of writing a list can plant ideas in your subconscious that will stir around even after you've left the office, and you won't even feel it! This is the magic of the subconscious mind. Come Monday, you'll somehow be full of creative solutions to problems that seemed insurmountable the week before. While you're at it, make a list of your key accomplishments during the week. A little pride never hurts.

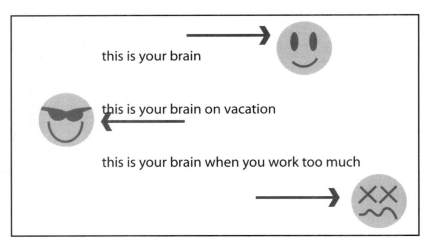

this is your brain

this is your brain on vacation

this is your brain when you work too much

Keep 'Em To Yourself

Speaking of weekends (or whatever your regular days off are), we suggest you keep them to yourself. A normal full-time schedule is not supposed to encompass a full seven-day week. Whenever you're tempted to go into the office on a Saturday or a Sunday or, even worse, you think about taking work home, repeat the anti-deadline mantra: "There is nothing, and I mean nothing, that can't wait until Monday."

Really think about it. How many times have you panicked over some fire at work and realized later that, with a little reflection, you could have come up with a more efficient solution?

If a short-term deadline makes it imperative that you work on a weekend, trade out that weekend day for a weekday off. If your corporate culture doesn't support that, rally your colleagues together and see if you can't change the tide.

Use All Your Vacation Days

Tragically, Americans on average squander a total of 20-30% of their vacation time per year, and about a quarter of them take no vacations at all. Vacation days should be enjoyed, not stockpiled or wasted. If you're fortunate, your manager will feel the same way.

"One owes it to themselves, their family and their company to plan—and take—their vacation," says Bill Coleman, co-founder of BEA Systems, Inc., a large California-based software company. "While I was CEO of BEA, I encouraged my staff to take a two-week or longer break at least every other year, during which their business voicemail and email were turned off. Vacation time for me is where I can get perspective. In fact, my best epiphanies came when I was off for at least two weeks." BEA's use-it-or-lose-it vacation policy backs this up: employees cannot accrue more than 150% of their allotted annual vacation. Once they hit that ceiling, they don't earn more days until they stop and take a break.

Although there are plenty of trips you can't take while fully employed, you can still cover some ground in the typical two weeks off. Whether or not you have a trip planned, spend some weekdays out of the office. Better yet, tell everyone you're taking a trip but then

ask for unpaid leave

Many companies will be amenable to granting you extra vacation days—if they're unpaid. One single mother we know has negotiated an extra week's leave into every job offer she's ever had, and she spends it with her kids during their summer vacation.

If you didn't negotiate time off up front, ask for it now. Propose a couple of unpaid weeks off at a time when your department is trimming its budget. What boss could say no to that?

Keep your ears open for sabbatical packages, too. Scott Phillips accepted his company's offer of a twelve-month leave at 20% pay. During his break, he finished writing a novel while living with his wife in her native city of Prague, where 20% of a U.S. salary goes a fair distance.

stay at home. You'll enjoy completely unscheduled time to yourself, and you'll be able to relax and enjoy your own city for a change. "Commit to your vacation days at the beginning of the year," Coach Garfinkle advises. "Make them as important as you would the birth of a child."

FOSTER A CULTURE OF LEISURE

All these suggestions sound great in theory, but could be hard to implement if you can't get others around you (your boss, maybe?) to buy into the concept. Peace of mind starts with you, to be sure, but to change more than yourself, you'll have to win over others to the cause. Don't be shy about sharing your philosophy with your friends, your co-workers and even your boss. Big changes can happen when people band together. Here are a few ideas to inspire your colleagues to adopt the leisurely 'tude at work.

TOTE YOUR LEISURE GEAR

Relaxation is infectious, so dress for the part. Keep a scrapbook open to the best photo from your last trip. Surround yourself with symbols of leisure and your hobbies. Co-workers are bound to wonder why you always seem so relaxed. At a minimum, it will give pause to those who constantly feel the need to escalate a crisis.

"Scuba didn't make the work go away," says Marlo Sarmiento about his job overseas near the dive-haven of Palau, "but it sure did make me happy." That showed in the underwater photos he displayed in his office. Licensing attorney Karen burned scented candles while she worked. "I got some grief from the salespeople for it," she said, "but it sure kept the room from getting too gamey during those marathon contract negotiations."

Build Your Own "Leisure Team"

Hoard your techniques, and you'll be a leisure team of one. Share your leisure insights! Although company perks like in-house massage therapy and pool tables might be part of a bygone era, creating an atmosphere of camaraderie will always be in vogue. "Workers who care about each other want to support each other," says Coach Garfinkle, "which creates an atmosphere of, 'I want to be here.'"

John Greene, a software support engineer and rock keyboardist, was recruited on his first day of work by his company band, the Low Hanging Fruit. "We played several company parties including a couple of cruises on the Bay," John recalls. "While the management-promised soundproof room never materialized, we do still have a piano and a drum kit in the rec area. LHF got the crowd dancin' and the bodies shakin'."

Socializing with people you like to work with (and can get things done with) will only bring more leisure to your day. Friday afternoon Happy Hours aren't too hard to pull off—rotate sponsorship of them through different departments to foster some friendly competition.

office exercise

You want to keep your blood pumping at work, not raise your blood pressure. Stretch in the doorway. Dance around. Stand up (sit down, fight fight fight!).

Does your company have a gym? Use it in the morning to get your energy up and your endorphins going, and invite others to join you. No gym? Never fear.

"I used to lie on my back and do stretches while talking on the phone," says Dane Larson, an avid surfer. "It helped a lot when my back hurt, and often sparked some good conversation."

Office Yoga by Darrin Zeer seeks to "inspire you to take good care of yourself at the office and throughout the day" with all kinds of tips on how to relax and keep breathing at work. May all its readers reach the promised Office Nirvana!

In fact, choose any activity or topic of conversation that takes you away from work for a moment. "I keep a lot of toys in my office," says Jeremy Cantor. "Balls, hacky-sacks, other things to toss around. People play with them when they come in to visit." Needless to say, Jeremy's got a lot of companionship at work.

This kind of grassroots effort is bound to be more effective than any top-down, contrived team building exercise—plus, it's free. What manager could say no to that? On that note, make sure your team includes your boss. If your boss isn't an ally, try to get one who is.

LINGO BINGO
and other reindeer games

The heyday of office pinball machines, pool tables, and aromatherapy might have passed…

…but that doesn't mean there aren't still games to be played.

If you can't convince your boss to officially endorse games at work, how about a rousing round of Lingo Bingo—a sure way to pass the time in a boring meeting. Players stay tuned for meaningless blather like "stakeholder," "think out of the box," and "step up to the plate." As soon as you hear five in a row—BINGO!!!

Find four pre-printed gamecards at **Working Wounded** (*www.workingwounded.com, scroll to the bottom*). See also the **Web Economy Bullshit Generator** (*www.dack.com, click "web" then "web economy bullshit generator"*), where users can combine any number of verbs, adjectives, and nouns to create true "bullshit." Unfortunately for most of us, these phrases will sound eerily familiar.

Petition Management

You can change your own workstyle and you can speak out individually or in a group, but systemic change has to come from the top. If you're not a decision maker yourself, press your case with those who are. Did you know that MRI scans of fatigued brains look exactly like ones that are sound asleep? Slip that factoid into your next conversation with your boss, then make a request for a leisure-friendly policy like company-wide meeting-free hours.

Find more ammunition in *Work to Live* by Joe Robinson, founder of the Work to Live campaign.

LEISURE TEAM'S COMPANY HALL OF FAME

Fortune magazine ranks their best every year. So do numerous other publications. But based on what measure—how good the coffee tastes? Many companies' generous benefit plans are designed primarily to keep you working there longer and harder. We say the number one benefit is time, whether in the form of reasonable work hours, ample vacation, or a formal sabbatical policy.

U.S. Companies That Consistently DELIVER THE LEISURE

Patagonia *(Ventura, California; www.patagonia.com)*
Patagonia epitomizes cool. Offices near the beach and a flex-time work policy allow workers the ability to surf during daytime hours. Paid environmental sabbaticals and on-site yoga keep employees coming back for more.

FedEx *(Memphis, Tennessee; www.fedex.com)*
Forget about the image of Tom Hanks' character as a workaholic FedEx employee in the 2000 film *Cast Away*. In real life, FedEx employees have plenty of reasons to smile; overwork isn't one of their ills. Free plane rides on its U.S. flights keep workers travel-happy and in 2003, the company spent $17 million on tuition reimbursement—meaning employees are definitely getting "schooled" on FedEx's dime.

American Express *(New York, New York; www.americanexpress.com)*
In the financial services sector, perks don't get much better than at AMEX. They offer paid six-month overseas rotations and sabbaticals that benefit local communities, and are famous for their generous tuition reimbursement program.

SAS *(Cary, North Carolina; www.sas.com)*
Talk about leisure: employees get to set their own hours! In addition, on their corporate campus is a self-contained recreation center with a ten-lane swimming pool, volleyball courts, tennis courts (lessons included)—even a putting green.

Google *(Mountain View, California; www.google.com)*
Sure, it helps that a substantial portion of the company's employees are millionaires, some of them hundreds, even thousands, of times over. That extra spring in everyone's step isn't just because the company cafeteria's blueberry muffins are so good. But Google is a survivor from the dot-com go-go days, and has been providing serious recreation at its world-famous Googleplex even before its bally-hoo'ed IPO, providing bicycles, musical instruments, pool tables, foosball tables, on-site massage and roller hockey (twice a week), among other perks.

[and the winner is...]

Your Own Company, Inc.

Okay, so maybe this is cheating, but we contend that the most leisurely organization (in a fulfillment sense) to work for is your own. Remember—that includes being an independent contractor or consultant, too. The upside? You like your boss (you), you report to yourself, and you set your own hours. The downside? Although you might be doing something you love, entrepreneurs consistently work longer hours than full-time employees, which can significantly impinge on your time off. So be fair to yourself. Make sure you give yourself time off!

LEISURE EVERYWHERE

We'll consider this chapter a success if any of its ammunition helps you make the case for more leisure at work. Speak up and speak often: leisure belongs everywhere, even in the office.

CHAPTER 13
THE LEISURE MOVEMENT

"It has been computed by some political arithmetician that if every man and woman would work for four hours each day on something useful, that labor would produce sufficient to procure all the necessaries and comforts of life, want and misery would be banished out of the world, and the rest of the twenty-four hours might be leisure and happiness."

~ Benjamin Franklin

A REVOLUTION of sorts is taking place around the world. It may be quieter than the discontents you read about in the World section of your morning paper, but it's gaining momentum nonetheless. This uprising is about work, and the time that we spend there. If forty hours a week is full-time, what is sixty hours a week? The Happy Unemployed in Germany don't want to know. Neither do the freeters in Japan or the Slow Food aficionados in Italy.

Recognizing that the work ethic has been hijacked by an overwork ethic, politicians in many industrialized countries are broadening their base by proposing family- and time-friendly legislation such as a four-day workweek. Even in the productivity-obsessed United States, those who favor more balance are organizing and speaking with a more cohesive voice. We call the force behind these global groups the Leisure Movement.

The core advocates are striving for shorter work hours, but the Leisure Movement circle encompasses campaigns aimed at creating a healthier work-life balance for all. The broadest rings include environmentalists, recreationalists, simplicity-seekers, slow movers, slow cities, and even enthusiastic nappers. ¡Viva la siesta!

If you're looking for leisure for your amigos as well as for yourself, these grassroots initiatives are calling you home.

SHORTER WORK HOURS

With a world of leisurely pursuits out there to be discovered, it's only natural to want more hours in the day. Alas, the workweek in the United States is 20% longer than it was in 1970. The average working American now spends just under 2,000 hours a year on the job, a full 30% more than the average German. Thank goodness for the folks lobbying for a shorter workweek!

The Basic Gist

According to its proponents, a legislated shorter workweek would ease unemployment, increase wages and improve productivity. If forty people working a 30-hour week can produce as much as thirty people working a 40-hour week, you've created ten more jobs and forty people who are more rested, happier at home and more efficient in the office.

"People working about six hours a day are the most productive people around!" reports Tracy Geraghty, a Master in Public Policy and board member of **Take Back Your Time** (www.timeday.org). Indeed, entire books have been written on the success of Kellogg's six-hour day (see *Kellogg's Six-Hour Day* by Benjamin K. Hunnicutt). Initiated at the time of the Great Depression, the company policy remained until the late 1980s, when it died a political death even though it remained a clear success for employer and employees alike.

Despite the success of these experiments, the Shorter Hours Movement in this country could use some help catch-

shorter hours, better results, no extra cost

Kellogg's
Replaced eight-hour shifts with six-hour shifts, which created jobs, increased production, raised morale, and lowered accident and insurance rates. Six-hour pay rose to eight-hour pay in just one year. The six-hour day survived until 1984.

Ideal Industries
A four-day, 38-hour week at 40-hour pay decreased absenteeism.

United Service Automobile Association
As hours went down, so did turnover and mistakes. Sales, morale, and efficiency all went up.

Medtronic
Paid employees at the 40-hour level for 36 hours of work. Even without hiring more workers, output increased.

Nestlé
Ending the workweek at 2:30pm on Fridays gave employees more time to see the doctor, drop by the market, or skedaddle out of town for the weekend.

ing up with the movement in Europe. There were certainly enough overworked Americans in the last boom economy—surely some of us who've taken sabbaticals are now sold on having a better balance in life.

Productivity

Many European countries have enacted shorter workweeks during the last half-century. Opponents cite productivity declines in Europe since World War II as evidence that a shorter week doesn't work.

"Come again?" say the shorter hours folk. If you divide hours worked by total output, you'll find that Europeans are *more* productive per hour. They do produce less in absolute terms than American workers, but only because they work a shorter year. Danes, Fins and the Dutch work notably short weeks; all are more productive per hour than Americans. Interestingly, workweek declines in Northern Europe coincide almost perfectly with steep declines in religious observance. Bye bye Protestant work ethic, hello leisure!

HE HAD A DREAM

"This country is changing. We had a 58-hour week, a 48-hour week, a 40-hour week. As machines take more and more of the jobs of men, we are going to find the workweek reduced, and we are going to find people wondering what they should do. I want to make it possible, and you do—make it possible for them to see green grass, to travel throughout this great, rich country of ours, not just in other parts of the world, but here in the United States, where I have seen parts of this country which are second to none, to any in the world, and where too many people east of the Mississippi are unaware of what golden resources we have in our own United States."

~ *President John F. Kennedy*
remarks at the dedication of the
Whiskeytown, California, Dam and
Reservoir, September 28, 1963

i could do this in my sleep

It should come as no surprise that rested employees perform better than zombies. Fatigue studies have been documenting that fact since the 1920s. Most people who work seven 50-hour weeks in a row accomplish nothing more than when they work seven 40-hour weeks in a row, one work-time study found.

Sounds like a lot of wasted time to us.

What's worse, those long weeks create domestic discord. "The '40-hour week' was enacted at a time when most families had one wage-earner," notes shorter work fan Pat Hallihan, a systems administrator in Chicago, Illinois. "When both spouses work, it becomes eighty hours per week per family. Daycare has become the norm and weekends are when you clean. Vacations are when you fix your house and car."

That's why Pat favors a *six*-day workweek: each spouse works three 10-hour days.

Pat's solution could give us a bit more shut-eye *and* turn domestic diss back into domestic bliss.

Yes, time off is productivity's friend, as scads of evidence show. Even in the U.S., numerous companies have breathed new life into their workers by granting them at least three weeks' vacation. A generous vacation policy can conquer high employee turnover and chronic overtime in a single stroke. Vacation goes up, profits balloon, morale skyrockets—it's the classic win-win-win.

Shorter work aficionado Erik Rauch points out, "The most important thing is not how fast productivity is growing, but that productivity is already high enough to sharply reduce working hours while maintaining a high material standard of living. We don't need to wait for future productivity increases—the necessary increases have already happened." In other words, we actually *could* have more hours in the day.

The Health Costs

Downsizing, long hours and unrealistic demands lead to overwork, which burdens the public health care system to the extent that a recent Canadian study recommends governments should consider tax incentives for employers who promote healthy workplace practices. And you can see why—health problems resulting from work overload cost the Canadian provincial governments six billion Canadian dollars a year. "Oh yeah?" says one shorter work time advocate. "I recently read that U.S. companies lose four *hundred* billion annually due to stress related to overwork." However you count, it doesn't add up.

GAME BOYS (& GIRLS)

The *International Game Developers Association* *(www.igda.org)* sponsored a white paper after a quality of life survey uncovered some alarming findings: "crunch time" was rampant (more than 35% of workers logged in between 65 and 80 hours a week, but only 50% or so received overtime pay), and turnover was crazy (only 3.4% of respondents had co-workers with more than ten years' experience).

The survey gave the gaming industry a big wake up call on keeping their workers animated.

U.S. video game studios are now morphing one by one from notorious sweatshops where game bangers sleep under their desks into more responsible companies that focus as much on keeping employees healthy as they do on keeping them at work. *BioWare* *(www.bioware.com)*, *Firaxis* *(www.firaxis.com)*, *Blue Fang* (www.bluefang.com) and *Cyberlore* *(www.cyberlore.com)* are among the growing number of game companies who realize that a happy developer will develop a better game, stick around longer, and maybe even train some new recruits.

The Shorter Work Time List

Robert Bernstein, coordinator for the **Shorter Work Time** email list, read Bertrand Russell's *In Praise of Idleness* when he was a college student in the 1970s and has been hooked on work hours ever since. "I see it as a fundamental issue that ties together all of the other issues I consider to be important," he says. "I wrote a one-page summary of the interconnections of these issues about ten years ago and I think they are as valid as ever." If you'd like to join the cause, Robert invites you to join the **SWT List** (www.swt.org).

Take Back Your Time

It's widely known that Americans work more than Europeans—350 more hours a year, on average. Translate that into workweeks (about nine), start from the end-of-the-year holidays and count backward. You'll hit October 24th, the date that workers around the world will celebrate "Take Back Your Time Day."

the time to care agenda

- 🖐️ Guaranteed paid child-birth leave for all parents

- 🖐️ Guaranteed paid sick leave of at least one week for all workers

- 🖐️ Three weeks of paid annual vacation leave for all workers, guaranteed

- 🖐️ A cap on compulsory, employer-imposed overtime

- 🖐️ Parity and prorated benefits for part-time workers

- 🖐️ A holiday on Election Day

"Let's bring the United States up to the standards already in place in all other industrial countries," the *Time Day* agenda reads *(www.timeday.org)*, "thereby creating more jobs and improving our health, families, community and civic life and environment. We call upon elected officials and candidates of all political parties to support this free time agenda."

The activists who organize this annual consciousness-raising event hope to challenge the "epidemic of overwork, overscheduling and time famine" in this country by encouraging folks to celebrate with barbecues, family-friendly events, and plenty of conversation on the topic of time poverty. Of course, you may have to play hooky to do so....

Similar to Earth Day, which brought so much attention to environmental causes, Time Day is fast becoming the stage on which to speak out in favor of more free time, and the Take Back Your Time organization has already brought several time groups under its umbrella. The "It's About Time!" coalition and its "Time To Care" public policy agenda propose protections for overworked Americans that they say are long overdue. The coalition urges public officials to put their "family values" mumbo jumbo where their mouths are and seriously address the critical issue of time poverty, as the American public policies protecting our family and personal time fall far short of those in other countries.

Time Day is gaining ground in large part due to the appeal, competence and straight talk of Take Back Your Time's National Coordinator John de Graaf and Program Director Gretchen Burger. "It's time America caught up to the rest of the world in terms of balance for working families, which in the end benefits everybody," says Gretchen. "Time is a value that builds strong relationships and strong families, which in turn create strong communities."

For more information, check out www.timeday.org and the book *Take Back Your Time*, edited by John de Graaf.

The Work to Live Campaign

"There's no rest for the weary," says Joe Robinson, author of *Work to Live* and founder of the **Work to Live** campaign (www.worktolive.info). The guilt, fear and lack of support that keep employees from taking vacation—sometimes vacation that they are contractually entitled to—has motivated Robinson to crusade for sensibility.

In addition to the many tips Joe arms his readers with ("break the Office Commandments that fuel overwork" for example), Joe lobbies single-mindedly for anyone who has been employed for more than a year to have the right to three weeks of paid vacation. Other industrialized nations have at least that—why shouldn't the world's "superpower" be powerful enough to guarantee the same? Robinson says that reforming the Fair Labor Standards Act to entitle workers to paid vacation is the only way to curb the mindtrip that has many believing they'll lose their jobs if they take time off.

Work to Live campaigns in cahoots with the Take Back Your Time team to lobby politicians like Senator Ted Kennedy, who, along with Senator Orrin Hatch, introduced winning legislation declaring October 2003 "National Work and Family Month."

The legislation called for discussion and action to improve the balance between work and family time in America. We hope politicians, from mayors to the President, finish the "discussion" part soon—and get on with the action.

Politricks

As well-organized and charismatic as the shorter-work-time activists are, you might have noticed a deafening silence from inside the D.C. beltway. Yes, the declaration of National Work and Family Month was passed unanimously, but politicians are all too aware that one of the biggest obstacles to gaining a shorter workweek, as well as more flextime and part-time work, is the cost to U.S. employers for employer-provided healthcare coverage. Hiring more people working fewer hours apiece would add a bundle to a company's cost of providing standard employee benefits, as things work right now. Thus, systemic work-hours reform touches on one of the most contested political issues of the day: universal healthcare.

"It is no coincidence that the European countries have universal healthcare and shorter work time," one shorter-work advocate notes. Making healthcare administration a public service would go far in paving the way toward a shorter workweek in the U.S.

But it's not like shorter-work-time advocates haven't claimed *any* political victories. Activists did succeed in derailing proposed changes to overtime laws that would have enabled employers to extract overtime work without overtime pay. The extra work would have been compensated for with more time off, which sounds reasonable—until you read the small print, which says that comp time could have been deferred for up to thirteen months, at the employers' discretion.

For every one letter or email they receive on a particular issue, politicians assume a hundred or more voters feel the same way but didn't write. In other words, your message to your senator about family-friendly work legislation carries weight. So pick up that pen! For a list of U.S. senate committee members and contact information, go to www.senate.gov, "Committees." For national congressional representatives, search by your zip code at www.house.gov.

The Genuine Progress Indicator

Did you know that Simon Kuznets, the man who invented the concept of the Gross National Product, warned against using it as a measure of national welfare? We didn't either. But seeing as how the GNP (which evolved into the Gross Domestic Product, or GDP) counts natural disasters as good for the economy, you can bet something's all wet. Recovery and rebuilding activity means money is changing hands, which makes cash flow look good, but what about the balance sheet? Floods and hurricanes destroy a lot of assets, something that GDP doesn't reflect.

Enter alternative measures of national welfare that move away from using cash churn to measure well-being and instead take into account the fact that a dollar in the hands of someone in poverty is worth more to that person than that same dollar in the hands of, say, Bill Gates. Not to get too Socialist here, but a little Robin Hood action could actually make everyone happier.

One such alternate measure is the Genuine Progress Indicator, or GPI. The GPI shows the number of hours per week that an average full-time employee's workweek could be reduced if productivity were applied to time rather than increased output. In other words, it shows how much time you could spend somewhere other than work if your boss took into account that you were actually producing more in fewer hours.

From there, you can calculate the Disposable Time Index (DTI), which shows how much worktime could shrink if consumption stayed the same from year to year, rather than continually growing, as it does now. Note that it has risen faster, cumulatively, than the Consumer Price Index (CPI) over recent years.

Year	Work Reduction Equivalent	DTI	CPI
1996	1.2 hours	2.8%	3.0
1997	1.0 hours	2.3%	2.3
1998	1.1 hours	2.6%	1.6
1999	1.1 hours	2.6%	2.2
2000	1.3 hours	3.0%	3.4
2001	0.5 hours	1.1%	2.8
2002	2.1 hours	4.8%	1.6

"People fail to realize the enormous potential of productivity," says Erik Rauch, who tabulates the DTI. "Think of the material standard of living in 1990—do the improvements since then make you that much happier? Then consider that, with productivity having gone up forty-four percent since then, it now takes twenty-nine hours to produce the goods and services that it took forty hours to produce in 1990. So people should be able to work twenty-nine hours a week with hardly any material disadvantage. Every single year, the increase in productivity makes it possible to shave one or two hours off the workweek while keeping the same living standard."

Nice work if you can get it. Erik freely admits that not everyone has the flexibility to work less than full-time, not to mention the cost to employers. Still, he sees the DTI and GPI as a "preview of what could be more widely available with this bonanza of increased productivity that technology has brought us over the last hundred years—if only our economy would get its priorities straight."

Sunday	Monday	Tuesday	Wednesday	Thursday	Friday	Saturday
					1	2
3	4	5	6	7	8	9
10	11	12	13	14	15	16
17	18	19	20	21	22	23
24	25	26	27	28	29	30

The Work Less Party

Spearheaded by colorful Canadian Conrad Schmidt, The **Work Less Party** (www.worklessparty.ca) is Canada's newest political squad, complete with candidates for office. They campaign for shorter work hours from their headquarters in Vancouver—and insert a large dose of play into their activism.

They celebrate Leisurely Yours Day at least twice a year, more often if they can. Laudatory activities include enforcing the pace (the Work Less Constable, accompanied by his pet turtle on a leash, cites those who are rushing down a busy shopping street "at scandalous speeds") and relaxing in their "living room" (complete with sofas, easy chairs, magazines, lemonade, cookies and a coffee table—smack dab in the middle of the business district).

Send a "Leisurely Yours Day" e-greeting any day of the year by visiting their home page, then "Past Events," "Leisurely Yours Day," and "Send A Leisurely Yours Day Greeting."

leisure today, leisure everyday!

Consecrated in San Francisco, the now-international *Day of Leisure* marks a once-a-year commemoration of leisure and leisurely pursuits. Mark your calendar for the fourth Friday in June and enjoy a day of relaxation and personal fulfillment. Take the afternoon off—heck, take off the whole day! Nothing's wrong with playing a little hooky now and then.

International Day of Leisure (www.dayofleisure.com)

If you've been feeling like a cog in a wheel or a rat in a cage, act out by joining in on a Work Less Party Rat Race. The Rat Race courses through a number of obstacles such as being scolded by a supervisor with managerial aspirations, and traveling down the Boulevard of Lost Dreams. You don't have to train for this event. Just arrive at the starting point wearing business attire. Whiskers and tails will be provided.

Operating under the slogan "Alarm Clocks Kill Dreams," the Work Less Party has created a three-day weekend calendar, the first of its kind in the world, and is the first political party whose platform favors personal growth versus continued industrial growth as a better solution to the world's social and environmental problems. "Instead of working so hard to make an endlessly growing stream of consumer goods that just land up in landfills polluting the environment and destroying our lives," they say, "it's now time for things that are not only good for us but good for the planet as well; music, art, leisure, community, family, sanity and what's wrong with a little clean air?" Yep, breathing works for us.

Work Your Proper Hours Day

Due to weaker laws, lack of enforcement, increased "white collar" work where overtime is not paid, and a "long hours culture," workers in the United Kingdom log in the longest hours in Europe. That's why the Trades Union Congress (TUC, the umbrella for Britain's trade unions) created **Work Your Proper Hours Day** (www.workyourproper hoursday.org). The holiday usually hits in late February, marking the first day of the year when the average employee who works unpaid overtime stops working for free. Many managers don't start earning money for their time until closer to the end of March.

The cousin to Take Back Your Time Day, Proper Hours Day brings the "It's About Time" campaign across the Atlantic. It's about time to remind your boss how much firms rely on unpaid overtime, the TUC's **workSMART** website (www.worksmart.org.uk) points out. On proper hours day, arrive on time (not early), eat a decent lunch (at a table, not a desk), and leave when you're meant to—preferably off to somewhere where your boss will buy you coffee or a cocktail. "More than five million people at work in the United Kingdom regularly do unpaid overtime, giving their employers £23 billion of free work every year," says the TUC. "If you're one of them, why not take some time to reflect on how well (or badly) you're balancing your life?"

A festive short-time site, workSMART offers e-Cards and free poster downloads, and invites employees to trip the Boss-A-Gram machine to remind their bosses—anonymously, of course—of the holiday. Their unpaid overtime calculator will help you figure how many days you work for free. Send it to a friend, then ring them up and go for a pint. After all, it's up to you to lead the charge: work your proper hours!

i am leisure, hear me roar

Arm yourself with advice from the experts and you'll be in the best position to work less and live more.

"Seriously consider, and prepare how to handle, how work itself might change if there's less of it—as in, 'What's the chance my boss will relegate me to the filing closet after a few months of this?'" time expert Tracy Geraghty counsels.

"Since our culture and work-places require work-leisure choices to be arranged through private and often personality-driven negotia-tions," she says, "as opposed to in the U.K., say, where certain workers have a right to flexible hours and a shortened workweek, the more strongly centered and clear a person is about what they want and need, the more likely that negotiation is going to go well."

Working Mothers and Fathers

Lack of free time hits families with young children and two working par-ents the hardest. Should that problem be solved privately, or should something be done on a larger scale? Tracy Geraghty undertook her Masters studies to re-search that very question.

"A few years ago," Tracy told us, "af-ter becoming a mother and living the battle of working-motherhood—while working for the State Legislature, ironi-cally—I decided to go back to school to research and understand the work-life balance problem, figure out if it's a pub-lic problem and therefore a matter for public policy intervention."

Tracy realized early on that the con-cerns of working mothers, of fathers, even of non-parents, is actually a big con-versation about time and who has con-trol over whose. "From there," she says, "it was a short step to the time move-ment where I found really smart people already working the policy angle."

According to Ann Crittenden, con-tributor to the *Take Back Your Time* book, the situation for working parents is not changing much. "All kinds of evidence shows that families are really suffering from work-related stress," she says. "The more parents are stressed out, the more they take it out on their kids. People don't know who to turn to or how to organize. There's not a single day of sick leave guaranteed for sixty-two million people. It's amazing that we put up with it."

Many working mothers groups don't plan to. **Mothers Ought To Have Equal Rights** (www.mothersoughttohaveequalrights.org) is fighting tirelessly for Paid Family Leave for each parent, as well as for guaranteed flex-time and a shorter workweek for parents of infants and toddlers. The 2005 Mother's Day campaign led by **Mothers &**

More (www.mothersandmore.org) and its many thousands of members know that the real story is about time. Both groups coordinate their efforts with the **National Partnership for Women & Families** (www.nationalpartnership.org), the education and advocacy non-profit founded more than thirty years ago as the Women's Legal Defense Fund. Highlighting issues such as the epidemic of "presenteeism" (when workers with no sick days are forced to go to work) the National Partnership promotes policies that help parents meet the dual demands of work and family.

In 2004, California became the first state to offer wage benefits for employees who take time off from their jobs to care for a new child or a family member with a serious health condition. The California law, known as Paid Family Leave, creates a Family Temporary Disability Insurance program within the State Disability Insurance program. Employees can receive partial reimbursement of their pay for up to six weeks during any 12-month period. California also finally granted new fathers paid paternity leave. New mothers were not forgotten: paid maternity leave was extended from six to twelve weeks. We challenge the other states to pass similar legislation!

Downshift Yourself

Are you convinced but can't wait for the political winds of change? Ready to step off the corporate treadmill and plan a new way to work, starting today? You'll be part of the movement towards downshifting, a term used to best effect by psychologist John Drake, founder of the worldwide human resources consulting firm Drake Beam Morin, and author of *Downshifting: How to Work Less and Enjoy Life More*. A corporate dropout himself,

---

a, b, c, downshift

The successful downshifts of consultant John Drake and other former execs are proof that it can be done, but remember that downshifting isn't all play and no work. You'll need to study up first. The good news is that the ABCs of downshifting are as easy to learn as the alphabet:

Acknowledge that the time is now.

Begin again in a career that truly interests you.

Cash? Fuhget about it.

Whether you're leaving an architecture firm to become a potter, stepping off the sales ladder to open a gallery, or turning in your security card at the brokerage firm to pursue your dream of being a landscape designer, if you know your ABCs, you will already be steeled for the downshifting challenges that lie ahead.

Drake now counsels others on how to do what he did—leave a tenured executive position for a less traditional career by drawing on income from several sources and sparing plenty of time for personal interests.

WORKOPTIONS.COM

While the wheels of public progress slowly turn, Pat Katepoo of *WorkOptions.com* (www.workoptions.com) helps individuals negotiate shorter workweeks and more vacation. "You're a trained and experienced employee who wants to stay at your current job and who can be more focused and productive with a work schedule that allows for time to attend to outside responsibilities," Pat says. "The employer who recognizes your value as an employee doesn't want to lose you, and spend more time and money recruiting and training someone else. So, having you three days a week or four days a week is better than not having you at all. A shorter workweek is a reasonable solution to meet your need and theirs." Pat creates template proposals to help people make non-standard requests of their employers—such as asking for an additional week off from work. Her newest new template explains how to request three to four weeks off when you get only two, and should be available as a free download by late Fall 2005.

THE BROADER CIRCLES OF LEISURE

Okay, enough talk about work. Let's turn to the flip side of the work-life seesaw—the living part.

Simplicity

More a community than a political movement, voluntary simplicity caught hold in the Pacific Northwest in the early 1990s and has since spread throughout the country. Researchers say one in ten Americans now practice some form of voluntary simplicity and predict that this number will continue to rise. Some practitioners believe that simplicity requires the rejection of consumerism, a commitment to social justice, or the embracing of a low-environmental impact lifestyle. We prefer—well, a *simpler* view of simplicity.

"I like to clarify simplicity," says Cecile Andrews, long-time simple-living proponent, "because people have this view that it has to do with going back to the land; that we're asking people to give everything up because they're shallow; that simplicity is deep, and if you're deep, you're not enjoying yourself. But you can be deep *and* fun! You can focus on laughing, smiling. This is what life's supposed to be about." In the U.S., Cecile has spearheaded Simplicity Circles based on a Swedish form of adult education and change, where people come together to share ideas and talk openly about an issue like time. "A lot of people immediately understand what simplicity is all about but other people just go blank," she says. "They believe they're already having the most fun in the world. That's why it's important to talk about it, to learn that there is another way. In the U.S., we've lost so many of our social skills, and our skills of sitting still and not feeling like we have to get up and do something. The practice of getting together to talk, even for talk's own sake, is itself a step toward a more leisurely way of living." See the **Simplicity Network** (www.simple living.net) to join a circle in your area, and for all other things simple.

Center for a New American Dream
(www.newdream.org)

The Center for a New American Dream conducted a Labor Day survey in 2003 and found that more than half of American workers would trade a day's pay in exchange for a day off from work. The rest couldn't afford even a small pay cut. Both parents and non-parents—greater than 80% of each group—want more time for family. Three out of four feel pressure to spend too much. What do you do when you can't cut your time because you can't cut your income? Spend wisely. Replace the pressure to buy more than you can afford with the satisfaction of knowing that you're making every penny count. Yes, it's better for the environment. Yes, it helps keep you out of debt. But the biggest bonus of buying only what you need is that with all the money you *don't* spend, you're buying time. By both lowering the income you need to support yourself (and your acquisitions), and lowering the amount of time you spend managing your "stuff," stepping off the consumption treadmill will free up your most treasured commodity—your time. Fewer possessions means fewer repairs, fewer spring cleaning sessions, more space in your closet, and more time to fully enjoy what you do have. Who knows, you might just discover an extra gear on your mountain bike and an extra key on your piano!

just in time living

Just as simplicity is not about getting rid of all your things, the Slow Movement is not about doing everything slowly. "Sometimes you do something fast because it makes sense to," says Carl Honoré, author of *In Praise of Slowness*.

"Personally, I'm not working any fewer hours," Carl says, "I just work them differently. At the moment, we've got a one-size-fits-all culture, which is, 'be busy all the time.' I wouldn't want to swap that for 'be slow all the time.' To me, slow is about people working at their own tempo, doing the work we like, getting out of that roadrunner mode we've collectively gotten stuck in."

In other words, give things the time they deserve. Take ten minutes to meditate and refresh, for example. Make sure you take a lunch break. Mix a little play into work. "It doesn't mean you have to go live in a shack in the Rocky Mountains and grow organic carrots—although you can. I live in London, a very energetic city, but I do things slow here."

Interviews should be slow but getting to the airport has to be fast. Carl has to run now—he's off to Iceland and his taxi is downstairs.

Slow Movement

Common lore has it that after a certain point, people don't get any happier as they get wealthier; they just get more fed up.

Now there's a growing body of scientific evidence to match the anecdotes. You can read all about it in journalist Carl Honoré's *In Praise of Slowness: How a Worldwide Movement Is Challenging the Cult of Speed*.

"There is very much a Slow Movement," Carl told us. "That's the essence of the book." Its popularity—translated into eight languages, slated for at least fourteen more, and a bestseller in Spain—shows the world's need to take a breather.

Carl sees people pulling together around the brand "slow," and thinks it's a wonderful way to sum up a whole lifestyle. "I hear things like, 'I've been slow but I was ashamed to admit it. Thank you for making it okay to be slow,' and 'Now I know what the word is. Slow is a word to be proud of!'" He sees the Slow Movement as "a broad church in a big tent," part of the same culture quake that recognizes it makes sense from all angles to work a bit less—or at least work differently.

Of course, some people crash and burn before they change gears. But once people see the light at the end of the tunnel, they come back with one hand on the brake. "They might even go back to the same job," Carl says, "But they'll never work the way they did. Nobody ever has two burnouts."

The naysayers insist things can't change. "You get them any time a social revolution starts happening," Carl says. "We are battling the prejudice that says as soon as you slow down, you're road kill. You're boring. You're lazy." But believers see the pace slowing. "People are starting to say, 'I can live better.'"

If you'd like to be a believer too, take some tips from around the world. The Poles have set up a chat room, **Slow Now!** (www.slownow.org), to help launch the Slow Movement in Poland. Canberra, Australia held the first ever Slow Festival, with workshops, meals and talks to get people thinking. The **Slow Biz Group** (www.slowbiz.org) in Toronto was formed to push the idea of slowness in corporate North America.

Nothing slow in your part of the planet? Start your own initiative. But take your time about it....

MORE FROM THE GODFATHER OF SLOW

"We've been accelerating pretty unremittingly since the industrial revolution," Carl Honoré told us. "In the last fifteen years, we've made amazing advances in technology that accelerate the speed of everything. Yet all the way along there's been a countercurrent of people trying to preserve the slow culture. For the most part, those people have been steamrollered, but they're now a large and growing minority. We can feel it in our bones that we've hit the wall. Everything is about racing against the clock. It's folly. It's bad for our families, for our communities, bad for our health, bad for everything. People are starting to do something about it in the form of what I call the Slow Movement."

Slow Cities

The Slow Movement has inspired other decelerated movements, like entire cities of slow folk. The Slow Cities agenda has won the backing of municipal officials in more than 100 towns and cities in Europe, Japan and Brazil, with their policies to reduce noise and traffic, preserve the local aesthetic and gastronomic customs, and establish more pedestrian zones and green spaces. Find out how to receive a certification for your own town at **Città Slow** (www.cittaslow.net, click on "How to become a Slow City").

The European Lifestyle

Any economist will tell you that people consume normal goods in greater amounts as they become richer. Leisure is a normal good. So why shouldn't its consumption increase with income?

The Europeans are doing it. They like their summer holidays, and for the most part don't complain about paying higher taxes for a higher level of government-provided services. If their shorter workweeks mean they won't keep up with the Joneses, they don't care. The Jacques, Bachs and Giovannis of Western Europe have less child-poverty, a higher literacy rate and a longer life expectancy than the Joneses do, which makes you wonder which nation is really falling behind. The Europeans aren't even in the race—and that's exactly the point.

One would expect no less from the region that's home to the **World Database of Happiness** (www.eur.nl/fsw/research/happiness). Run by Professor Ruut Veenhoven at Erasmus University in Rotterdam, The Netherlands, the database surveys reveal that happiness in the United States and Japan has been flat over the past thirty years but has risen in most West European countries. "The main difference from the U.S. is that we spend more time enjoying life," said Jorgen Ronnest, director for international affairs at the Danish Employers' Confederation, which represents about 30,000 companies. "And if you look around, maybe we don't need more refrigerators and more cars."

Sometimes "hard work" is all a matter of perspective. Iceland's Tourist Board claims, "We work a long work week in Iceland, about 40 hours. But our summer holidays are for example longer than they are in the U.S. Under the age of 30 people that have worked one whole year with the same company have 24 days summer holiday and between 30 and 40 years old have 27 days vacation."

Must be n-ice!

Downshifting in Australia

Support for a 35-hour workweek in Australia has risen greatly in the past five years. Why? Work takes up too much of life, say more than a third of employees asked.

Most Aussies predict they'd be just as productive in a 35-hour week, and would take on average a 13% cut in salary to be able to work fewer hours. Indeed, in the past decade, nearly one in four Australians between 30 and 60 years old voluntarily took a pay cut to adopt a better lifestyle.

Yes, downshifting has caught on strong Down Under. The trend goes hand in hand with the Australian rep for valuing friends, family and a good lager over burning the midnight oil ("Midnight Oil is a *band*, mate!").

effortless

The Japanese prefecture of Iwate was tired of trying to keep up with Tokyo, so they quit. Now they're slow—and they like it. "We don't make an effort in Iwate," declared Governor Hiroya Masuda. "In Tokyo, people are chased by speed, and life consists of working, eating and sleeping. Here, I want people to go home early in the evening, take a walk with their family, and talk to the neighbors."

It wasn't just an off-the-cuff remark. Mr. Masuda's administration launched an entire "no effort" advertising campaign, printing the we-don't-make-an-effort slogan on their business cards and explaining that "no effort" is about rethinking values, not about goofing off; about taking pride in what you have instead of focusing on what you lack. "No effort" means living closer to nature and away from the economic pressures of the city. "We don't make an effort in a normal way," says a happy Iwate resident, "but we're very busy. It's just not the kind of busy-ness where you feel stressed."

The ad campaign propelled Mr. Masuda to a third term—he won 88% of the votes cast—and spurred nearly 25,000 laudatory emails.

Neo-Leisure

There's another way to work fewer hours yet fly under the radar, and that is to show up and just pretend like you're working. Do you exercise at work? Well, at least you're at the office. Have "business meetings" at Starbucks? Yeah, that counts. Maybe your company has a ping-pong table in the lounge, or a meditation room, or even a room filled with hundreds of conga drums and other percussion instruments, like Toyota's training headquarters in Torrance, California.

This is neo-leisure—spending time at the office on activities other than business. It's a counterculture that blends leisure into work (or adds a little work to your free time, as you prefer). The non-cynical view is that fusing work with recreation leads to greater creativity, nurtured by friendly competition and the spirit of play. Work becomes fun and energized in nothing but the healthiest of ways.

Then the cynic comes knocking. Hello, laziness!

Corinne Maier, the French author of *Bonjour Paresse*, has become a countercultural icon of another type by encouraging her compatriots to "actively disengage" to pass hours at a job that seems more like a prison sentence. Look busy by always carrying a stack of files, she says, rather than trying to con yourself into thinking you like what you do.

This tract, whose title translates into "Hello Laziness," contains more than a whiff of the Dilbert mindset, compared to other pro-employee advice. Still, it makes the valid point that we shouldn't just sit back and take it. Or would that be recline back? Whatever it takes, it's time to drop the pretense that we all live to work.

Freeters—Twixters—Kippers—Mammone—Slackers

Twenty-something, unsalaried, with no idea what to do with themselves or their lives. Are they slackers, or just ordinary kids facing a modern world?

Young "non-regular" employees have come to be known as freeters in Japan, a term derived by coupling the English word "free" with the German word for worker, *arbeiter*. These men and women between 15 and 34 work only part-time, or in a series of temporary gigs. Known as "twixters" in Australia, "kippers" in the U.K., "mammone" in Italy, and of course "slackers" in the U.S., they are viewed by the establishment as perennial temp workers with no motivation to get "real" jobs.

There's more to the story, of course. Sure, those who live to ski in the winter and surf in the summer will never tie themselves to a salary. The rest of us may *want* a stable job, but have to deal with a nagging recession, more middle-aged and elderly workers in the job market, and the ever-more-popular trend of outsourcing. This leaves many young people working part-time or in side jobs despite their desire for conformity.

Still, many young grads are just not attracted by prospects of full-time employment right after high school or college. Studies in Japan define three types of freeters: the "okay for now" types who have no immediate plans; the "freeters with a dream" who want to break into show biz; and the "dead-end freeters" who no longer have a choice because they've never had regular work. About a third of freeters surveyed said that they didn't know what they really wanted to do, but at least a fifth were glad to be only semi-employed—and more than a tenth felt free to do what they liked.

The Happy Unemployed

In the summer of 1996, a couple of unemployed Berliners penned the *Happy Unemployed* pamphlet. Within a few months, it had reached at least 150,000 people. An informal network of Happy Unemployed sprung up across Germany, and then some groups protesting unemployment in France declared themselves Happy Unemployed. Now in Europe alone, the Happy Unemployed say they number nearly twenty million.

breaking the slacker stereotype

"Steve" doesn't want us to use his real name. He doesn't even want us to mention his industry. That's because he doesn't want employers to know that he quits his job every year to take three months' vacation. He calls himself a serial long-vacationer.

Yet he has no problem getting hired when he returns. "Even though I'm sneaky about my serial vacation lifestyle," Steve says, "it's not like I'm a slacker. In my industry, a lot of people do it. They are the most competitive and the most in demand, they just don't admit to how much time off they take. I tell them, 'I thought you were a workaholic!' and they tell me, 'No, I just work efficiently.'"

Sounds like they're all on to something. Why should you log in 10-hour days if you can get your work done in six? Why *not* take off to travel every summer if you can keep your skills up and contribute the other nine months of the year?

Don't worry, "Steve." Our lips are sealed!

This cheerful clan sent a message that caught on like wildfire—the very sensible declaration that an unemployed person is no more than a worker without work, and no less a poet, traveler or human being. Not lazy, not irresponsible, not the sole source of blame for the situation they find themselves in. They set down on paper a few truisms not often said out loud, such as that workers are publicly woeful to have been laid off but privately ecstatic to finally have time to go to parties every night or cook a decent homemade meal. If the unemployed are unhappy, they point out, it's not because they don't have any work, but because they don't have any money.

Although fans of leisure, the Happy Unemployed don't promote shorter work hours per se. They do see a day, though, when people would be less afraid of unemployment if they admitted they could be happy even without a job.

Amen to that!

GRADUATION

*To be for one day entirely at leisure
is to be for one day an immortal.*

~ Chinese proverb

WE'RE *almost* ready to confer your Leisure Connoisseur degree. But first, a critical question: Have we inspired you to take a break? If you've been plotting your getaway from the confines of your cubicle during your lunch hour, we have succeeded. We've done our job, too, if your layoff was easier to handle or your sabbatical a little jazzier. If you've discovered something new about yourself, your friends or your hometown—bonus points!

We hope you'll practice the Art of Leisure both at work and at play. Plan vacations with your friends and take them. Host leisure parties. Share this book!

Are you still not persuaded to lose a job at least once in your life? Then we'll leave you with some words of inspiration from our friends. Instead of overworking, you could be reaping all sorts of benefits from leisure—like they and countless others have.

FIND YOURSELF
like Nelson Hyde Chick

"Unemployment is a time to find yourself. Some people are so fixated on their jobs that it's their whole personality. Find a goal or objective and work toward it. Time is precious. Don't get caught up in just looking for work. Have a project."

TAP INTO YOUR CREATIVITY
like Rachel Karagounis

"You become more creative when you're not working. Your thoughts change, your routines change, you figure out ways to make your money last longer. You find things that cost less. You become a temporary artist until you go back into a schedule."

GET SOCIAL
like Gina Clark

"Take a visit to your childhood and do something fun, light and silly. Get out and meet people. You'd be surprised how many opportunities are just a 'hello' away."

HAVE SEX
like Joani Blank

"It's free and it's not fattening."

TRAVEL, REFLECT AND DISCOVER
like Michael Shapiro

"We can lose our direction when we don't take time off. I've gained clarity and perspective in my life during what some call 'downtime.' But for me it's 'up time'—I feel most alive when traveling; I feel I'm learning, connecting, growing, exploring myself, exploring the world. I don't see any substitute. As wonderful as armchair travel is, there's no replacement for getting out of that comfortable chair and hitting the road."

CHECK YOURSELF OUT
like Jeanette Watkins

"Your body reacts to overwork by having brain fog, acne, rashes.... You need sleep! If you're vain, don't work so much. You'll look better."

TRY A NEW ROLE ON FOR SIZE
like Mike Norman

"I've been working pretty steadily since I was about eleven or twelve years old, mowing lawns, shoveling snow, then having a paper route, then entering the regular workplace the day after I turned sixteen. Now that I'm forty-three, I'm ready to take a break from what has been a topsy-turvy attempt to make it big in this free-wheeling economy, with limited success. I'll tell ya, I love this stay-at-home daddy stuff. It's the best career move I've ever made."

REJUVENATE
like John Donnewald

"Unemployment should be viewed as a unique opportunity to right-click and refresh your screen, so to speak."

TAKE IT SLOW
like Chinyan Wong

"I got to spend more time at home in Hong Kong, playing with my dog and experiencing traditional Chinese festivals, luxuries I haven't had since I went to boarding school when I was eleven."

FALL IN LOVE
like Ann Marsh

"We have an over-employed society in general. People who work too much don't have the time to be good significant others. When that changes, people have time to fall in love, like I did!"

TIE THE KNOT
like Lynn Yuen

"When I first got laid off, I was a wreck. So sad, depressed, and the world was one black cloud. After a year and a half of travel, surfing, going to the gym, lounging, seeing friends and a therapist, reading, having time to date—and now with Mr. Right who just went ring shopping last night—well, it all worked out."

INSPIRE OTHERS
like Tess Roering

"Last night, I spoke with a really good friend who'd been talking for months and months about starting her own business, but was afraid to take the risk. She said it wasn't until I called her to tell her I quit my job that she was like, 'What am I waiting for?' She quit her corporate job and started her own company, working out of her home. Life's about liking what you do and how you spend your time and who you spend it with. That's what makes it good and that's what makes you successful, in my mind."

SHARE THE LEISURE
like Leisure Team!

We look forward to hearing about your own time off adventure. Life is short. Share the leisure!

ACKNOWLEDGMENTS

THANKS to the Leisure Team players! This book would not be here were it not for your help, and it's better thanks to all of your efforts.

Our All-Star Staff

★ **Jennifer Birch,** editing, writing, research, proofing, wow ★ **Nalani Jay,** proofreading, fact checking, sanity checking ★ **Eddie Foronda,** all kinds of stuff ★ **The Balinese Gigolo,** say no more ★ **Sara Irvin & Romnee Pritchett,** the illustration duo ★ **Jamie Leap,** cover design ★ **Kathryn Otoshi,** savior ★ **Paul Nemeth,** one great moment after another ★ **Jennifer Jeffrey,** editing, good vibes ★ **Adrienne Biggs & Debra Amador,** publicity

Most Valuable Players
Thanks for your valuable expertise and keen insights!

Cecile Andrews • Dick Bolles • Alayne Brand • Po Bronson • Neil Brown • Gretchen Burger • Dr. Jan Cannon • Ann Crittenden • John de Graaf • Rob DeWaters • J.J. Dillon • Karin Dixon • Hope Dlugozima • John Drake • Jason Enea • Joel Garfinkle • Tracy Geraghty • Tom Haan • Dr. Dory Hollander • Carl Honoré • Jason Julian • Terry Karp • Dana Magenau • Odd Todd • Chris O'Reilly • Erik Rauch • Joe Robinson • Conrad Schmidt • Lesley Schwartz • Rochelle Teising • Chet Van Duzer • Jeanette Watkins • Ethan Watters • Ted Witt • Lynn Yuen • Steve Yung

Thanks to everyone we interviewed. Special thanks to Ernie Zelinski, for your help, humor and oh-so-leisurely attitude.

The Fans
Anne & Horace Enea • Sue & Peter LaTourrette • our loyal friends

The Coaches
Tracy Fortini • Chris Schraeder • PGW
Thanks for drafting us!

The Owners
Bill Ralph • Jeff Stamper • the whole crew at Malloy

The Stadium
The Canvas Gallery (www.canvasgallery.com)
Thanks for the Internet access, eternal patience and tasty 'ffeine!

LEISURE LINGO

WHAT *is* Leisure Lingo, exactly? It's an attempt to remedy the serious lack of on-the-mark definitions for many of the concepts described in this book. Clearly, time off—whether planned, forced or otherwise—is a poorly defined notion in our work-centric culture. Leisure Lingo adds some clarity and fun to those non-working times.

ART OF LEISURE		
(mainstream) None. Leisure is not an art.	*(Leisure Team)* The skill, craft or phenomenon of creating a fulfilling life of leisure; making the easy way appear even easier.	*(example)* Although it took a lot of hard non-work for him to master it, Alex felt he was well-schooled in the *art of leisure* after traveling the world for a year.
ASPIRING RETIRED		
(mainstream) None.	*(Leisure Team)* Someone who's waiting for their options to vest or has saved up money and when the time is ripe, will jet off the job for good.	*(example)* The company committee on Functionally Allocated Business Processes was chock-full of *aspiring retireds*.
ASPIRING UNEMPLOYED		
(mainstream) None.	*(Leisure Team)* Someone who's working way too much, observing their unemployed friends and thinking the grass seems a whole lot greener on the other side.	*(example)* Mary, an *aspiring unemployed*, spent long afternoons staring out of her downtown office window at the sailboats drifting by on the Bay.

CASUAL EMPLOYMENT

(mainstream)	(Leisure Team)	(example)
Employment that is not permanent but not necessarily temporary. Exempt from sick leave, holiday leave, parental leave and unfair dismissal provisions.	The best kind!	Because Ken was on good terms with his former employer, he was allowed to maintain his prior health insurance coverage, yet pursue the *casual employment* that he found so much more fulfilling.

COASTER

(mainstream)	(Leisure Team)	(example)
A round object, preferably composed of semi-porous stone, upon which to set a cold drink to keep it from sweating into the table.	Someone who has enough money to sustain a healthy period of time off but not enough to retire, so is mastering the art of leisure before returning to a paying job.	Karen and Isidro had so many *coaster* friends, they decided to get married in Hawaii. The reception lasted three weeks.

CONSULTING

(mainstream)	(Leisure Team)	(example)
Offering your expert opinion or advice in exchange for pay.	A loosely conceived term used to describe a multitude of activities including volunteering, networking, traveling, meeting with friends to drink coffee and discuss new business ideas, and meeting with friends to drink beer and pontificate on the lagging economy.	Six months after getting laid off, Tara had accumulated so much *consulting* work that the local brew pub started charging her rent for her barstool.

FLUIDLY EMPLOYED

(mainstream)	(Leisure Team)	(example)
None.	A nebulous state whereby the distinction between work and non-work is blurred, usually applying to individuals who work for themselves or within the creative arts.	On any given weekday morning in Hollywood, most cafés are packed full of entertainment types. Are they working? Are they taking the day off? It's hard to tell, as most are *fluidly employed*.

FRICTIONAL UNEMPLOYMENT

(mainstream)	(Leisure Team)	(example)
Short-term joblessness associated with mobility. A person who leaves a job to find something better is considered frictionally unemployed. This type of unemployment also characterizes workers in industries subject to seasonal fluctuations, e.g., construction, agriculture or winter recreation.	Unemployment that causes unnecessary friction within one's family or oneself. Common among Type A personalities and those who don't plan ahead. Can be increased by pressures imposed by others.	Jerry realized how *frictionally unemployed* he was when his father asked him repeatedly at Thanksgiving, "So what *are* you going to do with your life, son?"

JOB CHURN

(mainstream)	(Leisure Team)	(example)
Jobs are created and destroyed all the time. If more jobs are being created than destroyed, the unemployment rate goes down and we feel good because it looks like our economy is growing. If fewer jobs are being created than destroyed, we head to the unemployment office.	The feeling you get in the pit of your stomach when you think about going back to work. Can be cured with heavy and continuous doses of leisure.	When he thought about how close to the end of his sabbatical he was, Scott got a serious case of *job churn*. Fortunately, bringing leisure back to work with him kept his *job churn* in check.

LAYOFF BLUES

(mainstream)	*(Leisure Team)*	*(example)*
None.	When you play them backwards, you get your job back.	Janice used to croon the *layoff blues* but she changed her tune once she started practicing leisure.

LEISURE CONNOISSEUR

(mainstream)	*(Leisure Team)*	*(example)*
None.	One who's gained wide experience in the various classes of leisure, including world travel, creative self-employment, music and athletic challenge. Most comfortable on sabbatical, in the company of other ladies or gentlemen of leisure, or spreading the word on the art of leisure.	Sam knew he'd become a true *leisure connoisseur* when he could no longer remember what day of the week it was.

LEISURE PATRON

(mainstream)	*(Leisure Team)*	*(example)*
None.	A patron of the art of leisure. Can come in the form of a rich uncle, a government grant or a corporate sponsor.	Sarah was able to extend her on-location study of fine Bavarian beers when her German uncle donated to the cause, becoming her *leisure patron*—and new favorite uncle!

LEISURE SEEKER

(mainstream)	*(Leisure Team)*	*(example)*
None.	One who pursues a life of relaxation and personal fulfillment. An enlightened one!	Bill knew he'd become an advanced *leisure seeker* when he chose to take a year off to travel instead of accepting a promotion.

LIMBO-EMPLOYED

(mainstream)	*(Leisure Team)*	(example)
None.	Not quite working on a career but stymied in the full-time practice of leisure by the need to pay bills. Related terms: underemployed, misemployed.	Tom's on-again, off-again consulting gigs left him stuck in the mire of *limbo-employment*.

McJOB

(mainstream)	*(Leisure Team)*	*(example)*
None.	What a writer, actor, or musician has to finance a creative career.	Until Caleb's band gets a record deal, he's keeping his *McJob* at Starbucks.

MISEMPLOYMENT

(mainstream)	*(Leisure Team)*	*(example)*
Forced career change or temporary work taken just to pay the bills.	Settling for work that is unsatisfying and unfulfilling.	An artist at heart, Sheara was suffering from a horrible bout of *misemployment*—working long hours at a law firm with no time to spend the beaucoup bucks she was making.

NON-EMPLOYED

(mainstream)	*(Leisure Team)*	*(example)*
A non-factor or non-contributor to the gross national product.	Unemployed and loving it!	Jason began competing in triathlons and got in the best shape of his life while *non-employed*.

OVERWORK OGRE

(mainstream)	*(Leisure Team)*	*(example)*
None.	The boss who won't let you take a vacation even after a long stint of long hours, or claims offense anytime real life interferes with your job.	Rachel found herself offering her *overwork ogre* an apology that her grandmother's sudden illness had not come at a more opportune time.

POST-SABBATICAL BLUES

(mainstream)	(Leisure Team)	(example)
None.	A type of dirge, commonly performed on a 12-string guitar and most emotionally played when dealing with the harsh reality of going back to full-time work.	Working with headphones on at his new desk job, Carter suddenly realized he'd been singing the *post-sabbatical blues* out loud while his co-workers listened in.

PRE-RE-EMPLOYED

(mainstream)	(Leisure Team)	(example)
None.	Not looking for a job right now but expecting to do so in the near future.	Rob frequented Baker Beach more and more as he entered his *pre-re-employment* stage, bagging rays and thinking deep thoughts about leisure.

PROTESTANT LEISURE ETHIC

(mainstream)	(Leisure Team)	(example)
A moral mandate to avoid idleness and convert all downtime into so-called productive leisure, such as a hobby.	A well-intentioned but incomplete ethic that reflects an American obsession with output and success.	The *Protestant Leisure Ethic* drove Amy to squander her European sabbatical marching diligently through museum after museum taking copious notes.

PROTESTANT WORK ETHIC

(mainstream)	(Leisure Team)	(example)
A term coined by Max Weber to describe the productivity-oriented culture giving rise to capitalism in Western Europe and later the United States. The ethic that spawned what Weber called the "spirit of capitalism."	Does not compute.	Leisure connoisseur Carey stared blankly from the bow of the boat as her friend, Blythe, recited the history of the *Protestant Work Ethic*. "Huh?"

PURITAN SOCIAL ETHIC

(mainstream)	(Leisure Team)	(example)
An ethic prevalent in the Massachusetts Bay Colony, which dictated that wasting time was evil. Its more benign tenets include living simply and being thrifty.	Say again?	Not applicable. Incorrect when used in writing or speaking, according to the grammar of Leisure Lingo.

REAL JOB

(mainstream)	(Leisure Team)	(example)
A job with regular, daytime hours where you work for someone else and no one questions your job title.	A job you can get fired from.	Rex was tired of worrying about layoffs so he quit his *real job* and went into business for himself.

RE-EMPLOYED

(mainstream)	(Leisure Team)	(example)
Would you believe it? This word is not in the dictionary yet. We'll take a leap of faith that it would be defined as "employed again."	Entering back into the workforce, and dealing with the "culture" shock that comes with it. Not unlike a spacecraft re-entering the earth's atmosphere and heating up from the friction and stress.	Jeri was having trouble getting to household chores like laundry now that she was *re-employed*, so she stocked up on a lot of new underwear and socks.

RETIRED

(mainstream)	(Leisure Team)	(example)
Withdrawn from one's occupation, business, or office; having finished one's active working life.	Happy! Leisurely! Free! Hallelujah!	Jamie threw a hearty fiesta in celebration of his newly *retired* status after his technology startup went public. Unfortunately, he quickly had to become *re-employed* six months later when his stock dove underwater.

SABBATICAL

(mainstream)	(Leisure Team)	(example)
A leave usually taken every seventh year. In Jewish antiquity, it refers to the sabbatical year in which the Israelites were commanded to suffer their fields and vineyards to rest or lie without tillage.	A godsend!	Sharon awarded herself a masters degree in Leisure after her long-awaited *sabbatical* studying at a culinary school in Tuscany—and threw some stellar dinner parties for her friends, too.

SELF-EMPLOYED

(mainstream)	(Leisure Team)	(example)
Earning one's livelihood directly from one's own trade or business rather than as an employee of another.	Fulfilled! Self-actualized! Free! (But possibly working too much.)	Darryl couldn't have been happier now that he was *self-employed* as a landscape architect. His only challenge was keeping up with his growing client list!

SELF-UNEMPLOYED

(mainstream)	(Leisure Team)	(example)
None.	Refers primarily to someone who has started a business but is not making any money yet.	So Neil, howz work these days? Oh, well I don't do it any more, I am *self-unemployed*. Neil, did you get laid off? No, I made a choice, I am *self-unemployed*. How are you paying the bills without a job? Well, *self-unemployment* brings a whole new perspective to bills.

SIT

(mainstream)	(Leisure Team)	(example)
To rest with the torso vertical and the body supported on the buttocks.	A verb describing the placid state of someone who's "between jobs." A primary pastime of a leisure connoisseur.	LC: "Yo, whassup?" Slave: "I'm workin'. You?" LC: "I *sit*." Slave: "True."

SLAVE

(mainstream)	(Leisure Team)	(example)
Unpaid and involuntary worker. One who works extremely hard. One bound in servitude as the property of a person or household.	Paid yet reluctant worker. Someone who works for The Man. In Leisure Lingo, to "slave" is to work extremely hard at a job that you don't like.	Alyssa tried to convince herself that her new software job would look good on her resume but deep down, she knew she was just a *slave*.

THE GRIND

(mainstream)	(Leisure Team)	(example)
A crunching or pulverizing action, often used in reference to the fineness of coffee grounds, or to the clenching and gnashing of one's teeth.	The endless churn of the industrial machine, which sucks in and consumes all that crosses its path, including well-intentioned but unsuspecting workers.	Sophia couldn't take one more day of *The Grind*, so she summarily quit her job and took the summer off to practice yoga and learn how to play the guitar.

THE MAN

(mainstream)	(Leisure Team)	(example)
The "it" person, the master. To be "The Man" is to be a person who's hip, happenin' and in charge.	The Orwellian presence of the powers that be in a structured employment environment, which inhibits its workers' freedoms in order to achieve its objectives. To be working for "The Man" is to be restricted to doing only what someone else wants you to do. See *Slave*.	Alejandro realized that unless he took a chance and started his own graphic design business, he'd probably be working for *The Man* the rest of his life.

UMU

(mainstream)	(Leisure Team)	(example)
Misspelling of the word for the large, flightless Australian bird related to and resembling the ostrich.	Urban, middle-aged and unemployed.	Harrison was pleasantly surprised to meet so many other *UMUs* in the brownstone where he lived.

UNDER-EMPLOYED

(mainstream)	*(Leisure Team)*	*(example)*
Someone who wants to work but has stopped looking, or is employed part-time but wants full-time work.	A term that reflects the misconception that everyone should work full-time; a malaprop brought on by peer pressure or financial constraints.	Michael thought he was *underemployed* until he learned to stop overspending; then he realized that his work paid more than enough to finance his leisure.

UNEMPLOYED

(mainstream)	*(Leisure Team)*	*(example)*
Out of work, especially involuntarily. Jobless. Not being used. Idle.	Blissful! At ease! Emancipated! (But maybe a little worried about money.)	Leo was *unemployed*. Leo was happy.

UNEMPLOYED HONEYMOON

(mainstream)	*(Leisure Team)*	*(example)*
None.	The euphoric period immediately after leaving a job when the world is new again, every sight and sound speaks to you and the leisure possibilities are boundless.	Liam and Marissa left their jobs at the same time and shared substantial bliss during their *unemployed honeymoon*. Unfortunately, once the honeymoon ended, so did their relationship.

UNEMPLOYED ODYSSEY

(mainstream)	*(Leisure Team)*	*(example)*
None.	The quest one embarks on after leaving full-time work, whether by choice or circumstance. A journey to the promised land.	Trevor took off from work for several "mental health" days so he could plot his upcoming *unemployed odyssey*.

WASTED LEISURE TIME SYNDROME

(mainstream)	*(Leisure Team)*	*(example)*
A particular kind of work spillover in which exhausted and drained workers can do little more with leisure time than engage in undemanding, unfulfilling and empty activities, as coined in 1973 by the late Swedish Professor Bertil Gardell.	*Wasted* leisure time?!	Join Leisure Team to help eradicate *wasted leisure time syndrome* from every city and town on the planet!

WORK INHIBITIONS

(mainstream)	*(Leisure Team)*	*(example)*
Social norms, specific to formal working environments, that keep workers from doing anything unconventional.	Career planning blinders, usually in the form of the ill-conceived pursuit of salary or status.	Once Jenny shook her *work inhibitions*, she more easily mustered the courage to leave her investment banking job and follow her dream of becoming an interior designer.

THE LEISURE LIBRARY
SELECTED SOURCES & FURTHER READING

21st Century Leisure: Current Issues by John R. Kelly and Valeria Freysinger (Allyn and Bacon, 2000).

ABC of Getting the MBA Admissions Edge by Matt Symonds and Alan Mendonca (The MBA Site Ltd., 2001).

The Art of Napping by William Anthony (Larson Publications, 1998).

The Art of Napping at Work by Camille and William Anthony (Larson Publications, 1999).

The Art of War by Sun Tzu (Clearbridge Publishing, 1999).

A Sense of Place: Great Travel Writers Talk About Their Craft, Lives, and Inspiration by Michael Shapiro (Travelers' Tales, 2004).

The Back Door Guide to Short-Term Job Adventures: Internships, Extraordinary Experiences, Seasonal Jobs, Volunteering, Work Abroad (3rd Edition) by Michael Landes (Ten Speed Press, 2002).

The Bartender's Bible: 1001 Mixed Drinks and Everything You Need to Know to Set Up Your Bar by Gary Regan (HarperTorch, 1993).

Beating the Success Trap: Negotiating for the Life You Really Want and the Rewards You Deserve by Ed Brodow (HarperCollins, 2003).

Bed & Breakfasts and Country Inns (16th Edition) by Deborah Edwards Sakach (American Historic Inns, 2004).

Blindsided: Financial Advice for the Suddenly Unemployed by Edie Milligan (Alpha Books, 2001).

¡Burritos! Hot on the Trail of the Little Burro by David Thomsen and Derek Wilson (Gibbs Smith Publishers, 1998).

The Complete Idiot's Guide to World Religions (3rd Edition) by Brandon Toropov and Luke Buckles (Alpha, 2004).

The Complete Medical School Preparation and Admissions Guide (3rd Edition) by Andrew Goliszek (Healthnet Press, 2000).

Consumer Reports Travel Well for Less, ed. Consumer Reports (Consumer Reports, 2003).

Critical Mass: Bicycling's Defiant Celebration, ed. Chris Carlsson (AK Press, 2002).

Downshifting: How to Work Less and Enjoy Life More by John D. Drake (Berrett-Koehler Publishers, 2001).

Educational Travel on a Shoestring: Frugal Family Fun and Learning Away from Home by Judith Waite Allee and Melissa L. Morgan (Shaw, 2002).

Everything a Working Mother Needs to Know About Pregnancy Rights, Maternity Leave and Making Her Career Work for Her by Anne C. Weisberg and Carol A. Buckler (Main Street Books, 1994).

Find a Job: 7 Steps to Success by Dr. Jan Cannon (Cannon Career Development, 2004).

Finding Funding: The Comprehensive Guide to Grant Writing by Daniel M. Barber (Daniel M. Barber, 2002).

The Fun Seeker's North America: The Ultimate Travel Guide to the Most Fun Events and Destinations (2nd Edition) by Alan Davis (Greenline Publications, 2003).

Go Away: Just for the Health of It by Mel Borins, M.D. (Wholistic Press, 2000).

Histories of Leisure: Leisure, Consumption & Culture, ed. Rudy Koshar (Berg Publishers, 2002).

Hobbies: Leisure and the Culture of Work in America by Steven M. Gelber (Columbia University Press, 1999).

How to Live Your Dream of Volunteering Overseas by Joseph Collins, Stefano DeZerega, and Zahara Heckscher (Penguin Books, 2002).

How to Retire Happy, Wild, and Free by Ernie J. Zelinski (Ten Speed Press, 2004).

I Could Do Anything If I Only Knew What It Was: How to Discover What You Really Want and How to Get It by Barbara Sher (Dell, 1995).

I'll Grant You That: A Step-by-Step Guide to Finding Funds, Designing Winning Projects, and Writing Powerful Grant Proposals by Jim Burke and Carol Ann Prater (Heinemann, 2000).

In Praise of Idleness: And Other Essays by Bertrand Russell (Routledge, 2004).

In Praise of Slowness: How a Worldwide Movement is Challenging the Cult of Speed by Carl Honoré (HarperSanFrancisco, 2004).

Internet Travel Planner: How to Plan Trips and Save Money Online (2nd Edition) by Michael Shapiro (Globe Pequot, 2002).

The Joy of Not Working: A Book for the Retired, Unemployed, and Overworked (21st Century Edition) by Ernie J. Zelinski (Ten Speed Press, 2003).

Kellogg's Six-Hour Day by Benjamin Kline Hunnicutt (Temple University Press, 1996).

Law School Admissions Adviser (2000 Edition) by Ruth Lammert-Reeves (Kaplan, 1999).

The Lazy Person's Guide to Happiness: Shortcuts to a Happy and Fulfilling Life by Ernie J. Zelinski (Thomas More Publishing, 2001).

The Lazy Woman's Guide to Just About Everything by Judie O'Neill and Bridget Fonger (Elephant Eye Press, 2001).

Life After Baby: From Professional Woman to Beginner Parent by Wynn McClenahan Burkett (Wildcat Canyon Press, 2000).

Life or Debt: A One-Week Plan for a Lifetime of Financial Freedom by Stacy Johnson (Ballantine Books, 2001).

Living Well On Practically Nothing by Edward Romney (Paladin Press, 2001).

Lonely Planet China (9th Edition) ed. Damian Harper, et al. (Lonely Planet Publications, 2002).

Lonely Planet Eastern Europe (8th Edition) by Tom Masters, Lisa Dunford, and Mark Elliott (Lonely Planet Publications, 2005).

Lonely Planet Southeast Asia on a Shoestring (12th Edition) by Kristin Kimball, China Williams, Marie Cambon, and Mat Oakley (Lonely Planet Publications, 2004).

Lonely Planet Travel With Children (4th Edition) by Cathy Lanigan (Lonely Planet Publications, 2002).

Making a Living Without a Job: Winning Ways for Creating Work That You Love by Barbara Winter (Bantam, 1993).

Moon Handbooks South Pacific (8th Edition) by David Stanley (Avalon Travel Publishing, 2004).

Money Troubles: Legal Strategies to Cope With Your Debts (9th Edition) by Robin Leonard (Nolo, 2003).

The Odd Todd Handbook: Hard Times, Soft Couch by Todd Rosenberg (Warner Books, 2003).

Office Yoga: Simple Stretches for Busy People by Darrin Zeer (Chronicle Books, 2000).

The Overworked American: The Unexpected Decline of Leisure by Juliet B. Schor (Basic Books, 1992).

Pay Nothing to Travel Anywhere You Like by Eric W. Gershman (Great Pines Publishing, 1999).

The Price of Motherhood: Why the Most Important Job in the World is Still the Least Valued (2nd Edition) by Ann Crittenden (Owl Books, 2002).

Rick Steves' Europe Through the Back Door 2005 by Rick Steves (Avalon Travel Publishing, 2004).

Road Trip USA: Cross-Country Adventures on America's Two-Lane Highways (3rd edition) by Jamie Jensen (Avalon Travel Publishing, 2002).

Rough Guide to Europe 2005 by Rough Guides (Rough Guides, 2005).

Scenarios for Success: Directing Your Own Career by Rochelle Teising and Catherine Joseph (Rudi Publishing, 1998).

Six Months Off: How to Plan, Negotiate, and Take the Break You Need Without Burning Bridges or Going Broke by Hope Dlugozima, James Scott, and David Sharp (Henry Holt, 1996).

Small Business Taxes Made Easy: How to Increase Your Deductions, Reduce What You Owe, and Boost Your Profits by Eva Rosenberg (McGraw-Hill, 2004).

The Story of Leisure: Context, Concepts, and Current Controversy by Jay S. Shivers and Lee J. deLisle (Human Kinetics Publishers, 1997).

Take Back Your Time: Fighting Overwork and Time Poverty in America, ed. John de Graaf (Berrett-Koehler, 2003).

The Theory of the Leisure Class by Thorstein Veblen (Dover Publications, 1994, originally published by Macmillan, 1899).

Time Off From Work: Using Sabbaticals to Enhance Your Life While Keeping Your Career on Track by Lisa Angowski Rogak (John Wiley & Sons, 1994).

Vagabonding: An Uncommon Guide to the Art of Long-Term World Travel by Rolf Potts (Villard, 2002).

What Color Is Your Parachute? A Practical Manual for Job-Hunters and Career-Changers (2005 Edition) by Richard Nelson Bolles (Ten Speed Press, 2005).

Work to Live by Joe Robinson (Perigree, 2003).

Work Your Way Around the World (11th Edition) by Susan Griffith (Vacation Work Publications, 2003).

Your Rights in the Workplace by Barbara Kate Repa (Nolo, 2002).

INDEX

C

D

E

G

F

P

O

Q

JOIN THE LEISURE TEAM!

GREAT MOMENTS IN UNEMPLOYMENT

12

LEISURE TEAM FOUNDED!

Leisure Team Productions (LTP) produces books, events and other media to promote the art of leisure.

LTP came to life in 2002, founded by two unemployed former classmates over several rounds of cask-conditioned ale at the Black Horse London Pub (coincidentally, the site of their original corporate headquarters). Tired of misguided perceptions of unemployment and the national obsession with work, Leisure Team decided to join hands with other organizations and individuals who have found more balance in life, to feature them in a deservedly flattering light, and to throw some raucous fiestas in the process.

Time Off! The Upside to Downtime is LTP's second celebration of leisure, and is the second in a series of leisure team[tm] guides.

Do *you* want to join the Leisure Team? You can! All it takes is an address. Sign up now at *www.leisureteam.com*. To give us feedback or to talk about working together, contact us at:

Leisure Team Productions, LLC
1392 La Playa
San Francisco, California 94122

feedback@leisureteam.com
www.leisureteam.com

ABOUT THE AUTHORS

The founders of leisure itself? Well, not quite.
Kristine Enea and Dean LaTourrette attended K-12 together and have lived
in San Francisco since finishing college—Dean in points West and
Kristine in points East. They rode the dot-com wave (both up
and down) and have been successfully non-employed
since 2001, pursuing creative interests and
attempting to perfect the leisure lifestyle.
Leisure Team Productions and
*Time Off! The Upside to
Downtime* were born
during this
time.

Kristine Enea

Kristine used to negotiate deals for a large software company but she saw the light and decided to take off and travel. Her subsequent trek to Panama City, Panama, and back—by car—led to the expansion of her family in the amount of one dog and several cats. She is a film-fest junkie who has been known to deplete her bank account to make it to Telluride around Labor Day. In addition to co-authoring the *Time Off!* series, Kristine heads up operations for Leisure Team Productions, producing the books and paying the bills.

Dean LaTourrette

Dean has worked in marketing on and off for the past 15 years—"on" during periods of full-time employment with a variety of companies, and "off" during extended hiatuses to travel, surf and write. He has written for several publications, including *Men's Journal*, *Surfer Magazine*, and *The Surfer's Path*. Dean swears that the idea for this book came to him while he was sneaking a nap at work, which only reinforced his desire to quit his job and write it. Dean is responsible for sales, marketing, and schmoozing for Leisure Team Productions.